THEOLOGY AND SCIENCE AT THE FRONTIERS OF KNOWLEDGE

NUMBER FIVE

EINSTEIN AND CHRIST

A NEW APPROACH
TO THE
DEFENCE OF THE CHRISTIAN RELIGION

THEOLOGY AND SCIENCE AT THE FRONTIERS OF KNOWLEDGE

THEOLOGY AND SCIENCE AT THE FRONTIERS OF KNOWLEDGE

GENERAL EDITOR — T. F. TORRANCE

EINSTEIN AND CHRIST

A NEW APPROACH
TO THE
DEFENCE OF THE CHRISTIAN RELIGION

RALPH G. MITCHELL

SCOTTISH ACADEMIC PRESS
EDINBURGH
1987

Published in association with the
Center of Theological Enquiry, Princeton
and
The Templeton Foundation Inc.
by
SCOTTISH ACADEMIC PRESS
33 Montgomery Street, Edinburgh EH7 5JX

First published 1987

ISBN 0 7073 0453 9

British Library Cataloguing in Publication Data
Mitchell, Ralph G.
    Einstein and Christ: a new approach to the
    defence of the Christian religion.—(Theology
    and science at the frontiers of knowledge; v.5)
    1. Religion and science—1946–
    I. Title   II. Series
    200   BL240.2

ISBN 0-7073-0453-9

Printed in Great Britain

Lord God,
you made Saint Albert great by his gift
for reconciling human wisdom with
divine faith.
Help us so to follow his teaching
that every advance in science
may lead us to a deeper knowledge and
love of you.

(From the Divine Office for the
memorial of St. Albert the Great)

To my friend and mentor

Archbishop Sir Guilford Clyde Young, D.D., K.B.E.

Nihil Obstat: Bishop E. J. Cuskelly, M.S.C., D.D.
Censor Deputatis

Imprimatur: Bishop J. J. Gerry, D.D.
Vicar General

Archdiocese of Brisbane
2nd January 1985

CONTENTS

INDEX OF DIAGRAMS AND TABLES

GENERAL FOREWORD

A VAST shift in the perspective of human knowledge is taking place, as a unified view of the one created world presses for realisation in our understanding. The destructive dualisms and abstractions which have disintegrated form and fragmented culture are being replaced by unitary approaches to reality in which thought and experience are wedded together in every field of scientific inquiry and in every area of human life and culture. There now opens up a dynamic, open-structured universe, in which the human spirit is being liberated from its captivity in closed deterministic systems of cause and effect, and a correspondingly free and open-structured society is struggling to emerge.

The universe that is steadily being disclosed to our various sciences is found to be characterised throughout time and space by an ascending gradient of meaning in richer and higher forms of order. Instead of levels of existence and reality being explained reductionistically from below in materialistic and mechanistic terms, the lower levels are found to be explained in terms of higher, invisible, intangible levels of reality. In this perspective the divisive splits become healed, constructive syntheses emerge, being and doing become conjoined, an integration of form takes place in the sciences and the arts, the natural and the spiritual dimensions overlap, while knowledge of God and of his creation go hand in hand and bear constructively on one another.

We must now reckon with a revolutionary change in the generation of fundamental ideas. Today it is no longer philosophy but the physical and natural sciences which set the pace in human culture through their astonishing revelation of the rational structures that pervade and underly all created reality. At the same time, as our science presses its inquiries to the very boundaries of being, in rhacrophysical and microphysical dimensions alike, there is being brought to light a hidden traffic between theological and scientific ideas of the most far-reaching significance for both theology and science. It is in that situation where theology and science are found to have deep mutual relations, and increasingly cry out for each other, that our authors have been at work.

The different volumes in this series are intended to be geared into this fundamental change in the foundations of knowledge. They do not present 'hack' accounts of scientific trends or theological fashions, but are intended to offer inter-disciplinary and creative interpretations which will themselves share in and carry forward the new synthesis transcending the gulf in popular understanding between faith and reason, religion and life, theology and science. Of special concern is the mutual modification and cross-fertilisation between natural and theological science, and the creative integration of all human thought and culture within the universe of space and time.

What is ultimately envisaged is a reconstruction of the very foundations of modern thought and culture, similar to that which took place in the early centuries of the Christian era, when the unitary outlook of Judaeo-Christian thought transformed that of the ancient world, and made possible the eventual rise of modern empirico-theoretic science. The various books in this series are written by scientists and by theologians, and by some who are both scientists and theologians. While they differ in training, outlook, religious persuasion, and nationality, they are all passionately committed to the struggle for a unified understanding of the one created universe and the healing of our split culture. Many difficult questions are explored and discussed, and the ground needs to be cleared of often deep-rooted misconceptions, but the results are designed to be presented without technical detail or complex argumentation, so that they can have their full measure of impact upon the contemporary world.

This contribution to our series on *Theology and Science* is as distinctive as its author, Fr. Ralph Mitchell of

Queensland, Australia. Before entering the priesthood of
the Roman Catholic Church late in life as a married man,
he had a varied and colourful career, in life assurance and
actuarial work, as a soldier throughout World War II, in
civil engineering construction, as a business manager, as
Chief Estimator of a company which was then Australia's
largest Civil Engineering enterprise and finally as a Project
Manager of an International Consortium of Railroad
Contractors. But between various appointments he made
time to study scholastic philosophy and theology. On
retiring from his last appointment in 1962 he spent several
more years assisting his son in the development of a cattle
station in Western Queensland, before a late vocation
claimed his services for the Church. This unusual book
represents the kind of ministry he has been pursuing, in
helping his younger contemporaries to reach a deeper
understanding of the Christian Faith within the perspective of the Einsteinian revolution in scientific knowledge.
While Fr. Mitchell, like the other authors in this series,
seeks to establish the emerging convergence of thinking
between theologians and scientists, unlike them he writes
with an avowedly apologetic objective in seeking scientific confirmation for Christian convictions independently
reached on the ground of divine revelation. The arguments are engagingly worked out both in deference to the
compelling claims of scientific knowledge and within the
Thomist tradition of the Roman Catholic Church, with
special attention to the immortality of the soul.

                                        Thomas F. Torrance

Edinburgh,
Advent, 1984

INTRODUCTION

IT must be anticipated that any prospective reader of this book might reasonably ask, "What are the qualifications of this unknown author that enables him to write under the title and sub-title displayed on the cover?"

To this the author would reply: primarily a sincere love of Christ and his Church, coupled with a deep-seated conviction that acceptance of Christ's teaching and the Church's role is a matter of extreme urgency in the present world-climate, if civilisation is to be preserved and peace attained. At this point in time, annihilation of mankind in his mortal state on earth, in a matter of minutes, is not only possible, but not at all improbable. It is a time for decisions. Christianity through the Church has an immediate answer to both issues. If the call to return to Christ through his Church is answered positively and sincerely there will result "peace on earth to men of goodwill". Brothers and sisters in a truly loving family do not concentrate on how to kill each other with speed and certainty. On the contrary they help each other in every possible way and at expense to themselves.

Faith in Christ through the Church can remove the fear of death deep in every human being. This problem is dealt with in chapter 2. Of course the quasi-instinctive urge for self-preservation common to all terrestial life persists but there is no fear of annihilation, for to the Christian there is no such thing as far as mankind is concerned. In the first eight chapters of this book with one or two exceptions the evidence for man's immortality is taken from the work of modern empirical scientists and is based strictly on scientific methods.

This is just as important to the atheist as to the Christian — perhaps more so. That is why the study of modern scientific thinkers is so important. Hamlet's famous soliloquy; "To be, or not to be, that is the question" can now be answered scientifically. No! You will not die. The obvious reply to this affirmation must surely be: "Then what is mortal life all about and how should I live it?" This book attempts to answer the quandary.

A long life, coupled with study in various disciplines, leaves the author convinced that atheism cannot be defended on any truly logical basis. On the other hand orthodox Christianity can be demonstrated to be entirely reasonable.

Let it be clearly understood that faith in God, in Jesus Christ and his Church can never be obtained by study or work. Faith is a dynamic personal relationship between God and man. It can be had by any man or woman who asks God for the gift sincerely, and it can be fully worked out only in his Church.

However, faith, or trust, or confidence requires an object. One cannot just believe — one must believe in something. There is no more concise or simple summary of the content of Christian faith than the Nicene Creed, a copy of which can be found on page 227.

This book is addressed to any person interested in having a look at the Christian religion, to Christians who have lost touch with the Church, to people who are interested in Christianity but don't like the Church and to young people around about the matriculation/undergraduate standard who may be perplexed. It could possibly serve as a discussion stimulant in homes and schools. It does not pretend to be a scientific text-book or a manual of theology. It is written by a Roman Catholic priest and it is consequently inevitable that this should become apparent from time to time. Only towards the end of the last chapter is the Catholic position dealt with specifically.

The following remarks are addressed primarily to young people, but as the problems outlined could arise at any point in life it is hoped more mature readers will also find them of interest.

The age span from 16 to 26 is critical in any life as it is the period in which a young person moves out from the protective influence of the home, and sometimes a religious school, into the world in which individual life-styles are to be formed.

It is a period which is particularly difficult where the young person has made most of his friends amongst peers from a similar environment, and where parents have restricted their friendship to relatives and friends from the same circle.

Quite suddenly, and usually with little or no preparation the young person is plunged into today's secular environment, an environment which is often hostile to religious values and traditions.

For the first time the young student may encounter lecturers and professors who have quite honestly adopted one of the materialistic philosophies, some of which, by their nature, are opposed to all forms of religion. He may find himself among peers who are either indifferent to or scornful of his Christianity. The student then encounters for the first time trained minds, sometimes brilliant and far more experienced in the art of argument, perhaps minds which have sincerely found religious beliefs irrelevant or even absurd. For the young Christian this is a crisis, and unless careful and skilful support is found in his home and from his friends he tends to move in one of two directions. Either he becomes fascinated by the new ideas he hears and deliberately rejects his faith, or subconsciously he allows a dichotomy to develop in his thinking: his religious beliefs and moral standards are relegated to one level of cognizance and his "scientific" knowledge to another. It is hard, from the pastoral point of view, to judge which is more damaging — the outright rejection, or the schizophrenic condition occasioned by keeping basic Christian beliefs and scientific knowledge in separate and separated compartments of the mind. While in many cases the divorce from Church becomes absolute, there are quite a number of instances where, disillusioned with the vacuous despair of atheism, the developing young mind reembraces the Christian faith with a true conviction. This grace when it is given and received certainly presents the Church with the cream of its membership. The overall situation raises very sharply the question of the adequacy of religious education in our secondary schools. A further question which must be faced reverts to the family and home. Is regular attendance at Church in childhood simply a passive form of obedience or are Christian values and doctrine discussed, practised and defended in the family circle? In other words does the young person's Christianity mean more than just going to church?

The Church too has some serious and urgent self-questioning to do. Is it's preaching relevant to the true situation in the secular world? Are its pastors and teachers up to date in their knowledge of what is going on in the scientific world? Are they humbly sharing concern with leading scientists in considering the deep philosophical questions that new physics, biology and astronomy are raising? Has the Church yet realised the limitations of Newtonian physics? Have we faced up to what the Incarnation of Jesus really means i.e. that he was and is true flesh — yes, atoms, nuclei, electrons, protons, that the DNA phenomenon was part of him. In other words are we presenting the WHOLE Christ to our people? Are our seminarians bogged down in Newtonian or even Aristotelian physics? Do we realise that what we call space and time are merely co-ordinates of a limited part of total reality? Do our people still think eternity is a "long time" or that infinity is "very big" (or small)? Do we know anything about the hierarchies of reality — the macro-universe, the mini-universe, the micro-universe?

Do we realise that while classical physics work very well with large concepts like the molecule up to our solar system, they are quite inadequate in the sub-atomic world or in the "bent light" areas of macro-cosmic measurements and that these areas constitute by far the greater part of known realities?

Most important still, is the Church aware that our leading scientists have discovered and stand in awe before the "mystery" (in the true theological sense of the term) of the universe? Here, of course, is a possible meeting point.

As late as October 1972 the National Academy of

Science Meeting in the United States resolved *inter alia* and I quote "Religion and science are therefore separate and mutually exclusive realisms of human thought whose presentation in the same context leads to misunderstanding of both scientific theory and religious belief".

Out of fairness it must be said that this resolution arose out of a conflict between certain biblical fundamentalists and scientists as to the use of the first chapters of the book of Genesis in text books for school children, interpreted in a strictly literal sense as a record of the earth's origins and the emergence of life.

The resolution was in substance a restatement of a paragraph from Francis Bacon's *"Advancement of Learning"* (1605) which reads: "Let no man think or maintain that a man can search too far or be too well studied in the book of God's word *or* in the book of God's works; divinity *or* philosophy and again, that they do not universely mingle or confound these learnings together" (italics mine).

This dichotomy upheld by Newton has resulted in the still existent gap between empirical and theological scientists. However, important signs are emerging from both disciplines. Both sides are rapidly beginning to realise that the "book of God's word" and the "book of God's work" have a common author — God. Scientists are moving this way from their re-discovery of "mystery" and "awe". At the top level, modern scientists and modern theologians have re-established dialogue. Despite areas of difference they have reached a stage where they genuinely respect each other's views and are open to discussion even conviction.

The reader will notice many apparent inconsistencies in the units of measurement used in this book particularly in chapters 2 and 6. The method used in producing this work is to present an emerging picture to the general reader. To further that end units of measurement have been used which it is hoped will accomplish that objective. The inconsistent use of different units has been influenced by the fact that tracing the closing of the gap between the philosophy of science and the Christian religion, which is taking place in this century, chapters 5 to 8 inclusive consist of reviews of books written by scientific authors over the period from 1938 to 1981. During that time, particularly in the English speaking world, there has been a movement towards general adoption of the metric system. However, the speed of the movement has varied considerably from country to country, particularly in measurements of distance and mass.

The author, faced with the problem of inconsistencies amongst the reading audience to which the book is addressed, has tried to be true to his aim of presenting an overall picture rather than anything approaching text book accuracy; hence the wide use of approximations and variant units of measurement. These are, as far as possible, consistent with the units used in the books which have been chosen for review.

Very important work establishing international standard units of measurement has recently been done by our physicists and chemists in creating an "International System of Units", commonly referred to as "S.I.". This system is based on the metre (m) as the unit of length, the kilogramme (kg) as the unit of mass, the second (s) as the unit of time, the ampere (A) as the unit of electric current, the Kelvin (K) as the unit of temperature, the mole (mol) as the amount of substance and the candela (cd) as the unit of luminous intensity. The relationship between the units is obtained by simple multiplication and division. For example the S.I. unit of energy, the Joule, is defined in terms of base units as $kg\ m^2\ s^{-2}$.

To enable comparisons to be made, a table is given at the end of the book relating the principal units given in the text to their S.I. equivalents.

Again, in the interests of presenting an uncomplicated picture, speeds, for example of sound, have been given in their generally understood medium, in this case through dry air at a temperature of 25 °C.

In chapter 2 we have presented a view of the concept of "eternity". Eternity is a theological mystery which has been and is the centre of philosophical and theological discussion. As the notion is outside mortal experience, it raises a mystery in God which we cannot fully understand. It is inevitable therefore, that we use pictures and analogies to convey our meaning, and these are never fully definitive. The outline given in chapter 2 is based on the definition of Boethius (*circa* 500 A.D.), later adopted by St. Thomas Aquinas. The critics of this approach are concerned that it can give a view of God as a static point of reference and a non-dynamical concept of eternal life. There is, of course, nothing static about God whose very nature is to create; nor is there any doubt that those of us called to eternal existence with him will participate in eternal activity. This is the excitement we hope for. If the author's presentation creates the idea of inertia in eternity in the reader's mind, he is asked to attribute this to the limits of analogy rather than as a fact presented for acceptance.

Most unusual words used in the text have been defined where they are used, or their meaning has been clarified by the context in which they occur.

In the writing of this book I must acknowledge with thanks unstinted help from so many people that to list them all would be impractical. I must however, record the kindness of Sir Guilford Young, Archbishop of Hobart, who graciously gave me leave to spend the summer of 1979 at Cambridge, to Dr John Wall who not only facilitated my acceptance as a visiting scholar to that University but later gave me valued help in the reading of my manuscripts. My thanks also to Father John Coventry S.J. then Master of St Edmund's House whose hospitality and help I will never forget. Amongst my Tasmanian friends especial thanks go to Dr Laurie Dunn and Dr Penny McCartney. This short list would not be complete without acknowledgement of the loyal and patient co-operation of Marjory Mitchell for the great work she did in typing, re-typing and correcting this work and last but not least warm thanks to Professor Tom Torrance of Edinburgh for his consistent and kindly encouragement.

CHAPTER I

THEOLOGY AND SCIENCE

CHRISTIAN theology stems from a belief in God, an eternal, infinite, omnipotent being existing without reliance on any preceding cause — the Creator of all that is, seen and unseen. From this Creator all things have their being but unlike God everything else depends on God for its creation and sustenance. Amongst the immense numbers of God's created beings, there exists on the Earth (which is a relatively tiny sphere in the universe) an animal called "man" — a sexual creature requiring a male and female component to establish his completeness and to enable him to reproduce.

This creature possesses an animal body combined with an element that cannot be seen, measured or investigated by any known scientific method. It is referred to in various terms such as soul, spirit, mind, self and so on. It interacts with man's remarkable brain. It can accept messages from the brain, reflect on them, accept them, reject them or modify them. It is an entity in itself: it has no component parts; so it is obviously indestructible and immortal.

Destruction as we understand it occurs when the order or nature of the components of anything is varied to the extent that the thing we are examining no longer presents to us those characteristics by which we know it and name it. If something has only one invariable component it must be indestructible or immortal. Every human being's soul or mind is different. We refer to this difference as the "character" of the person concerned. Theology delves into the relationship between God and mankind and all that flows from the fact that such a relationship exists. It is very interested in the ultimate explanation of things and their origins. Modern science looks at reality in another way. Up to the era of Copernicus, Galileo, Descartes and Newton (late 16th to early 18th centuries) science, theology and philosophy were inter-connected disciplines, and harmony and unity were sought, even insisted upon, in Western academic circles. All forms of knowledge were subordinated to theology, which was of course Christian in origin. Copernicus, Galileo, Descartes, Newton and others moved right away from this method in their scientific work and concentrated on accurate descriptions and measurements of things and reactions that they could observe and measure. They were not really interested in ultimate explanations. Newton was a genius in mathematics and his works on light, colour, mechanics and gravity are still basic in modern science.

His *Principia Mathematica* placed him amongst the greatest geniuses the human race has produced. Newton's research laid the foundations of the empirical method of scientific investigation and he taught us how to calculate with workable accuracy the results of experiments.

For practical purposes the design of our machines and engineering works and construction, knowledge of our solar system, and most other sciences today rest on Newton's principles. At this time in the development of human thinking, scientific attention was directed to things, their properties, reactions and uses. The question of their ultimate origins was eclipsed by the excitement of putting knowledge to practical use. This attitude was greatly stimulated by the fact that new applications and machines that would perform tasks hitherto deemed impossible often rewarded the inventor with quick acquisition of enormous wealth and power. Interestingly enough Copernicus, Galileo, Descartes and Newton were all theists (they believed in God), but it is highly probable that each of them would attempt to define the word God in different terms.

From the early nineteenth century (starting from 1801) theology and science for practical purposes drifted apart. The frenetic pace of scientific discovery, coupled with the ultra-conservatism of theologians at that time, resulted in a virtual dichotomy. Neither side understood the other and the desire for communication waned. In this atmosphere the mere idea that either side needed the other was considered untenable.

Newton had expressly stated that science and religion were two entirely separate phenomena and this idea was generally accepted by both sides. A sort of *decree nisi* was tacitly accepted between science and religion.

This *decree nisi* appeared to become "absolute" with the emergence, writings and theories of Charles Robert Darwin (1809-1882).

Darwin was born a wealthy man but never enjoyed good health. When he was 16 he was sent to the University of Edinburgh to study medicine. As he disliked these studies his parents sent him to Cambridge in 1828 to train for the Anglican ministry.

He did not obtain a degree but became very interested in science, particularly natural history. On leaving Cambridge he obtained an appointment as naturalist on a ship called the "Beagle" which was employed in mapping activities off the South American coastline. He had a brilliant speculative mind and extraordinary powers of observation and discernment. His work on the islands of Galapagos and Tierra del Fuego caused him to question the assumption his Christian training had given him that God had created every creature in a direct act and complete with its own distinguishing characteristics.

He noticed and recorded with accuracy the unique changes in species of birds and reptiles which made them ideally suited to the environments in which they lived. From Darwin's work supported by distinguished contemporaries and predecessors (going back at least as far as St. Augustine) "The Theory of Evolution" came into prominence. More will be said of this in a later chapter when we consider the phenomenon of man. In its extreme form the Theory of Evolution does away with the necessity for a Creator altogether. It proposes that life developed from the chemistry of the Earth by chance and in assuming various forms, from simple living cells through sea weeds, land plants, invertebrates, fishes, reptiles, birds, animals, mammals, primates, hominids and finally *homo sapiens* (mankind as we know it now). Development occurred through "survival of the fittest" and natural progressive adaptation to the environment. "Natural Selection" it was called. An atmosphere developed in which man could look to science for an explanation of the origin and purpose of all things including himself. This was the great period of "*A*-theism" which persists strongly to this day. Established Christianity and established science in that era found themselves irreconcilably opposed.

Both sides became intolerant of each other, dialogue broke down and views were expressed with vehemence and bitterness. The "de-cree nisi" between Religion and Science appeared to become "absolute". Let us remember that over half the world's population today lives in countries where religion is either proscribed or its practice severely inhibited. Out of the heat of battle a state of mind which we will now refer to as "fundamentalism" grew in both camps — a state of mind where certain ideas (fundamentals) are held in a kind of obstinate certitude; and logical discussion and argument about them are not tolerated. Worse still, both sides seemed to distort, bend or ignore any evidence which proved inimical to their "fundamental" tenets. This strange, illogical and depressing mental attitude persists among numbers of theologians and of atheistic scientists today. In countries ruled by Marxist governments the minds of the people are to a great extent locked in to this inhuman attitude.

It must be remembered that both theology and science have the same ultimate and common goal, the search for truth. The dullest and most counter-productive periods both in the history of Christianity and the history of science have always been when free discussion has been inhibited. On the contrary, advances always occur when free rein has been given to Isaiah's principle: "State your case and bring your proofs". Never in the history of mankind has there been a greater need for open mindedness and exchange of ideas than at this period when our knowledge of things and their causes is expanding at a pace analogous to an explosion. In this climate science needs theology and theology certainly needs science.

The question can be raised as to whether theology is in itself competent to relate to science. Theology's answer to this is that it is *per se* a science — the Queen of sciences. It depends on a presumption of the existence of God and the validity of what it refers to as "revelation". Modern theology would include scientific discoveries as a form of revelation but the Christian idea of "revelation" goes a lot further than a restriction to anything empirical science can offer. The "God problem" and related concepts will be dealt with in the next chapter.

Right at the outset let it be said that one of the main problems in communication between the scientist and the theologian is that of language. Our human thought-patterns and words have naturally evolved out of the situation in which we live. Our human lives are fulfilled in a world where everything has a beginning, a duration and an end. When we try to understand such concepts as eternity, infinity, omnipotence and so on we have problems. While mathematics has crossed some bridges in this area many people are not able to use the mathematical approach. The reader must realise that as soon as we find ourselves considering concepts outside time and space our language becomes analogical, picture language, and falls short of absolute precision. In the following chapters use has been made of diagrams and analogies to try to give a reasonable "picture" of the concepts under discussion. Some of the ideas fall into the category of what the theologian refers to as "mystery". These situations occur when it becomes obvious that the idea concerned can be entertained legitimately but its ultimate explanation lies clearly beyond the reach of a human brain. The prime and obvious example is God. In this area both the Bible and the teaching church have shown useful and remarkable consistency in speaking ordinary human language; not that either ignore the value of stories and pictures as Christ used in his parables and men like Milton, Dante, Bunyan (*The Pilgrim's Progress*) have used as teaching aids in later times.

Sometimes to get an idea across, both the Bible and the Church have talked about God as though he were human. This device theologians call "anthropomorphism". As a general rule it is wise to accept that "analogy" is the device used immediately we leave the sphere of everyday worldly experience.

As the very existence of theology depends on acceptance of the validity and value of revelation it poses a challenge first of all to the Christian to enable him in any company to argue for its reasonableness. It simultaneously poses an even greater challenge to the non-Christian, for if it is a valid fountain of truth emanating from the Creator it is basically and ultimately the source of all knowledge. Unless the Christian is able to see the confirmed validity of scientific laws and discoveries as part of the *corpus* of revealed truth he too will find himself in trouble. The fundamentalist Christian will tell us that God revealed himself in Christ and no further revelation is necessary. At the same time he must concede that scripture tells us Jesus Christ was a man like us in all things but sin. Now a human body like any material is fundamentally of atomic/ molecular structure; so surely for a study of this aspect of Christ's nature we may turn to the biologist, the chemist, the physicist who are qualified to teach us the wonders of modern scientific discovery in these and associated sciences.

That is, of course, if our honest approach is to ascertain the truth. Again we cannot cut off communication between God and his creation. It is easier to admit this since Einstein broke down any separation of geometry and physics, thus paving the way for the theoretical and empirical components of knowledge to operate together inseparably.

It seems absurd to think of God as the Creator of the universe, including that highly intelligent, inquisitive creature man, and then standing aloof from his creature to let him flounder in ignorance. Conversely if as the psalmist says "the heavens declare the glory of God", then surely this is sufficient motivation for the study of astronomy.

Naturally the best source of knowledge in this field is a qualified astronomer.

It is useless quoting scripture as a guide to an atheistic fundamentalist scientist but there is a passage in St. John's Gospel which can be tossed into the ring between the fundamentalist Christian and the fundamentalist scientist and it is where Christ says: "But when the Spirit of Truth comes he will lead you to the complete truth".

This places a sort of prophetic halo round the genuine scientist who honestly and without preconceptions is seeking the truth about things. It also poses the question to the scientist: "Whence this driving force, this vision, this peak of intelligence in certain men from time to time, and above all how does one explain the steady orderly development of scientific thinking?" Plato, Aristotle and the Greeks paved the way for Aquinas and the scholastics, who with their icy logic opened the way for deductive syllogistic reasoning in our age.

Copernicus and Galileo stimulated Newton who in turn fired the mind of Einstein. Teilhard de Chardin brings out this point dramatically in his book *The Phenomenon of Man* where his movement from geosphere to biosphere to noosphere has a prophetic ring about it. The acceptance of a "revealing God" also opens up the idea of our talking to him, as a created intelligence communicating with the Creator of intelligence.

Many of the ideas hinted at so far will hopefully be given deeper meaning in subsequent chapters.

Here however it is necessary to insert a word of warning. In these days of expanding knowledge in science and of remarkable developments in theological thinking one must avoid being too dogmatic in either field.

By comparison with the total field of Christian thinking the area of dogma is quite small; similarly it is noticeable that really eminent scientists are equally slow to designate discoveries as involving immutable laws.

It could be proposed as a principle that the greater the competence of either theologian or scientist so is his open-mindedness.

CHAPTER 2

CLEARING TERMS AND CONCEPTS

Eternity

THIS chapter is an attempt to clarify some important concepts as simply as possible in a way that may prove acceptable to both theologian and mathematician.

Every effort has been made to avoid the "trade language" of either discipline. The hazards of this approach include what might appear to one party to be unnecessary wordiness or perhaps to the other, over-simplification.

The last line of the Nicene Creed, "We believe in the life of the world to come", is for the individual Christian the most exciting proposition in the Creed.

We humans can be certain of only one thing, and that is that each and every one of us is going to die. As no one can die when he is dead, death is the last and final experience of every mortal life. If we consider death to be an utter and final dissolution of all we are or hope to be it is certainly a terrifying prospect. It is understandable that people who think this way do not want to think or talk about death.

For them it is a final and complete catastrophe.

For a Christian who believes in "the life of the world to come" the outlook is entirely different, for in this case death is not an end but a beginning. The interesting fact is that most Christians also seem to think very little about death and certainly seldom talk about it.

It is suggested that this is because few of us seem to have any clear ideas of what we mean by the concept of eternal life. Let us then try to generate a working idea of this. First of all it is absolutely essential to clear our minds of a generally held misconception that the "life of the world to come" — eternity — means a long time. Eternity has nothing to do with what we think of as time (or space either for that matter). Eternity means another level of existence outside the confines of space and time as we know them.

The great difficulty in trying to elucidate a concept like eternity lies in the fact that all our language and thought-patterns are generated from our experience in our mortal existence where everything, including life itself, has a beginning, a duration and an end.

Pre-Christian thinkers like Plato and Aristotle tried to define the idea. To Plato there were certain forms which simply *are* rather than were or will be. Aristotle considered eternity as the perfect all-at-once existence of God. Plotinus came nearer to later accepted definitions when he described eternity as the unchanging life of Intellect possessing all things, all at once in the present. St Augustine further expanded the view: because God is his own existence he is immutable and eternal. Hence eternity is the total presentness of the one immutable being. About the year 520 Boethius wrote his simple classic definition: "Eternity is the perfect possession of interminable life held wholly all at once."

These are hard concepts to understand; so let us use analogy to illustrate some aspects of their meanings. Look at the drawing on page 41.

Let us suppose you were standing with a friend at a street corner surrounded by tall buildings, the one behind you being the tallest of them all. Up a side street invisible to you, a procession of floats is being marshalled to represent all the major events of your friend's existence. Your view is limited by the surrounding buildings and the route of the procession so that you can see only a few metres of the road. The procession, however, is some kilometres long. At five past one the first float comes into your field of vision, and you make a note in a book: Birth 1.05 p.m. The second float follows five minutes later and you write down Baptism: 1.10 p.m. At 1.15 you note first day at school; and so on until your book reads: 3.00 p.m. death. Then follow the after-death experience expected by a Christian who dies in a state of friendship with God, one who has not by unrequited word or deed placed himself at enmity with the Heavenly Father. These experiences might be represented by floats picturing individual judgement at 3.05 p.m. followed at 3.10 p.m. by an experience of purification known as purgatory.

Death is an intermediate state leading from mortal life to eternal life. Both personal judgement and purgatorial experience are best thought of as part of this process.

At 3.15 p.m. a float goes by, representing eternal happiness or as St Paul describes it seeing God "face to face", until at 4 p.m. a float is seen representing bodily resurrection.

At this point you would be able to declare that between the tableaux of your friend's death at 3 p.m. and his resurrection at 4 p.m. an hour had passed when he existed in various situations without a body. Let us now suppose that your friend who had been standing beside you, immediately he saw the float representing his death come into view, went into the very tall building outside of which you were standing and took the elevator to the roof-garden; from this vantage point he could look down on the whole procession. Ahead of you he could clearly see the Birth, Baptism and other "pre-death" floats and equally he could see not only the floats representing his death but also those representing his resurrection and beyond. The result of this would be that simultaneously and equally present in his consciousness would be his birth as a man, and his resurrection as a man; so in *his* view of all the events, he would always be conscious of his existence as a man. The floats between his death and resurrection would merely be experiences in the total consciousness of his continued humanity-body/soul. His view, as distinct from yours, as you still stood at the street corner would be caused by a different level of being. In the analogy he could be 200 metres higher than you.

Inevitably the use of analogy has its limitations, but what we want to emphasise is the legitimate difference in the view of the same reality as seen from different levels. You get quite a different impression of any city standing on the top of a mountain overlooking it from what you get in any square or park in the city confines. In both cases what you see is the city. If I asked you as you stand at the street corner in a limited time/space view of the procession, "What did you see at 3 p.m.?" you would rightly reply, "the death float". If however the same question, "What did you see at 3 p.m.?" were asked of your friend he would reply with equal truth, "The sum total of experiences of my life wholly all at once." The definition of Boethius would apply.

Now let us look a little closer at the implications of this picture. If, in eternity, there is no past or future, we find ourselves existing in an eternal "now". Meditation on this thought can produce very beautiful pictures in the context of Christianity. For the Christian who dies truly sorry for his sins we know that his transgressions are blotted out of existence by the saving power of Christ who is the remedy for them. So our experience — our procession — can consist of the beautiful and the good things of our lives. This thinking leads us to one most important conclusion that in eternity my individuality consists to a great extent of the sum total of my experiences; your individuality is largely distinguished by yours. Now each Christian who dies will share with Our Lord the wonder of the resurrection of the body. This fact becomes part of all of us, so that in eternity each of us will, living in the eternal present, be just as fully aware of his resurrection as he is of his death. In other words, you and I will always know ourselves as men and women. While those of us who mourn a departed brother or sister, see a lifeless body and from that fact assume a disembodiment of the soul, this is not the *eternal* truth, for the departed person is instantly aware of his resurrection, of complete manhood and womanhood. This hope is well founded in Scripture. Our Lord himself says in Luke 20:35, "Those who are judged worthy of a place in the other world in the resurrection . . . can no longer die, for . . . being children of the resurrection they are sons of God. . . . Now he is the God not of the dead but of the living; for to him all *men* are in fact alive". St. Paul in his first letter to the Corinthians says (Cor. 15:4), "It is the same with the resurrection of the dead, the thing that is sown is perishable but what is raised is imperishable . . . when it is sown, it embodies the soul; when it is raised it embraces the spirit." In St. Paul's second letter to the Corinthians in the *Good News Bible* we have a translation reading (2 Cor. 5:2), "And now we sigh so great is our desire that our home which comes from heaven should be put on over us: by being clothed with it *we shall not be without a body*." Again if my individuality is shaped by the sum total of my experiences and if you have been kind and good to me; if during my life and after my death you pray for me; then these events become part of my total experience ever vividly present in an eternal now. These events are then recorded as floats in my procession. You actually become part of *me*, and I have the same opportunity to become part of you — to enter into your total experience. Here is a dimension of the doctrine of the "Communion of Saints" we seldom hear mentioned. Whatever experiences may fall to me, what a glorious consolation will be the prayers and concern which my friends contribute to become part of my eternal experience, part of me. St. Paul expresses this well when, writing to the Romans (14:8), he says, "If we live we live for the Lord; if we die we die for the Lord . . . so that he might be Lord both of the dead and of the living."

When we start to talk about eternity it is necessary to stress that the concept has a different meaning for the Christian than it would have for anyone outside the Christian faith. Full initiation into the Christian Church is a new birth, or rather a new conception, of a creature vitalised anew by being given a germinal share in the life of the risen Christ, which is, of course, the life of God. We become actually, not figuratively, sons and daughters of God. Union with Christ becomes the most important float in our whole procession. Communion with him in the Eucharist helps the human embryo to grow in the womb of Mother Church until in the Creator's wisdom the child of God is ready to break through the placenta of the time/

space confines into the reality and wonder of the eternal NOW. One hates to contemplate the situation, which is of course possible, where the individual's encounter with Christ in this life results in that person's deliberate and full rejection of the Saviour. This float of course becomes part of the eternal experience, part of the person who makes the rejection.

It is hard for us to realise that sin need never have intruded into human experience. We are so used to living with it. God gave mankind freedom of choice for one purpose only; that his creature might have the ability to love in the divine sense, which is to give oneself completely to the object of one's affection. Let us suppose that instead of using his God-given gift of freedom to grab, to take, to sin, man *had* used it to love — to give himself wholly to the service of good with complete integrity and utter dedication. In that case a miracle would follow; he would find himself in a state of complete repose, he would have achieved a state of perfect being. Perfection is an absolute — no beginning, no development, no end, a *perpetual now*, in other words, ETERNITY.

One might conjecture some experience such as this as being what might have happened but for the intrusion of death, as the wages of sin, into human experience. Nevertheless, when one considers Christian death, St. Paul's words dramatically emphasise the effect of Christ's salvific action: "Death, where is your sting? Grave where is your victory?" (1 Cor. 15:55). One can see that if there existed a being whose whole purpose was absolute goodness and at the same time this being were as powerful as he were good obviously there could be no change or striving in such an existence. Such a being there is — it is God. Eternity then, is God's mode of existence, so here Christianity becomes all important because obviously our sharing in eternity depends on our relationship with God. If, at our death, we have retained the Father/son, Father/daughter relationship established at Baptism we enter our eternity at the level of members of the Divine Family — members of the Mystical Body of Christ. Our process of divinisation, however, does not entail our absorption into the Godhead in a sort of Pantheism but comes about through the planned destiny God has for each of his children individually.

Only God is truly eternal, God is pure act. He has neither beginning nor end. Our eternity does not approach this level because we have a beginning in time. Our death is a transition. The Scholastic philosophers call our experience of entering eternal existence "aeviternity". It follows from God's perfect love for each and every one of his children and the child's love for the Father purified through grace. Thinking on these lines, "time" becomes short-lived, ephemeral. Eternity becomes the centre of all things. From it all things proceed, or to it all things return. Time, to a human being, is a convenient idea applicable to a finite and material condition — it relates to the speed of the Earth's revolution on its North–South axis and to its circuit around the sun. Imagine yourself on a spaceship well out into our solar system. There would be no day or night; merely the spectacle of a number of spheres revolving and moving round our sun at different speeds. The recordings of your wrist-watch would have no relationship at all to the position in which you found yourself.

It would be much easier for us to assume that only the "spirit" component of man moves into eternity, but the Church has always rejected this idea throughout her history. Christ rose from the dead as a true, complete man, is that man now, and will be throughout eternity, and all Christian hope rests on that fact. The fact of man's resurrection, body/soul complete, is not a scandal but a dramatic pointer to God's purpose in creation. From the soil of this earth has evolved under God's creative guidance and will, a creature, "the phenomenon of man", chemically a sort of conglomerate rock, some might say, a mud pie, composed entirely of the stuff of the earth. From the human point of view, when he dies every milligram of his body resolves into the dust of the earth. Yet this creature has freedom; he is capable of the divine creative power of

love. God is love: so immediately we have a relationship —
a common "denominator", as it were with the Creator.
This relationship moved to another plane at the first
Christmas when God became incarnate in Jesus Christ
who was born as we are, except for sin, and who grew up,
worked, taught, suffered and died as we do. The difference
between Jesus Christ and mankind generally is that in his
human life in time and space he obeyed God's commandments always. He made God's Will his will. In him the
"love" relationship was perfect to the extent that the
mutual love between God the Father and Jesus Christ
could not be broken by death, but, by his death and
resurrection Our Lord assumed humanity into the Divine
Eternity. His humanity required no change because it
was and is perfect. It is eternal. That is why the Athanasian Creed refers to Christ as eternally begotten of the
Father.

Against this background, what then are we to think of
death? As already stated it is certainly not an end because
the last thing is not death but life. As at death we each
become eternally, to a great extent, the sum total of all our
individual experiences, death gives man the opportunity of
posing his first completely personal act. As Ladislaus
Boros states in his book *The Moment of Truth*, "death is
therefore by reason of its very being for any man, the
moment above all others, for the awakening of consciousness, for freedom, for the encounter with God, for the final
decision about his eternal destiny". Our entrance into
Heaven does not affect our personality except in a positive
and constructive sense. Freed from the distortions and
inhibitions caused by sin, each of us is destined to become
completely that unique self God wishes him to be. As cells
in the human body, though basically the same in structure,
all perform actions peculiar to their position and purpose
in the body, so we, as cells in the Mystical Body of Christ,
in the Church Triumphant situation, will be called upon to
exercise in fullness our complete predesigned potentiality.
Each of us will have our duty and responsibility working in
complete harmony with the "cells" around us for our

mutual good and the health of the whole body. The nature of God is to create — mankind even on earth is called to *pro*create. In Heaven with that reserve of Divine Life and power given us at Baptism and realised in our assumption into Heaven doubtless we will, as members of the "Body" which has Christ as its head, immediately become involved in God's creative work. What this will be we do not know. I think St. Paul was given an insight into this condition when he said in 2 Cor. 12:2 "I know a man in Christ who fourteen years ago was caught up . . . into paradise and heard things which must not and cannot be put into human language", and again in 1 Cor. 2:9 where St. Paul quotes as his teaching "the things that no eye has seen and no ear has heard, things beyond the mind of man, all that God has prepared for those who love him".

Infinity

This word is derived from the two Latin words, "in" meaning not and "finis" meaning end, boundary or termination. Just as thinking of eternity as a long time can get us into all sorts of difficulties, so thinking of infinity as a long line can also lead to complete confusion because no matter how long a line is, one can always add a further length to it or "rub out" a determined length. Infinity really means immeasurable, not something big or small, but simply beyond the scope of measurement. Concepts like eternity and infinity are ultimately aspects of the nature of God. St. Paul reminds us that all we can hope for is "to see through a darkened glass". A helpful way to assist us in comprehension of "infinity" is to look westward on a dark clear night and ask what lies beyond the star on the horizon; then turning eastward perform the same exercise. Let us go to the extreme limits of size using Einstein's famous equation $E = mc^2$ (E being energy, m being mass or weight and c being the speed of light, 186,000 miles per second). Now if we make m the mass of the Cosmos we still have not reached infinity because although we will get an immensely large value for E it is still at least theoretically measurable. The universe cannot be infinite.

Now if we stick to our definition of infinity as beyond the scope of measurement we are really thinking of a state of "perfection", we are thinking of a concept to which nothing can be added and from which anything can be taken away while still leaving the concept valid. Of course the idea could be posited also of a void because nothing can be added to a void or it simply ceases to exist as such, and nothing can be taken away from a void because there is nothing to take. The question then arises as to whether there is such a state as a void.

If one believes in God the word infinite can be understood because God is omnipotent, eternal, infinite and perfect. Nothing can be added to or taken away from God. The non-believer — the a-theist must have considerable problems with the term infinity. Now let us consider the problem of the concept "void". Immediately we have to face the age-old philosophical question, "Why Existence, why not nothing?" Well we are sure we exist or we could not be examining this problem, for as Descartes expressed it *"Cogito ergo sum"*. Immediately we admit existence we rule out the validity of the idea "void", except in a relative sense. We must be careful not to confuse the idea of "space" with that of "void". Space implies that at least two things exist and it pertains to the idea of the distance between them. Void on the other hand means the absence of all things. It is really a metaphysical term. From this we conclude that infinity denotes a "perfection"; it cannot mean a void or "imperfection" simply because the concept "void" is meaningless in the absolute sense.

The believer has no worries about the fact of his own existence because he attributes it and indeed the existence of everything that is seen and unseen to God. Thinking along these lines many men have come to the conclusion that God consists of all that is. This idea is called Pantheism, but developing our line of thought as we have expressed it Pantheism is an obvious illusion because it means that we can add to or subtract from God as more or less things come into being or alternatively cease to be. We can also alter the character or "shape" of God by our own activity or thinking. If we can add to, subtract from, or alter God, then he ceases to be infinite or perfect. This brings us to a most important conclusion that is, that all things must be created by God *ex nihilo*. They can have no origin except from God who created them from nothing, for if God created them "out of himself" he diminishes himself and ceases to be infinite and perfect. In dealing with the concepts of eternity and infinity we are faced with a great difficulty in expression because all human language develops from our existence in time and space. Now we can't lock God in a box consisting of time/space co-ordinates nor can we lock *our minds* exclusively into physical problems. Our senses and our brain can feed all sorts of information to our mind but the "phenomenon of man" is not completely limited by his sense-experience; he can speculate, he can conceive abstract ideas and within his limitations, look out into the eternal and infinite. As the writer of Genesis so perfectly expresses it, "he is made in the image and likeness of God". Man can conceive in his "mind" a level of existence superior to his, where the terms "eternity" and "infinity" have real meaning. It is not suggested for a moment that we can by our unaided efforts know and "see" God. This, however, does not prevent God from revealing himself to us in a way we can understand, and this is exactly what he has done, not by compelling us to grope and search with our limited powers to try to find him but by himself becoming man, being born among us, living with us, dying for us and rising from the dead. The Incarnation of the Son of God in time/space limitations, his living in this constricted area, and above all his resurrection from his human death and his ascension into heaven and into eternity have revealed in a dramatic and clear way the purpose of God in creating man, and his unsurpassable love for his creature. In mankind we find the link between God's material and spiritual creations. The miracle is that man is not destined to become pure spirit. As Christ demonstrated by his resurrection, he retained a recognisable human body, but, in contradiction to his experiences when he lived among us as "a man like us in all things but sin" his resurrected person possessed spiritual characteristics not obvious before his crucifixion (See Luke 24:31, 36, 37, 51). The significance of all this is summarised in the Athanasian Creed. Speaking of the divine and human natures found in the one person of Christ the Creed goes on to say: "He is one indeed not by the conversion of the Divine into flesh, but by the assumption of humanity into God."

Love

Primarily because this work is written in English and because we have already established "love" as the relationship between God and man, it is imperative to clear our thinking about the meaning of this crucial term. The history of Western European philosophy has its origin in the pre-Christian Greeks whose thinking still has a considerable impact on current philosophical debate. The New Testament of our Bible was also written in Greek. Generally speaking the English language is extremely rich in giving us alternative words to describe a concept with all needed nuances. However in the "love" area it is barren. The Greeks have at least four words which when translated into English are usually rendered by the word "love". *Eros* for instance expresses the natural physical love of a lad for a lass (and vice versa!) with a heavy emphasis on sexuality. That great saint and doctor of the Church Gregory Nazianzus defined *eros* with starkly amusing honesty as "that hot and unendurable desire". Moving up the scale to higher concepts we meet the word *stergein* which is apt to describe that unique and lovely relationship evident, for instance, in a good family — the loyalty, trust and affection between brothers, sisters and parents. It can be used of course to describe the same idea between people who are not necessarily blood relatives. It can be used of a benign and respected ruler. Then there is *philia* a lovely warm word applicable to the affection developing from a deep and lasting friendship. At the top of the scale we find the word *agape*. The reader will have noticed that in the three words considered so far; *eros, stergein,* and *philia* emotion of some sort or other occupies a prominent place in the full understanding of each word, as it does, no doubt, in our English word "Love". *Agape* transcends these notions and indicates more a state of mind, an exercise of the will. It indicates a situation where the lover is prepared to forego all his "rights" if by so doing he can benefit the object of his affection. He, as it were, absorbs the beloved into his own being so his rights become the property of the beloved. It is in this sense St. John tells us "God is Love": God is *Agape*. In justice God is not obliged to give us anything, even our existence, yet he has given us everything, everything we have, even to the extent of giving us the life of his only begotten son as a propitiation for our sins. This is *agape*. This is what we mean in Christian theology when we use the term love. In simple terms "loving" in the Christian sense always embraces the notion of "giving" as against "taking" or "grabbing" and involves the exercise of the will as predominant over our affective, intelligent and imaginative abilities. Christ's commands to "love your enemies", "bless those who curse you" require the exercise of love at the full *agape* level.

Relativity

It is quite impossible to comprehend the understanding of the universe presented to us by contemporary physicists, mathematicians and astronomers without some understanding of the work of a genius of this century, Albert Einstein, and his brilliant disciples and contemporaries; men like Planck, De Broglie, Bohr, Schrödinger, Dirac, Heisenberg and others. The difficulty with the "Theory of Relativity" is not so much that it is hard to follow the reasoning nor for that matter the expression in mathematics of its basic tenets. The problem is rather one of accepting the mind-boggling revelations which follow logically from the theory.

It is beyond the scope of this book to present an elementary study of relativity. However there are readily available a number of books written for the layman which provide a very interesting and easily understood introduction to the subject. An excellent example is *Relativity for the Layman* by James A. Coleman (Penguin 1981). This book as originally published has the recommendation of Einstein himself. Any modern theologian needs it or some equivalent in his library. For the readers with some mathematical ability the subject is presented at a deeper yet quite lucid level in *Relativity: The Theory and its Philosophy* by Roger B. Angel (Pergamon, 1980). The mathematical section is developed excellently by a first class teacher and while one may wish to argue or even differ in the philosophical area, to do so is quite an exercise, but one well worth trying. This book is not recommended to a reader who has not had some training in both disciplines, mathematics and philosophy. To people keen to know more about this highly relevant subject a good idea might be to tackle Coleman first and then try Angel. The prelude to Einstein's work was the scientific interest taken in the phenomena of sound and light. For instance it was pretty obvious that lightning caused thunder, and that being so, it was observable, without the aid of instruments, that a time lag occurred between the lightning flash and the sound of the thunder. In cases where to the interested observer there was no time lag there was also simultaneously no interested observer as he would be killed by the lightning flash — for him at least there was no further problem. In the early seventeenth century a Frenchman named Mersenne, using intruments and methods which today would be considered primitive, assessed the speed of sound at 700 miles per hour. Today, and using much more elaborate techniques, we use a figure of approximately 770 miles per hour as the speed at which sound travels through the atmosphere. Light posed a much more difficult problem because it obviously travelled at enormous speed. To start with the argument centred upon whether the velocity of light was infinite or measurable. Great minds differed.

Descartes (1596–1650) claimed the velocity of light to be infinite while his equally brilliant contemporary Galileo thought it to be measurable. As a matter of interest Galileo tried to establish the speed of light but his methods and instruments were too crude and insensitive to yield consistent or acceptable results. One of Galileo's inventions was the telescope. Late in the seventeenth century a Dutchman, Roemer, using a telescope, measured the periods of the four moons of Jupiter firstly when the Earth's orbit round the sun placed him nearest to Jupiter and then again when the earth in relation to the sun was furthest from Jupiter. The times were different and he rightly assumed that the difference was caused by the variation in the distance light had to travel and from this he calculated by a correct method a speed of light. Unfortunately in his day the mean diameter of the Earth's orbit round the sun was assumed to be 172,000,000 miles. As the correct measurement has since been established as 186,000,000 miles Roemer's result was too low.

Following Roemer's estimate of the velocity of light much attention was devoted to the subject. Conspicuous work was done by James Bradley in 1727 and although his result was not accurate, his method was important as it foreshadowed the idea of relativity. In 1849 Fitzeau used an ingenious mechanical device and from his experiments proposed the speed of light at 194,600 miles per second; which, while about 5% too high was quite remarkable considering the nature of his equipment, which by our standards today would be considered crude. His work was still further confirmation that the speed of light was measurable.

In 1865 a radical discovery was made by James Clerk Maxwell. Clerk Maxwell was working on electric and magnetic experiments. He found he could cause electrical waves to be generated, and that these waves could travel outward into space at a velocity of 186,000 miles per second. Still more important was his identification of light waves as one type of electromagnetic waves. The difference between light waves, radio waves, X-rays, gamma rays and other similar phenomena is attributable to variations in the wave-lengths, or frequencies of the oscillations per second. For practical purposes the speed of all these waves is constant.

In 1926 an American, Michelson, used a refined mechanical method, similar in principle to that used by Fitzeau in 1849 and Foucault in 1850. His system was ingenious and accurate and again confirmed the velocity of light at 186,000 miles per second (300,000 kms approx).

Lucid explanations of the methods used in these experiments are given in Coleman's book already referred to, *Relativity for the Layman*. His explanations accompanied by amusing drawings make easy and interesting reading. The velocity of light strains the abilities of human perception to this day. For example light could travel round the world in about a seventh of a second. The sun is about 93,000,000 miles from the earth. When we see it rise in the morning we are looking at it, as it was about 8 minutes earlier. When we talk about a star it is common practice to express its distance from the Earth in light years, a term which as its name suggests, means the number of years its light takes to reach the Earth. When we look at the nearest star beyond our sun which we call Alpha Centauri, instead of saying it is a mere 24,000,000,000,000 miles away, we say it is approximately four light years from our Earth. This means of course that from observation we cannot say Alpha Centauri still exists; all we know is that it was certainly in position about four years ago.

The next problem to concern the physicist was, how is light transmitted over such enormous distances in space? It was known that sound needs an atmosphere to conduct it, and what our ears pick up are waves or vibrations in the air differing in length and intensity. We cannot transmit sound through a vacuum. As it was accepted that from a relatively short distance from Earth there was no air — simply a vacuum, the question arose, what is it that transmits light waves? As no substance could be detected, scientists invented an hypothetical medium which they called by the dignified title "lumeniferous ether". Having invented it, the ever curious human mind became engrossed in the problem of proving its existence and learning something of its properties. Great minds wrestled with this problem from the beginning of the nineteenth century to 1905 when Albert Einstein made his great "break through".

Having postulated the existence of "ether" the question immediately arose, if ether existed, then all our stars, planets and galaxies must be moving in it. Taking the analogy of a ship's movement through water, science began to look for evidence of "bow waves" or "drifts". More and more sophisticated experiments were made in the search for the proof of the existence of "ether" and for effects it might have on light waves transmitted through it. In 1881 Michelson and Morley used a highly sophisticated method which has attracted the attention of scientists ever since, culminating in work by Townes and Cedaholm in 1960. The results of these experiments verified the conclusion of Michelson and Morley that the ether, if it exists cannot be detected. Far more important than this conclusion, however were the possible explanations put forward from evidence derived from the experiments; one of which was that the velocity of light is independent of the velocity of the source which emitted it; that is, that no matter how fast a source of light is moving towards us or away from us (as long as the source is moving at less than the speed of light) the light still travels towards us at a constant velocity of 186,000 miles per second. All sorts of affirmations, denials and rationalisations were made. It was into this cloud of frustration and confusion that Albert Einstein emerged. His Theory of Relativity not only cleared the confusion but extended the boundaries of human thinking by solving a number of other tantalising problems not in any way connected with the problem of "ether". Einstein and his disciples went further and made predictions which seemed fantastic fifty years ago but which have since introduced the genesis of the atomic age. Realising the limits of his early work Einstein introduced his theory in two parts, calling the first in 1905 the "Special Theory of Relativity". Later after maturity of his thinking he announced the "General Theory of Relativity" in 1916. As already stated this book is not intended as a text book on Relativity, so this presentation will be limited to stating the postulates on which Einstein based his theory and some of the conclusions which follow. For details of the experiments confirming these conclusions please refer to the recommended text books or their equivalents. Simply stated, the Special Theory deals with objects which are moving at constant speeds in relation to each other or perhaps not moving at all. On the other hand the General Theory deals with objects which are accelerating in their speeds or slowing down in relation to each other. The General Theory really covers the entire problem if we think of the Special Theory as dealing only with the situations which occur where the acceleration factor is zero. Einstein proposed that all motion is relative. What do we mean by this? Suppose you were driving your car at 60 miles per hour in an easterly direction on a highway near the equator. A traffic policemen goes by on his motor cycle and gives you the thumbs up sign indicating you are within the law, as the speed limit on that section of the road had been set at 65 miles per hour. There is, out in space directly above you and stationary in relation to the earth, a space ship with an observer looking through a powerful telescope at you and the policeman. As far as he is concerned he sees you travelling at about 1100 miles per hour or the speed of your car plus the speed of the surface of the earth revolving on its own axis. At the same time another car, also driven at 60 miles per hour, is approaching you travelling westward. As far as the observer in the rocket is concerned if he sees you are doing 1100 miles per hour then the other chap is reversing at 980 miles per hour or thereabouts, so he observes your passing the reversing car at 120 miles per hour because when making that observation he is looking at your *cars in relation to each other*. Here we have an observer confidently giving two speeds by making the movement of your car "relative" to his stationary position for one observation and "relative" to the other car for his second assessment.

Einstein's first postulate was "ether cannot be detected". The reasoning is simple. There is certainly no reference point in our universe which is stationary. Every heavenly body we can see is in a state of movement relative to any other body. Now if the "ether" be stationary we get back to our concept of infinity (i.e. immeasurable) because nothing in the way of speed can be added to it or taken away from it. Therefore it comes into the "negative" or "void" view of infinity which is not only immeasurable but is a basically false concept. If we consider the "ether" as moving we have enormous problems because, if it has substance, we could hope to detect "its" influence on things moving through it. We might expect an orbital movement like the Earth's to accelerate when moving with the "ether" and slow down when moving against it. Science has not been able to detect any phenomenon of this nature. We are again left with no alternative but to agree with Einstein: "ether cannot be detected".

Einstein's second postulate was one we have already discussed namely "that the velocity of light is always constant relative to an observer." This postulate has been proved experimentally. Its acceptance has a profound influence on the theology of "light" outlined in the New Testament particularly by St. John. We will deal with that later. The exciting nature of Einstein's work is that it enables us to make predictions in many branches of science and then to verify them by experiment. All the wonders of modern age, like landing men on the moon, launching and directing space rockets, atomic fission and fusion, all were made possible to some extent by Einstein and his disciples.

Now let us just enunciate some of the "hard to believe" but nevertheless true discoveries revealed by application of Einstein's Special Theory postulates.

(a) Whenever one observer is moving with respect to another (whether approaching or separating does not matter) it appears to both observers that everything about the other (his space rocket, for example) has shrunk in the direction of motion. Of course neither observer notices any difference in his own system. The mathematics dealing with this phenomenon are called "Lorentz transformation equations".

(b) There is an increase in mass when velocity has to be considered. If A and B both have a mass of 1000lb and are at rest in relation to each other, and if they start to move in relation to each other, A will find B's mass has increased and vice versa. However, at the same time both A and B, disregarding the movement in relation to the other would maintain their masses at 1000lbs each. The mass increase equation states that when an object is moving in respect to an observer the mass of the object becomes greater; the amount of increase depending on the relative velocity of the object measured by the observer. Note! it is only the mass (weight) that increases; the object will actually appear smaller see (a) above.

(c) If you have found your credibility strained by statements (a) and (b) you will be more astounded by a deduction which logically follows and that is that there is an ascertainable velocity beyond which nothing can go. This follows from para (a) above which gives the principle of contraction occuring as a relative velocity is established. There is a point at which the size of the object contracts to zero and ceases to be measurable and this maximum velocity can be demonstrated mathematically as the speed of light, namely 186,000 miles per second. However if we apply the principle of paragraph (c) we arrive at the result that at the point at which our object ceases to have "size" its mass becomes infinite. By simple reasoning from this we can deduce that no material thing can travel at the speed of light, because if its mass becomes infinite then it would require infinite energy to propel it. Our universe is not infinite and therefore could not provide the necessary energy. All sorts of questions present themselves immediately. Supposing two objects each travelling at a velocity of 0.90c (c = speed of light = 186,000 miles per second) were approaching each other on a collision course: surely you will say the speed of approach will be 1.8c. The answer is no! Their approach speed would be only a little more than .9c and would never equal c.

(d) Now we have reached the stage where we accept that mass of an object increases with its velocity, therefore to continue the propulsion of the accelerating object we require more and more energy as its velocity increases. Now a heavier object has more momentum than a light object travelling at the same speed. It can be shown that the additional energy associated with additional mass is mass times the square of the speed of light. Thinking on these lines Einstein defined everything that has mass in terms of energy, with a simple equation $E = mc^2$ where $E =$ energy, $m =$ mass and $c =$ velocity of light. To illustrate the significance of this I quote an example from Coleman's book. A pound of coal if burned in a fire-place would release energy by chemical action between the coal and the oxygen in the atmosphere to heat a small room for a few minutes. But in fact that pound of coal represents 30,000,000,000,000,000 foot pounds of energy which would be approximately the energy produced by all the power stations in the United States in a month. This hidden energy can be released only by nuclear processes. Regretably interest in these techniques climaxed suddenly in World War II with the result that science gave birth to a monster — the so called "atom bomb".

Writing as a theologian one of the important corollaries to the Special Theory of Relativity is the Time Dilation effect caused by two observers A and B moving at a constant velocity in relation to each other. In this situation it appears to each observer that the other's time processes are slowed down. The equation:

$$t' = t\sqrt{1 - \frac{v^2}{c^2}}$$

gives the result where $t' =$ the time observer A reads for observer B's clock, t is the time A reads on his own clock, v = relative velocity and c the speed of light. This supports our findings earlier in this chapter when we were considering Eternity as another and higher level of existence outside the restrictions of time as we know it as earth bound mortals. Theological speculation runs as follows: Christ is the Light of the World: buried in Christ at Baptism the Christian becomes a member of his Mystical Body. At death when the mortal body ceases to exist in time the person takes on the dimension of light. Now if we assume the velocity of light for v in our equation the value of the equation disappears completely. In other words we, then "Children of the Light and of the Day", enter a timeless situation or eternity. This is of course on its own, pure speculative analogy but married to St. John's theology of light it becomes very significant. From the days of Newton, and even before, time has been tacitly and sometimes explicitly assumed as a universal constant. Relativity tells us time is not an absolute nor a constant in the universal application of the term but the velocity of light is. It is in this area shall we say of "time versus light" that the trouble causing divorce between theology and science began. As soon as we give a meaning to time and its corollary space, which contains a nuance of constants, absolutes or universals, we really become mentally and spiritually locked into a small segment of known reality which we call our solar system. In the mathematics of this century we are constrained to calculate in four dimensions, for length, breadth, height and *time*. To deal with the four dimensional problem a new branch of mathematics evolved called the "tensor calculus". This explanation accounts for the now common usage of terms like space/time and space-time continuum. It is interesting to note that the slowing down of time in relation to velocity overflows into biology; in fact, into every aspect of existence. Coleman gives an example of several men making a trip in a space ship travelling close to the velocity of light to a star 33 light years away. Immediately they land on the star they take off again to Earth at the same speed arriving back according to their wives and families about 66 years after they left. As far as the men on the space ship are concerned they will have the experience of being away for a short time and return to find some old ladies in their late eighties claiming to be their wives!! Worse still, their babies whom they kissed goodbye only a day or so ago are now 66 years old and doubtless have children and grand-children of their own, whereas the great grandfathers are hale and hearty young men! As stated earlier Einstein's proofs and subsequent experiments are easy to follow but immensely difficult to accept. However, that is how reality exists. How necessary it is to study the subject. The reader is again referred to the recommended textbooks. These not only expand on the ideas expressed above but give lucid descriptions of the ingenious experiments carried out to test and prove the assumptions. Theology must be expres-sed in terms relevant to the scientific knowledge of the era in which we live. There is a lot of work for theologians to do!

This little essay on Relativity is far from the complete picture. It is written merely to demonstrate the "hard to believe" facts of existence in our universe and to point up the urgency of the need for our theologians to grasp and grapple with those problems. It is also written to support the plea already made in this book to keep our minds open. The days when we could adopt a somnolent attitude of complete security, knowing all the answers are lost and gone forever — and good riddance to them.

One question which arises immediately is whether Newton's mathematics and all the physics and math-ematics that have flowed from that source are "wrong"? The answer is yes: but in nearly all applied physics and mechanics that we use in everyday life the dimensions of mass, speed and so on are in a range where the quantum of the error involved is so miniscule that it is of no practical importance. However in our researches into micro-physics and macro-physics we deal with masses so minute on one hand, and so enormous on the other hand, that the new mechanics, post Einstein become essential in these areas; hence the development of mathematical systems such as quantum mechanics, wave mechanics, the uncertainty and exclusion principles and so on.

Let nothing already said or to be said convey the idea

that knowledge of the material universe has anything to do with salvation of the individual. Sufficient to say that salvation depends on faith, and faith is an interpersonal relationship between God and an individual. It is a gift from God demanding a response from the person to whom it is given. It can be had for the asking.

What is said is that the theologian must talk to men in terms of the world as it is seen and understood in his day. The scientist on the other hand once he honestly concedes the existence of God and the immortality of the human soul sees himself in the great stream of revelation and development of doctrine. He is also led to admit that empirical science is limited to the study of material things. His science and its methods cannot be extended to immortal, eternal and infinite reactions. Further, as the assumptions on which our classical physics and mathematics are based are reasonably accurate only in a modicum of known reality, then their acceptance as infallible and universal locks any person who adopts this attitude into the prison cell of the time/space co-ordinates and binds his mind to a limited range of known material things, thus dehumanising him and confining his thinking to an unreal, tiny area of the total reality. Ultimately this must generate despair. A "fundamentalist" attitude to "empirical science" amounts to intellectual and spiritual suicide. Acceptance of Marxism and dialectic materialism in fact, places an "iron curtain" around and over the human mind. Let us allow one great physicist Erwin Schrödinger, the discoverer of wave mechanics, to speak for himself: "No personal god can form part of a world model that has only become accessible at the cost of removing everything personal from it. We know when God is experienced, this is an event as real as an immediate sense perception or as one's own personality." Knowledge of the material universe and everything in it is growing daily. In meditating on the significance of new discoveries both theologians and scientists must maintain a plastic type of philosophy or each may find himself locked in the paralysing mental state of "fundamentalism".

The Universe We Live In

Most Western civilisations tend to be Urban. By that I mean that the proportion of the total populations living in the country as opposed to the cities is becoming less and less. Mechanisation and efficient farming methods on the one hand and the relatively high wages and creature comforts in cities on the other are the principal causes for this development. City dwellers, however, are deprived in two important areas. It is very rarely that they can see the glory of the heavens on a dark night, because of smoke, smog and bright lights and they can hardly be expected to know the quality of deep silence. Both these experiences are profoundly awe-inspiring. Imagine a situation where the loudest sound you can hear is your own breathing and sometimes the gentle "dub dub" of your heart; at the same time lying on your swag you find yourself entranced by the sight of the stars, from the fast moving man-made satellites to the millions of far distant little points of light, way beyond the glory of the planets and the Milky Way. There is nothing more awe inspiring that man can look at than the star-filled sky and nothing more wonderful than silence.

If what we can see with the naked eye on a dark, clear night is majestic in itself, how much more wonderful is the universe as seen with the new "extended eyes" man has invented, from the crude telescope of Galileo, through modern optical telescopes, radio telescopes and now X-ray telescopes. For the serious minded non-specialist there exists a remarkable book from which one can gain the "feeling" of modern astronomical research and that is *The Cambridge Encyclopedia of Astronomy*. My copy which is the 1979 reprint, is almost certainly out of date by now. This remark is not made in any disparaging sense. Any scientific reference book written these days becomes more or less obsolete as the writer pens his last word.

The purpose of these few pages is merely to paint a picture. It is far beyond the competence of the writer to go into detail, and indeed detail would thwart the purpose of this book. It is interesting to note that in modern astronomy, the mathematical work of Einstein and his disciples is indispensible and it is in this area of macro-physics (as also in micro-physics) that so many of the predictions of Einstein and his successors have been verified.

Let us for a start try to get an idea of the range of sizes in our universe that scientists are studying today and the difficulties and methods of measurement of huge distances on the one hand and the incredibly minute particles on the other. The centres of the pupils of adult human eyes would be in the order of six or seven centimetres apart. This fact enables each of us to relate, subconsciously, the distance to an observed object to this base. Experience and practice enable us to gauge the distance to and the size of observed objects with a useful degree of accuracy within limited ranges of size and distance. The surveyor uses this principle, but extends his field of vision by using the telescope of his theodolite, its accurate protractor to establish his angle of sight, and a much longer and accurately measured baseline. Most of our maps have been compiled this way. If the baseline is long and accurately measured the probability of correctness of the surveyor's findings is increased proportionately. In astronomical measurements the system used is more complex. The objects whose distance we want to determine or even whose size to measure are moving in relation to the Earth and to each other at differing speeds and most of them are enormous distances from us. The method used is called trigonometrical parallax. Human beings, subconsciously, use this principle constantly. Driving along a highway, power poles seem to pass us quite quickly. The lighthouse we can see away ahead on a promontory approaches us at a slower speed, while the snow-capped mountain towards which we are heading for our skiing holiday hardly seems to move at all. In actual fact neither the poles, the lighthouse nor the mountain are moving. We are doing all the moving. However, if as we travel we want to look at a certain power pole we have to turn our heads quickly, less quickly as we approach and pass the lighthouse and very slowly as we look at the mountain, so here we have a basis for comparison of relative distances. Let us now spend a little time looking at the relative sizes of "all creatures great and small".

Big Things

The man we must listen to when considering the "large" aspects of present human knowledge is the astronomer, the space explorer. Immediately we must learn, or know where to find a dictionary concerning a strange language. Miles or kilometres and their accepted subdivisions work comfortably on our little planet, Earth. These units of measurement are quite impractical for space exploration. A number of more appropriate units of measurement have evolved, as modern technology enables us to probe further and further into the universe. Our sun and its planets (including our Earth) are part of a galaxy of stars we call the Milky Way. At this point of time we know of some 1,000,000,000 stars larger or smaller than our sun in *our* galaxy. The following list refers to some of the most frequently used terms in astronomical measurements. As metric measurements are universally adopted in astronomy they will be used in this chapter except for the definition of the velocity of light and the astronomical unit, where distances are expressed in both kilometres and miles. This is done to give any reader not familiar with the metric system the "feel" of the measurements concerned. A kilometre is about five-eighths of a mile, ·6214 to be precise:

1 Astronomical Unit (AU) equals 149,598,000 kilometres, about 93,000,000 miles. This is the average distance between the sun and the Earth.

1 Light Year (a measurement not used frequently in modern astronomy) equals 9,460,500,000,000 kilometres or 5,878,754,700,000 miles. This represents the distance a beam of light will travel in a year.

1 Par-sec equals 30,856,000,000,000 kilometres. This measurement is now generally used instead of the light year. It is equivalent to 3·26 light years and is the parallax of one second of an arc. (Abbreviation pc.)

1 Solar Mass (M⊙) $1 \cdot 989 \times 10^{30}$ kilograms is the equivalent of 1,989,000,000,000,000,000,000,000,000,000 metric tonnes. This represents the mass of our sun.

1 Solar Luminosity (L⊙) equals $3 \cdot 9 \times 10^{26}$ watts or in full 390,000,000,000,000,000,000,000,000 watts.

All these measurements are used in what we call macrophysics, the science of big things.

Small Things

Small things take us into an area of studies called microphysics. Let us consider the mass of a molecule of water (H_2O). The mass of an atom of hydrogen is one of the accepted constants of physics. It is $1 \cdot 6733 \times 10^{-27}$ kg. The mass of an atom of oxygen is $26 \cdot 56805 \times 10^{-27}$ kg. Therefore the mass of a molecule of water is $29 \cdot 915 \times 10^{-27}$ kg. You will notice that in all the figures shown above, we have written in the mathematical shorthand used in dealing with very large or very small numbers and that is to express them as a positive or negative power of 10. To allow us to get a more accurate "picture" we express in full the mass of our molecule of water as 0·000,000,000,000,000,000,000,000,029,915 kg.

There is a famous example which was used by Lord Kelvin to give his audiences an idea of the size of a molecule of water. Let us imagine that you took an ordinary kitchen tumbler of water and were able to put a distinguishing mark on each molecule. Having done so, you next poured your glass of water into any ocean and stirred it so that the water you poured in became distributed equally through the seven seas. If you then dipped your glass into any ocean anywhere in the world and filled it you would find it contained about a hundred of your marked molecules.

A commonly used unit of measurement in atomic physics is the angstrom (Å) which measures 0·000,000,000,1 of a metre. Atoms do not have sharp boundaries. They do not respond kindly to the mathematics of Newton. The modern tendency is not to talk of size of particular atoms but of the mean distances between their nuclei. This distance for most atoms would be between one and two angstroms. Now let us consider for a while the size of the universe as we know it today. The purpose of this book is merely to convey a reasonable and easily understood picture. If it is a little underestimated or somewhat over-simplified in some detail please treat this as a stimulus to further detailed reading in the area of concern. The extension of knowledge in the past fifty years has become so vast and fast that to be fully competent in any branch of science requires a lifetime of dedicated study. In the excitement of chasing the ever receding horizon of discovery in any scientific discipline there lies a real danger of overlooking the *significance* of what is found out, of overlooking the results, physical and philosophical, that the new found knowledge may have on humanity. Further as a few brilliant minds pursue some "will of the wisp" they perforce invent new words descriptive among themselves of things or circumstances they encounter, forgetting that their fellow men, who may be very interested in their work for differing reasons, find themselves unable to understand or communicate with the researchers in meaningful terms; a real Tower of Babel situation. Hence we find a sort of elitism growing in groups who may call themselves micro-physicists, macro-physicists, biologists, chemists or whatever. Few would quarrel with the notion that the pursuit of happiness is the ultimate goal of human mortal existence. If this goal is lost and *knowledge* is substituted for *happiness* the outlook for the mass of humanity becomes bleak and hopeless. One might suggest we need philosophers to walk hand in hand with our scientists, but of those who do, very few in these times have the gift of communicating their reflections in terms a yearning mass of people understand. The philosophers too, have in so many cases, fallen into the trap of developing their own "trade language". Our answer is that the solution lies in Christian theologians becoming better informed of current scientific thinking and developing their ability to convey the significance of modern knowledge to those in their pastoral care, and relating what they discover to the basic Christian Revelation. Only in this way can the Church regain her position as the divinely appointed "teacher" and carry out Christ's commission to "go teach all nations . . . to the end of time". There is no place today for the lazy or complacent theologian who has all the answers to everything. Again, let us in this field too, avoid the trap of "trade language". The Gospel must be preached to the world we live in today. Again it is emphasised the theologian *needs* the scientist and the scientist *needs* the theologian.

On page 45 you will find a diagram designed not to scale or purporting to be of particular accuracy. Its purpose is solely to stimulate a mental picture of things big and small of which we now have some scientific knowledge. It is an unorthodox form of graph. The lower horizontal axis has an arrow head at each end. The left hand end tends towards very small measurements and the right hand end to very large measurements. The vertical axis is scaled in probabilities upwards and downwards from a line drawn in the middle, parallel to the horizontal axis, which indicates, shall we say, "reasonable certitude". It is shown as a 1 in 1 probability. The little box in the middle of the centre-line represents where we live and the span of total reality in which our classical physics and mathematics (Newtonian) work with near perfect accuracy. Once we get clear of the box we need Einstein's system and derivatives like wave mechanics, quantum mechanics, the uncertainty principle, vector analysis, mathematical logic, Boolean algebra and many other ingenious extensions of the art of calculation. While in the area of large things, particularly astronomy, we need skills in the trigonometrical parallax, the Dopler principle and so on. These are subjects for specialists and mathematical experts; nevertheless excellent explanations for the interested reader can be found in such books as the *Cambridge Encyclopedia of Astronomy*. In simple terms the further we proceed away from our little box and beyond say a molecule at the small end of the scale and our solar system at the large end all our hypotheses and calculations must contain a factor representing the probability of accuracy. The probability denominator tends to grow proportionately as we move away in size or distance from our little planet. This phenomenon in the atomic area is the subject of Heisenberg's "uncertainty principle".

At both extremes of the spectrum, large and small, the scientists concerned are the first to admit that many current ideas are hypothetical and could be abandoned or modified as further knowledge comes to hand. This immediately raises some interesting points. First of all, that we have gone past the limits of pure empiricism. We cannot, with our senses extended in these times by all the highly ingenious instruments and methods available actually see, hear, feel, smell, taste, measure, analyse or dissect the objects of our investigation. What we can do, however, by use of our brains, our minds and our imagination, is to extend the patterns and orders satisfactorily proved by science to this date beyond the range of immediate observation. We then calculate the effects our hypotheses postulate. Next, we seek evidence from things we would expect to be affected should our "guesses" be correct. In a significant number of cases this method has proved fruitful. Very rarely however can we obtain a "certain" result. Almost invariably we are forced to test our findings by a balance of probabilities. Here again a Christian believer finds himself in a happy position when he accepts the validity and content of divine revelation. His source of infused knowledge is from the One Immutable Cause of all things. All truth is *available* to Christ's people, the only limitation being our ability to absorb it. As St. Paul says, "We are looking now through a darkened glass". Christ himself told us, "I still have many things to say to you but they would be too much for you now but when the Spirit of Truth comes he will lead you to the complete truth". Here we have both a warning about our limitations and an encouragement to continue seeking the full truth. Inherent human curiosity compels us to reflect on the "actor" who is progressively proceeding into an area which in strict terminology must be called metaphysics (beyond physics). It supports, not only the contention that the human mind and the human brain (which relies for its information on the senses) are separate entities which interact with each other; but that the mind self or soul, whatever you like to call it, is as already affirmed "spiritual". It is therefore indestructible, immortal, unique and unlimited in its ultimate potential. This argument will be developed in a later chapter. Let us go back to our schematic diagram. At first sight the range of human "exploration" seems enormous, varying approximately from something weighing 0·000,000,000,000,000,000,000,000,030 kilograms to our solar system with a mass of something in the order of 3,000,000,000,000,000,000,000,000,000,000 tonnes. On the "large" side, enormous as these figures are, they fade into insignificance when we consider that our galaxy alone contains in the order of 100,000,000,000 stars (suns), that the distance to the nearest of which is 4.1 light years away and that our probes into space beyond our galaxy extend to objects 3,258,000 light years distance and beyond. When we turn to the "small" side of studied phenomena we really pass the stage where the "mass" of the object defined is significant and our "measurements" for want of a better term resolve into miniscule assessments of energy such as positive or negative charges. Even the atom itself can hardly be defined as a mass but rather as a shape or a boundary of certain activity between the nucleus and the related electrons. Everywhere there are overlappings, "grey areas" and probabilities rather than certainties. In these early chapters the purpose as already stated is to paint a reasonable picture of the universe we live in as we know it today and to clarify certain concepts commonly misunderstood.

In later chapters we will try to show where "everyman" fits into the scene.

Time/Space and Eternity

The diagram represents a procession containing all the main events in a friend's life and after-life.

The two little figures at the corner of Time Street and Space Street represent you with your friend on your left. The little figure at the corner of the forty-storey building represents your friend at the position he took up on the roof of the very tall building just as his "Death Float" moved by.

The procession which was marshalled up Hope Street is moving down Hope Street into Time Street, turning right into Space Street then left into Charity Row.

The hatched area indicates the space in which you can see the procession from the street corner and the time during which any float remains in your field of vision.

The broken lines between the floats up Hope Street represent the many floats relating to the major events in this life and the "life of the world to come". The broken lines have been used solely to save space in the drawing. You can use your imagination to fill in the gaps, but it is suggested that you leave room for some floats covered by white sheets so you can't see what is underneath.

These can represent sins which, being contritely confessed, have been obliterated "eternally" by the saving mission and power of Our Lord Jesus Christ.

Any sinner thus reconciled with God can ensure that his "eternal procession" consists only of the beautiful and exalted experiences of his life.

TIME/SPACE & ETERNITY
Boethius' Definition: perfect possession
of eternal life, held wholly all
at once.

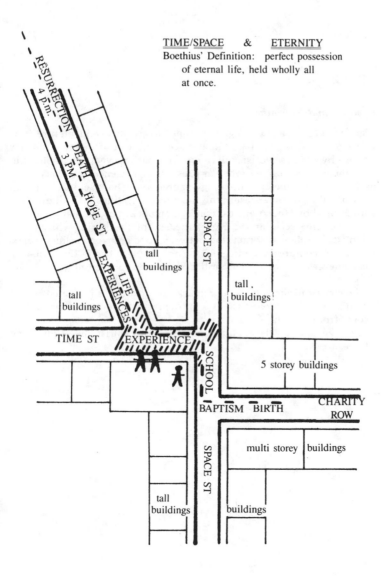

Creation and Revelation

The drawing on page 43 is again designed to give an overall picture. The lower pyramid shows the generally accepted idea of the evolutionary process by which scientists tell us modern man evolved. If we believe in God then the evolution of man as presented by science can be accepted as a divinely planned methodology of creation. The "faculties" of man shown in the sketch represent the amazing capabilities of the individual soul infused by God at or near conception of each individual.

In the time scale at the right, the age of the Earth, which most scientists estimate as something between 4000 and 5000 million years, has been compressed into one year. You will see that modern man emerges on the 31st December, sometime between 11.30 p.m. and 11.50 p.m.!

Revelation of himself to his remarkable creature is indicated by the upper inverted pyramid. It shows the degree of "gentleness" one would expect from a loving Creator.

Creation and Revelation both climax in Jesus Christ the "Alpha" and "Omega".

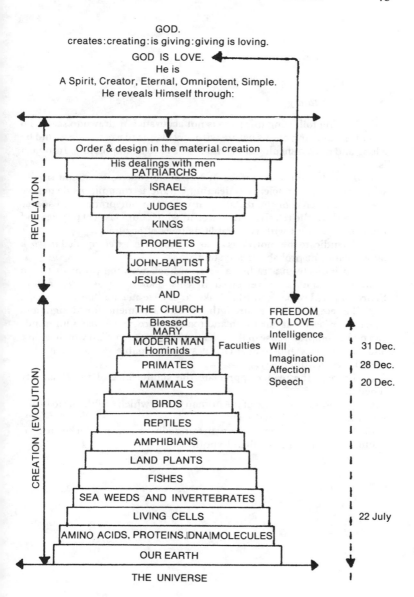

GOD.
creates:creating:is giving:giving is loving.
GOD IS LOVE.
He is
A Spirit, Creator, Eternal, Omnipotent, Simple.
He reveals Himself through:

REVELATION

Order & design in the material creation
His dealings with men
PATRIARCHS
ISRAEL
JUDGES
KINGS
PROPHETS
JOHN-BAPTIST
JESUS CHRIST
AND
THE CHURCH

CREATION (EVOLUTION)

Blessed
MARY
MODERN MAN
Hominids
PRIMATES
MAMMALS
BIRDS
REPTILES
AMPHIBIANS
LAND PLANTS
FISHES
SEA WEEDS AND INVERTEBRATES
LIVING CELLS
AMINO ACIDS, PROTEINS, DNA MOLECULES
OUR EARTH
THE UNIVERSE

FREEDOM
TO LOVE
Faculties Intelligence
Will
Imagination
Affection
Speech

31 Dec.
28 Dec.
20 Dec.

22 July

Size and Certainty

The drawing following this page is not accurate nor drawn to scale. To produce a drawing of this nature with any claims to exactitude would be a long and most difficult task. It might prove to be impossible. Its object is:

1. To indicate the difference in size of "creatures great and small" with which modern science is dealing. On the astronomical side to give the reader a sense of the distances involved in our probes into space.

2. To show the relatively tiny area in which our classical physics and mathematics work with acceptable degrees of accuracy.

3. To indicate the enormous areas in which we are compelled to work on a balance of probabilities system.

4. To indicate in a rather over simplified way the problem which prompts authors later reviewed in this book such as Sherrington, Schrödinger, Popper and Sheldrake to say we need a "new physics".

5. To emphasise the strength of our argument for design and "Designer" as far as our Earth and mankind are concerned. Our minds can make complete sense of the celestial "environment" in which *we* live and our physics and mathematical systems enable us to expand our knowledge continuously.

6. To help the reader appreciate the significance of the Relativity Theory.

7. To show the miracle of the human mind, which enables us to probe into the limits of created reality.

8. To stress the need for open mindedness and prudence in proclaiming theories rather than hypotheses.

Schematic Diagram only.

Very small things

Probability of absolute certainty using standard maths

1 in 1   1 in 10^6 1 in 10^{10} 1 in 10^{20} 1 in 10^8

Electrons	about 0·0005 mass of proton or neutron
Proton rest mass	$1·6726485 \times 10^{-27}$ kg
Neutron rest mass	$1·6749543 \times 10^{-27}$ kg
Atomic Nucleus	Almost all mass of atom
Hydrogen Atom	Mass $1·67333 \times 10^{-27}$ kg
	Molecule of water - Mass $3·0 \times 10^{-26}$

Within these size limits	classical physics and mathematics work well

Our Solar System $1·99267 \times 10^{30}$ kg	
Nearest star - Centauri	Distance from Earth 1·32 pc = 4·3 lt-yrs
Ursa Major cluster	20·9 pc
Pleaides	125 pc
Messioc 4	2,762 pc
Maffei	1,000,000 pc = 3,260,000 lt-yrs

Not to Scale

Enormous distances from earth column 1

Probability of certainty see column 1

Large things

1 in 1   1 in 10^6 1 in 10^{10} 1 in 10^{20} 1 in 10^8

CHAPTER 3

THE PHENOMENON OF MAN

BEFORE proceeding with this chapter it is suggested that reference be made to the diagram and comment on pages 42 and 43.

Obviously the lower pyramid of the chart indicates that we are assuming that physically mankind has evolved from the stuff of the earth. This assumption should be acceptable both to the "creationist" and the "evolutionist". The upper inverted pyramid is designed to show the gradual process of God's self-revelation to mankind which culminated in the incarnation of the second person of the Trinity, when the man-child Jesus Christ was born of Mary.

The line at the bottom of the drawing with an arrow head at each end represents the universe.

Unfortunately many Christians and some scientists have placed themselves in opposing and sometimes antagonistic camps. Briefly there are those believers who treat the first few chapters of Genesis as a scientific account of the creation of the universe and our solar system, which must be accepted literally. On the other side there are many Christians and quite a few scientists who take an equally uncompromising attitude which seems to elevate Charles Darwin's studies and writings and later developments from them as having an aura of infallibility about them. To the writer this is a storm in a teacup because, if as Christians we take the Nicene Creed (even with all the inbuilt problems that have lately been generated about credal formulas) as our touchstone of orthodoxy, all we commit ourselves to is the statement "We believe in one God, the Father Almighty, Creator of heaven and earth and all that is, seen or unseen". One can affirm this in good conscience from the stand of the so called "creationists" or as an "evolutionist".

46

Evolution can be accepted as a possible divine methodology of creating the animal "man", as far as his physical composition is concerned. However, as already postulated, mankind in the Christian view has a spiritual component which transcends the possibility of material evolution. Evolution is a material theory and its followers outside the religious members of the community, as a general rule, deny any spiritual element in mankind.

The time chart shown by a line at the right hand side of the lower pyramid demonstrates, approximately, times and ages as scientists would present them to us today compressed, to give a comparative picture, into the space of one year. A similar scale is shown on page 81. No highly qualified scientist in any discipline is dogmatic in these times for the simple reason that new techniques and extensions of knowledge are being presented constantly and of course, theories and hypotheses are subject to consequent revision. The "creationist" can vary this time and scale to suit himself. The end result which the diagram proposes is similar in each case. It is that *homo sapiens* is a relatively recent arrival on the world scene.

It is this end product that we intend to examine. Mankind is unique. Chemically it is not too outrageous to describe man as an animated mud pie. Certainly at death, if the body be buried, it's every particle resolves into the material of the Earth. In Genesis we are told "The Lord God formed man of dust from the earth and breathed into his nostrils the breath of life and man became a living being." It is doubtful whether any better description can be given of the origin of *life* from any source. Any person dealing with human beings at death cannot help but be mystified by the fact that at one moment he is holding the hand of a person, with all that human personality implies, and seconds later without moving he finds himself holding the same hand which has become a piece of lifeless flesh with no personality, vitality or consciousness. What has happened? Medicine can give us a clinical description of the functional changes which have taken place but who can tell us what has happened to the "life" *per se*. In this work, as already stated, it will be assumed that man has a metaphysical immortal element as part of his being. Of course this element is indestructible and eternal. For the Christian this fact is explicitly expressed both in the Old and New Testaments and in our creed we state our belief in "everlasting life". Eminent twentieth century scientists also subscribe to this fact and representative views will be given in later chapters.

In a preceding section on "Eternity" an explanation has been given as to how a man or woman will always be conscious of that identity before, during and after the process we call death.

Of course the life/death process occurs right through the entire hierarchy of life on earth from the simplest living forms up to and inclusive of mankind. We know that life is constantly coming into being from lifeless forms but the individual emerging is always a "bud" from a previous living organism. The great difficulty about human speculation concerning soul or mind is that, as it is metaphysical, the only apparatus available to examine it is itself. It resembles a situation where we are asked to do a detailed examination of a rock and the only tool, apparatus or reactor we are allowed to use is the rock itself. It is easy to see that the single available certainty we can arrive at is that the rock exists and its outward and visible characteristics can be described. The soul has no outward and visible characteristics but instead we can describe to a limited extent its functions. We must remember that the soul works with the brain which can be described as a very complex tissue. The many hypotheses put forward regarding the relationship between the soul and the brain can be classified into three categories: (1) that the mind and brain are identical, (2) that they work together in a sort of parallel relationship or (3) that they interact with each other. In this discussion we accept the principle of interaction. More will be said of this in a later chapter.

From now on the writer who has already warned you that he is a Catholic priest will use the ages and sequences proposed by scientists at this day and age and will accept a *directed* evolutionary process as the methodology by which mankind's physical nature came to its present state. However we hold that the "soul", the metaphysical component of every man and woman is "infused" (not "imposed") by God at conception. In taking this stand the author, who may disagree with others who think differently, in no way alienates himself from them. The purpose of the book as stated in the introduction is not to divide but to bring together as many views as possible in our search for the "Truth". As already argued the view that all that is, or has been, is created by God will be defended as axiomatic. There must be a first cause. The idea of creation as a continuing process will be defended. It is the nature of God to create, hence as God by definition must be immutable, creation is a process not an isolated act. By creation is meant constructive activity at different levels of existence and these at progressively higher levels. Evolution is the obvious example. Always the movement is upwards towards more complicated, efficient creatures with greater and greater potential. Man's ultimate destiny can be seen as unlimited, or in time/space language an immensely exciting prospect.

The Earth

The lowest line of our diagram represents the universe, as we know it now, and it is enormous. The first block above it represents our Earth and naturally we know more about this planet than any other cosmic body, though our knowledge is far from complete. It is one of a number of planets in orbit around a star which we call the Sun. At this stage of our researches we cannot positively identify any planet outside of our own solar system but there is weighty evidence that other stars may be similarly endowed. For a start the observable universe contains some 10^{20} stars, so that the chance of finding a planet-endowed star besides our sun immediately seems high indeed. Confining our attention to our own little planet we certainly find some extraordinary characteristics all of which are, to some extent, necessary for existence of life as we know it. For a start we don't know what life is. We know a good deal about the highly complex organisation of matter necessary before a creature can be described as living. Living things make use of a process called metabolism which means that they have the capacity to use energy to change materials available to them into their own forms. They also have the ability to reproduce their species. Let us then examine some of the remarkable (perhaps unique) characteristics of our Earth. First and foremost must be the existence of relatively large quantites of water in its liquid form. Except for clouds, the polar ice caps and the peaks of a few high mountains, wherever water exists on the Earth's surface it is in liquid form. Now water is essential to the existence of all terrestial life forms and water exists in liquid form only between 0° and 100° celsius. Very little if any terrestial life can exist at temperatures of − 90° or above 90° celsius. Temperatures in the universe in which we live vary over an enormous range. The coldest would be close to the absolute minimum of − 273·16c. On the hot side the surface temperature of our sun for instance, is over 5,500c, while its central temperature is estimated at about 15,000,000c.

Imagine a line drawn right across this book representing the variation of temperatures in our solar system. Suppose the span in which human life can be sustained to be 100 degrees. This span in relation to the line would be a small dot. What we need to realise is that not only is our life possible in a very small segment of the line but the dot must be positioned accurately. It is no use placing it at a position in the line where it would represent 100 degrees between a temperature of 1000c to 1100c nor at − 100c to − 200c. No active terrestial life could exist in these temperature ranges.

In studying remarkable features of the Earth it is essential to have at least a "handshake" with hydrology, the branch of geophysics dealing with water. Over 97% of the Earth's water is in the oceans and all this water is saline. In this state it is suitable to sustain marine life but is inimical to the production and sustenance of land based creatures. This leaves only 3% of the total water on Earth in its fresh state; of that 3% about 75% is ice, so nearly all living creatures on the face of the Earth depend for their existence on 0.75% of the total water supply on the Earth's surface. When we hear concern expressed at the "explosion" of the Earth's human and animal populations one cannot help but wonder whether the supply of fresh water available may be the limiting factor as far as the numbers of living animals are concerned. The effect of rainfall becomes obvious when we contemplate the proportion of the Earth's surface which is desert. Much desert country is basically fertile. All it lacks is a sufficient rainfall to generate and sustain life. There are two ways in which sea water is desalinated: one, by evaporation into the atmosphere and the second by freezing it into ice. Both clouds and ice are free of the mineral salts held in solution in the sea. Our supply of fresh water is obtained through the hydrologic cycle. The Sun's heat causes water to evaporate from the oceans into the atmosphere where it may form clouds. Much of this water is precipitated back into the ocean as rain but fortunately clouds also produce rain over the dry land, normally by one of three phenomena: by convection where hot moist air rises suddenly into the colder upper atmosphere where it condenses into rain; or by the orographic method, which occurs when moisture laden air as it travels is made to rise in order to cross a mountain range and thus again enters the cold upper atmosphere in which it condenses; the third phenomenon is cyclonic rainfall where enormous amounts of moist air are forced high into the atmosphere by the whirling winds of the cyclone and this usually produces very heavy rain. Almost all the rain which falls on land ultimately finds its way back into the sea by various routes. Remember that without the hydrologic cycle life on Earth could not exist. There are many other criteria superbly and minutely balanced which are essential to the maintenance of life as we know it. These include such matters as soil chemistry, the chemistry of the atmosphere, and the existence of the ozone layer of the upper atmosphere. The presence of ozone protects the surface of the Earth from much of the ultra violet radiation emanating from the sun. Again, without the ozone layer life on Earth would cease to exist. There is a most interesting chapter in the *Cambridge Encyclopaedia of Astronomy* entitled "Life in the Universe" in which certain plausible hypotheses are put forward as to the way the Earth we live on came to be in its present state.

These make interesting reading but must be taken for what they are, namely hypotheses.

Every one of these "explanations" could be wrong or alternatively they could all be correct. The search for the ultimate truth in both the macro- and micro-physical worlds must perforce go on in this manner. We work on the evidence we have and then project our hypotheses for the next step. Every now and then some verifiable discovery is made which results in a change in the balance of probabilities, abandonment of some ideas and the retention and strengthening of others. As far as the individual scientist or theologian is concerned the psychological danger is to become "hooked" for or against some reasonable hypothesis. This condition causes the mental blindness previously referred to as "fundamentalism" which is the greatest obstacle in our search for TRUTH. As those of us who can remember our soldiering days would say, "expect anything — it usually happens"!

Amino acids, proteins, DNA molecule, etc.

Now let us move up one block on our diagram to the box "Amino acids, proteins, DNA molecules etc". Scientists are fascinated by the problem of how the basic materials necessary to the origin of life came to be present on the Earth and more mystified still at the fact that somehow basic elements like carbon, nitrogen, oxygen and hydrogen became organised in the complicated patterns of the molecules forming the building blocks of life. This step could represent the most astounding stage in the ascending ladder before we encounter the phenomenon of mankind.

As this work is not a text book it would be a useful exercise to look up such references as amino and nucleic acids, protein, protein synthesis, hormones, metabolism, the DNA molecule and the suggested cross references in any modern scientific encyclopaedia, (useful books include the *Methuen Concise Encyclopaedia of Science and Technology*, the *Penguin Dictionaries* and similar aids). Let us consider a very brief outline of the argument supporting the proposition that evolution is a directed methodology of creation, at the same time developing an argument against the hypothesis of the atheist that life on Earth as we know it now is the result of blind chance. We will take the view that on the evidence available what we see now is the handiwork of an Intelligence of infinite ability.

Amino acids are organic compounds made of a complex chemistry of carbon, nitrogen, hydrogen and oxygen. By slight variations in the molecular construction we could reasonably assume the possibility of the existence of some hundreds of different amino acids. To form a protein we may require hundreds or even thousands of amino acid molecules but of the hundreds of different kinds available we require as a general rule only twenty select types. Now, not only must these twenty types combine, but they need to do so in a certain order of grouping for each type of protein. These groups are sometimes referred to as chains or rings. *Proteins* are found in all living organisms. In a human being our muscles and that part of our blood which is not water are, in the main, proteins. *Nucleic acids* are the vital chemicals required by living organisms. There are two main types DNA (deoxyribonucleic acids) and RNA (ribonucleic acids). The DNA molecule has a unique characteristic, *the ability to reproduce itself* (replication). It is therefore an essential element in every living cell and it imparts this same ability to reproduce, to the cell of which it forms a part. It is the DNA molecule which programmes the protein synthesis of amino acids to form various components of a living organism (viruses excepted).

DNA Molecule. A detailed description based on

current knowledge of the DNA molecule is far beyond the scope of this book or the competence of the author. It is submitted however that when one studies the order, design, function and complexity of this molecule one is faced with two alternatives. The first is to react with awe before the most ingenious mechanism known to man and to become a theist, or alternatively to classify oneself as an atheistic "fundamentalist" who will not admit the existence of the Supreme Intelligence despite the fact that the balance of probabilities points overwhelmingly at this point in human development to the DNA molecule as a Divine *design*. One could of course move even further and describe it as a planned development having as its ultimate intention the creation of *homo sapiens* and the environment and ecology in which he can live and reproduce. In dealing with the DNA molecule in this chapter the intention is not so much to describe it as a biologist would, but to outline only the most conspicuous components and their interrelated functions and then to show the moral impossibility of this molecule evolving without the direction of a governing and active intelligence. The method used will be an hypothetical compounding of probabilities. There is in the M.R.C. laboratory within the University of Cambridge a fine free standing schematic model of the DNA molecule. The sketch shown here relates well to this model. It is schematic only and has the appearance of two coiled springs which have been pushed together. Each "spring" is a long chain of nucleic acid molecules together with thousands of chemically linked sub-units called nucleotides. Let us now work backwards from the conception of a human baby and see where all the bits and pieces we have been talking about fit together and react to produce in 9 months the phenomenon of man. Once a month an ovum (or egg) leaves an ovary of every normal fertile woman. It travels down a duct called the fallopian tube towards the womb. It may be that the woman has had recent sexual intercourse with a man. If one of the millions of male sperm ejaculated into the woman's vagina during intercourse has managed to swim up to the top of the

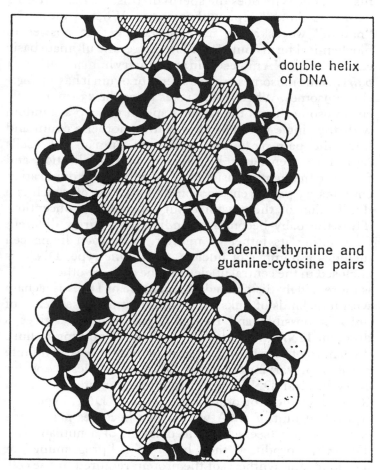

double helix
of DNA

adenine-thymine and
guanine-cytosine pairs

DNA MOLECULE

woman's womb and enter the fallopian tube containing the
ovum and if this sperm meets the ovum it may enter it and
fuse with it. Why does the sperm do this, we ask? "It is its
nature to do so" replies the atheist. What is meant by
"nature" we ask? We may perhaps get an answer in
biochemical terms but we will never get the ultimate basic
cause. Each DNA molecule in an ordinary human cell has 23
pairs of chromosomes but in a sperm or ovum it has 23 *single*
chromosomes. When fusion takes place the 23 single male
chromosomes from the father's sperm pair up at random
with the single chromosomes of the mother's ovum and
form the pair pattern of a normal human cell. Cells
reproduce themselves by division and duplication and
from the moment of fusion every division and duplication
contains 23 paired chromosomes, each one of which is a
duplication of the new structure formed at conception.
Thus the baby becomes an individual entirely different
from either its father or mother. Now each living cell
includes a number of nucleic acids. One type, DNA, is
enclosed in the central nucleus of the cell; the other, RNA,
is more widely distributed. A molecule of DNA is a chain
with four kinds of links. Any combination or sequence of
links is possible and each different sequence gives a
different DNA molecule. As we know of nothing to limit
the length of the chain it is possible that there is an infinite
number of varying kinds of DNA molecules. Now for
every kind of DNA there is a corresponding variety of
RNA. Somehow or other a molecule of DNA evokes an
equivalent unit of RNA which then becomes part of the
cell substance (see schematic diagram of a human cell).
The RNA produced then becomes a "programme" or
mould for the synthesis of the protein required by the cell.
As we have already noted a molecule of protein is also a
chain composed of 20 different kinds of amino acids. Now
each of the amino acids is attracted to one particular
sequence of three links in the RNA molecule. As already
explained the different kinds of protein produced depend
on the sequence of the amino acids. This is determined
primarily by the link sequence of the RNA molecule which

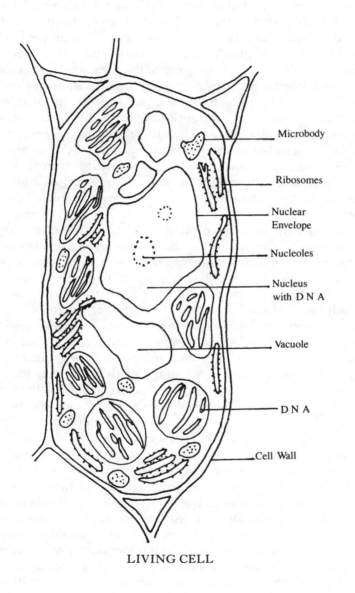

Microbody

Ribosomes

Nuclear
Envelope

Nucleoles

Nucleus
with D N A

Vacuole

D N A

Cell Wall

LIVING CELL

is itself programmed as stated above by the DNA molecule which is the master mind. Thus the whole structure of the body which is composed of cells is dependent on the kinds of DNA at its disposal. Thus we have the picture that every cell in a human body is a replica of that single cell generated in the fallopian tube and every cell contains in its nucleus a DNA molecule which is an exact reproduction of the original formed at conception. Now a living organism exists by metabolism which is the ability to use energy to convert selected parts of the surrounding ecological environment into itself as food or fuel to maintain its temperature and provide the material for its duplication. It must also have the ability to eliminate undesirable intake as waste.

Extending this complex idea further we can see that some cells form the physiology of the eye, a delicate and intricate structure; others may form hair. Yet the basic cell of each organ is a replica of the other. The protein pattern has been programmed to produce the variety required for each task. At the back of all this is the DNA molecule.

Let us remember we are putting forward the proposition that at this point in history all available evidence tends to indicate strongly that life on Earth reaches its highest form in mankind and that the ecology of this planet is ideally suited to the maintenance of human life. Further we propose that the DNA molecule alone shows, by its intricate and ingenious design, that to consider it the result of a random chance, a fluke, demonstrates a blind "faith" in the *non-existence of God* which flies in the face of reason.

We can commence our defence of our position by starting from a point of mutual agreement between ourselves and those who do not believe in God and that is that the DNA molecule is a truly remarkable phenomenon without which life on Earth as we know it could not exist. Some may say a virus can exist independently of the DNA molecule because it is based on the RNA molecule, but as far as we know a virus cannot continue its life cycle without at one stage entering a living cell and as all cells contain DNA in their nucleus the virus too, is dependent for its

existence indirectly on the presence of the DNA molecule.
This sketchy treatment of the DNA molecule has been
given as a stimulus for the reader to find a book from the
many available and become familiar with the elements of
biochemistry.

It is now proposed to examine again very briefly the
various theories put forward as the basis for the hypothesis
that life on Earth generated spontaneously and developed
or evolved independently, and that the direction and
organisation of an "outside" Supreme Intelligence is not a
pre-requisite for the biosphere as we now view it.

Unfortunately we are compelled to start with an unanswered problem. What is life from the scientist's point of
view? Let us review what we have already ascertained.

We can agree on what properties an object must possess
to be classified as living, and we can analyse the chemistry
and functions of the components of living matter in great
detail, but what is "life" by itself as distinct from the
properties it exhibits, and the conditions necessary for its
existence?

The problem we are facing is called "biogenesis". Until
the work of Louis Pasteur in the eighteen sixties many
scientists considered that living things could arise spontaneously.

Pasteur eliminated this idea, it was thought, once and for
all. However in 1960 John Keosian proposed his theory of
Neobiogenesis which proposes that life evolved and is still
evolving from non living to living matter. Consonant with
this theory, present day viruses are recently generated
organisms. However, it must be recalled that viruses
cannot reproduce outside a living cell. On this point alone
strong objections to his hypothesis have been put forward.
Most scientists today reject Neobiogenesis.

Other theories have been proposed such as the Cos-
mozoic Processes which, in brief, put forward the idea that
viable spores from cosmic space have accidently seeded
life on Earth when conditions were favourable. This of
course does not explain the origin of life, as such spores
would already be living. This theory is not widely held.

Problems with temperature, ultra violet radiation and vast distances create great difficulties for the acceptance of this proposition.

Biopoiesis

The theory most widely accepted currently is called Biopoiesis which proposes that the first living things evolved naturally from inorganic matter. It is a plausible and well reasoned hypothesis supported at certain important points by confirmatory experiments. It was put forward in 1924 by A. I. Oparin who proposed that the complex organisation of living things was a *natural* process in the evolution of matter. Basically the idea is that from the oceans of the Earth in its primitive condition, large amounts of complex organic compounds reacted with each other and in so doing produced more and more complex molecules until finally one turned up which could be classified as "alive".

Oparin did some brilliant work by mixing solutions of different proteins and other substances of high molecular weight and demonstrated he could produce droplets capable of absorbing organic substances from his primitive sea. In 1926 J. B. S. Haldane speculated that ultra-violet light acting on a mixture of water, carbon dioxide and ammonia could produce organic compounds in the early oceans. This overcame an enormous problem in that if a "live" molecule evolved it would have something to "eat".

Chemists, working on these principles, have actually produced the amino acids, adenine and guanine which are the purines peculiar to RNA and DNA acids and also some protein-like polymers. Other fascinating experiments are proceeding. We must always remember that all these experiments are designed by men of outstanding intelligence and that they take place in strictly controlled conditions in advanced laboratories — a far cry from the primitive "soup" in which they may have happened countless years ago. We constantly run up against the temperature problem already referred to. The acceptance of Biopoiesis at this stage of research appears to entail the assumption that the Earth's temperature range has remained approximately as it is now for a period of two billion years, the point of time at which the "Biopoiesians" think it likely that life on Earth came to be. There is a lot of evidence from geophysicists and astronomers, however, that the Earth's temperature range has varied over a wide scale in the period of time suggested above, a scale too large to allow life to continue to develop.

Let us have a look at the probability of the DNA molecule evolving by pure chance completely independent of a design or designer. Unrelated materials and situations we need simultaneously for the formation of a DNA molecule would include (the list is by no means complete):

1. A temperature range somewhere between oc and 7oc as outside limits (Note: water in liquid form is essential, though life once initiated, can exist at temperatures below freezing and for a short time at temperatures of 7oc).

2. The organisation and formation of nucleotides and nucleosides.

3. More or less simultaneous formation of the RNA molecules.

4. *Simultaneous* availability of the following complex organic chemicals.

  (*a*) Adenine as Adenosine and Adenylic acid.

  (*b*) Guanine as Guanosine and Guanylic acid.

  (*c*) Cytosine as Cytidine and Cytidylic acid.

  (*d*) Uracil and Uridine and Uridylic acid.

  (*e*) Thymine as Thymidine and Thymidylic acid.

  (*f*) Select enzymes.

5. DNA molecules from different species differ in the relative proportions of their purine and pyrimidine basis therefore we need an inbuilt or exterior "programmed" catalyst to effect these mutations.

6. Something to make the nucleotides pair up and form spiral spring type chains.

7. The sugar phosphate material to make the chains.

8. Something to make the two spiral springs of the DNA molecule come together in an interlocked situation.

9. Something to limit the diameters of the various spirals of the chains so that they coincide.

10. The hydrogen bonding "glue" which "sticks" the bases of the double helix of the molecule together on the same plane so the spirals can interlock.

11. Something to organise the DNA molecules in *double helix* formation.

12. Something to make the adenine-thymine and guanine cystosine pairs mate up.

13. Something to control the volume, mass and shape of the effect described in 6 above.

14. Some catalyst, power, or force capable of making the pairs of molecules split into single molecules of the same composition, shape and organisation in genital cells.

15. The source of the metabolic action of the single DNA cells in the mother and daughter units enabling them to build up into a paired system again.

16. The availability of suitable "food" for this metabolic action. Surely this food needs to be organic — then "which came first, the chicken or the egg?"

This list quite obviously is not the work of a qualified biologist. It was compiled from notes at least ten years old by the writer who is merely an interested spectator. The sole purpose in compiling it is to paint a picture, certainly not to give a course in micro-biology.

Let us assume that the chance of each of the above events happening simultaneously and spontaneously is 1 in a million for each event. (Actually in most instances the probability would be much rarer than that proposed.) This would give us a figure of the overall chance of DNA evolving from the "soup" or "stew" of the primitive Earth as 1 in 10^{132}. Expressing it thus, in mathematical shorthand, we really conceal the drama of the picture. As an exercise try writing 1 followed by 132 zeros and realise you are talking about the probability of one chance in that number occurring. Interesting support for this approach comes from the experience of Professor Sir Fred Hoyle and Professor Wickramasinghe of the University of Cardiff in Wales. Both were "fashionable" agnostic evolutionists until they applied the mathematics of probabilities to the proposition that life on Earth is a random chance phen-

omenon and that evolution of *different species* followed
Darwin's principles of "survival of the fittest" and "adaptation to the environment". By painstaking investigation
they both arrived at a probability of 1 in $10^{40,000}$ (that is 1 in
1 followed by 40,000 noughts) as the chance of Darwin's
hypothesis being correct. Wickramasinghe added "For life
to have been a chemical accident on Earth is like looking for
a particular grain of sand on all the beaches in all the
planets in the universe — and finding it." Both men are
now theists.

We propose that the atheist must have an enormous faith
in the primitive "stew" or "soup" of the forming Earth or
something that he naively calls "nature". Of course we
have nowhere near exhausted our long shot probabilities at
the DNA stage. To add to the problem we have now to get
the DNA, RNA and other components of a living cell
together. We have to account for the cell's ability to
replicate. We know the DNA molecule can do this but how
does it persuade the cell to do the same act? Add to the list
the formation of proteins, the functions of advanced
metabolism, with its digestive and waste elimination
systems, the organisation of the identical cells into proteins
capable of forming bones, muscles, sinews and organs as
potentially different as the eye, ear, nose, the skin and the
nervous system with its many functions, the incredible
tissue we call the brain and so on and we state without
reserve that the proposition that life on Earth came to be
without the intervention of an All Wise Creator is mathematically untenable. This is not to say that life on Earth as
we know it now did not evolve, but rather that if it did so, it
must have been under the direction and guidance of a
Supreme Intelligence. It is also suggested that it is far more
reasonable to hold the view that mutations were from time
to time directed. Of course the means used may have been
enormous or even delicate electric discharges, radiation in
one form or another, or any "natural phenomenon". We
have an excellent analogy in the laboratory experiments
already mentioned and in others at present being under-
taken in attempts to form living matter synthetically or to

effect mutations by cloning and other methods.
Suppose some scientific genius does succeed in creating
a living cell. What has happened? He has merely proved
that:
  1. the production of life or a mutation requires the
intervention of great intelligence.
  2. the "laboratory" concerned must be superbly
equipped and controlled.
*This is exactly what the believer proposes that God did and
does.*
   It is not at all unlikely that we may, in the reasonably
near future, be able to "build" a chemically complete cell,
though it must be admitted that this achievement would
probably be the most involved and complicated piece of
engineering ever produced by a human being. The great
unanswered question remains. Can we induce it to reproduce spontaneously without incorporating in its structure a "bud" of some already living organism? We keep
coming back to the critical question: what is life itself *per
se*? Great minds have exercised themselves with this
question in the twentieth century and a review of their
work will be attempted in a later chapter.
   Proceeding one step further up the ladder from the
miracle of the living cell with its inbuilt metabolism and
ability to reproduce itself by duplication we come to the
block named "Sea weeds and Invertebrates". This marks a
radical change of life-style from a single cell.
   It represents the first successful movement of cells to
form a colony with its own purposeful existence and
demonstrates the ability of the DNA molecule to direct the
formation of proteins capable of different tasks within the
one organism. Without going into detail it is obvious that
these colonies of cells which we call sea weeds or jelly fish
have the ability to reproduce *their own kind*. Why don't
they disintigrate and fall back into groups of unrelated cells
again or alternatively reform in some new species? The
materialist will tell you it is because the DNA molecule
programmes the reproductive system to reproduce its
own kind. *But why does it do this?* The materialist will

never answer the second "why". He is not interested in ultimate causes. He will tell you that you have asked a silly question. He will demonstrate how the "programming" works but will not tell you why. It is like an instructor informing his class how a computer works. Ultimately however the computer will not respond, no matter what you do to it *until someone turns on the power switch*. The scientist who is a theist, on the other hand, starts his work on the problem from the other end. He knows where the "power point" is and suggests what will happen once it is turned on. From sea weeds and invertebrates we move up our ladder to "fishes". Fish have a skeletal structure, brain, nervous system, sense organs and highly developed metabolic and waste disposal systems. They are also sexual in their method of reproduction. All sexual activity requires co-operation in some degree between compatible males and females. The "creationist" obviously has a strong case here for his stand for individual and direct creation of the species. The materialist evolutionist on the other hand is driven to extremes of speculation and rationalisation. This is so in every instance where massive mutation of pre-existing species would be required to produce the next upward step in the evolutionary procedure. Evidence from palaeontology is from its very reliance on fossils, both slight and fragmentary. However when we consider the massive effects that relatively minor mutations of combinations and permutations in the structure of the DNA molecule can effect, the case for evolution is far from demolished. It is suggested that if evolution be the methodology by which the *new species* is produced the case for direction and control by a Master Mind against pure chance is, on the basis of probabilities, overwhelmingly convincing. There are other similar and massive jumps in our ladder (in which, incidently, I have followed generally the sequence proposed by Michael H. Day in his book *Fossil Man* (Hamlyn). Typical examples are birds to mammals and mammals to primates. Finally of course is the inexplicable leap from hominids to *homo-sapiens*.

The theist who, in company with the author, is prepared

to accept a directed evolutionary process as a possible explanation of the emergence of a different species of life at this stage of our never ending voyage of discovery, has the privilege of being able to view the phenomenon of terrestial life from still another interesting point of view. Accepting as he does a Creator of infinite power and intelligence, and mankind as a recently arrived psychosomatic phenomenon he can view the development and multiplication of the life forms as an intelligently conceived plan to provide an ecosystem in which man can live, procreate and prosper. Let us summarise. There are so many finely tuned features about the Earth which are all necessary to support life (and particularly human life) that it is by no means an absurd hypothesis that our planet is unique. This of course does not in any way exclude the possibility that different kinds of life may exist on other planets or even stars, perhaps in gaseous forms or based say on silica instead of carbon or some entirely different and unknown chemistry. Such speculations at this point are really in the realm of science fiction. However, never let us forget that less than a century ago the works of Jules Verne were classed as science fiction and in that short period of time men *have* walked on the moon, the Earth has been circumnavigated in *hours,* men in a space ship have witnessed four sunsets in 24 hours and as for submarines they are so commonplace as scarcely to raise an eyebrow!

When we come to the building blocks of life, for example the DNA molecule, let it be asserted that to posit that such a miracle of design and planning came to be by chance out of the chaos of the forming Earth is to classify the person making that assertion as a "fundamentalist" of the scientific genre who is prepared to ignore the evidence of the balance of probabilities and indeed the structure of the molecule itself, simply because he wills not to believe in God under any circumstances. This attitude which is really a negative form of faith can be found right across the spectrum of human intelligence. There is, for example, the story of the philosopher Heidegger who, when lecturing, announced to his class a conclusion based on certain evidence. A student rose in his place and commented "But, Herr Professor, your conclusion seems at variance with what the facts reveal"; to which Heidegger replied "So much the worse for the facts!" Heidegger was a philosophical "fundamentalist".

Jelly Fish to Mammals

In the stand we have taken we find ourselves in the company of a growing number of thinkers and scientists. In his book *What is Life?* — *Mind and Matter*, Erwin Schrödinger, Professor of Physics at the University of Vienna and the discoverer of wave mechanics, says, in a discussion on the function of chromosome fibres (for which he is using the analogy of the cogs of a clock): "the single cog (a chromosome fibre) is not of coarse human make, but is the finest masterpiece ever achieved along the lines of the Lord's quantum mechanics". (My copy published by Cambridge University Press, 1977.) Having moved up our evolutionary pyramid on our diagram and observed the successive emergence in time of invertebrates, fishes, plants, amphibians, reptiles, birds, mammals, primates and *homo sapiens* we can find in any modern text book on biology weighty evidence that each species survived, failed, or underwent mutation according to "the survival of the fittest" principle. We have on the other hand considered the evidence against random chance as the way life came to be. There is of course no doubt at all that adaptation to the environment produces variations *within any species* of a lower order than mankind and that the factor making for those changes is "survival of the fittest". There is weighty evidence to support this view which was observed and described very well by Charles Darwin. In comparison, the existing direct evidence for one species evolving out of a prior species is really very thin. Admittedly from the point of view of comparative biology and using the existing specimens as our basis of comparison there are marked resemblances in the anatomy and physiology of many different species of life on Earth today.

Again, these coincide both in resemblance and difference in many instances with the proposed order of appearance of the various species suggested by the evolutionist. Obviously the combined evidence of palaeontology and comparative anatomy or biology could be used with equal validity as proof of two incompatible conclusions. First that the "evolution by chance and adaptation" theory may be correct or alternatively that the different species are the handiwork of the same single intelligence, the same "Master Craftsman", using similar design criteria where similar functions are required. The claim that mutations from one species to another were triggered by high voltage electric activity such as lightning or exposure to some form of radiation can be used either to support the "chance" theory or the "design" theory. In view of the fact that bolts from the blue either by lightning or radiation would of necessity require to be within strictly controlled limits certainly weighs in favour of the idea of guidance by a Supreme Intelligence. Working strictly within the rules of empirical scientific methodology the evolution of man, at this time and age, can neither be proved nor disproved. Again we can be guided only by a balance of probabilities. Let it also be said that there is considerable evidence in favour of the evolution of man's animal body. Where there is ample room for varied opinion is whether this evolution was directed or whether it occurred by chance. Many features of the human body are similar to those of primates and to the pictures drawn of hominids. But don't forget the hominid is a concept of a creature strongly resembling the *primates*; unfortunately there are none of them around for us to examine.

Modern Man

Modern man (*homo sapiens*) appears to be unique in many ways. He is certainly psychosomatic. This word means different things to different people. We all agree man has a body and relatively a very large brain. This is the "soma" part which can be, has been and will be examined by scientists in great detail. As already stated the mystifying area is called by the various names of mind, soul, spirit, self and so on. These different words amount in the final analysis to viewing the "psycho" aspect of man through the different coloured spectacles of the atheist, theist, psychologist, anthropologist, neurologist or other specialised points of view. As this component of *homo sapiens* is not material it is really outside the competence of the empirical scientist to deal with it at all. It becomes the prerogative of the philosopher, the theologian and the so called social scientist all of whom work with methodologies foreign to the empiricist.

The diagram on page 81 shows on the left side a table which designates the generally accepted classifications of the Earth's geological formation. The centre column is the time gap proposed currently, working backwards from the present to the Earth's origin as we know it. On the right of the time column is indicated the evolutionary history of life on Earth as it is currently taught.

People holding the "evolution by chance" approach to man's existence rely heavily for evidence on fossils and presently accepted dating systems for rock formations. Palaeontology combines the significance of fossil discoveries and geological dating. It is a relatively young science but has attracted a number of brilliant minds. It is a fascinating study and no doubt it should be encouraged and assisted as a most valuable aid in our search for our origins. However it poses traps for the "fundamentalists" both of the creationist and atheistic evolutionist camps. The creationist seems to consider it a challenge to his faith and ridicules the whole idea. His objections stem in the main from the relative paucity of material discovered and difficulties with geological dating. Other objections include the lack of evidence for mutations and some puzzling inversions of accepted geological strata. The "fundamentalist atheistic evolutionist" also creates difficulties by tending to ignore the obvious problems mentioned above and to come to conclusions on very flimsy evidence. If however we turn to sources which are not biased, the subject can be profitably examined. Michael Day's book *Fossil Man* details most of the important discoveries and the way palaeontologists have related their various finds to produce a tentative picture from the evidence so far available. The last two sentences in the book give an honest summary and are recommended as the correct mental attitude in dealing with a young developing science. Day says, "The best synthesis that can be offered, in honesty, is to indicate the major structural phases leading towards hominisation, with the warning that individual known fossils within those groups are by no means necessarily ancestral to each other. What is known of the evolution of man is still but a fraction of what there is yet to learn."

There is a lamentable tendency for "fundamentalists" of both camps to rush to conclusions which appear to support their preconceived ideas. This attitude is neither scientific nor honest. The classic example is the "Piltdown Man". In 1912 it was announced that some skeletal remains had been found in England at Piltdown, including the upper part of a human skull and a broken lower apelike jaw-bone with the teeth worn down the way human teeth age. One possible clue, an important canine tooth, was missing. Eight months later the missing tooth was found. Over the next few years other bone remains were discovered. The evidence was assembled, drawings made which purported to be primitive man 500,000 years old. The claim was made and it appeared quite rational that this find proved a sort of missing link between apes and modern man. This was fairly generally accepted. Years later however the skull was proved without doubt to be that of a modern man, the jaw proved to be from a recently deceased ape, the jaw-bone and teeth had been chemically stained and the teeth had been filed to give the appearance desired by the discoverer.

The biblical fundamentalists reacted by completely discounting the value of all palaeontological work while the evolutionist fundamentalist camp rationalised the deception as only a practical joke and proceeded on a "who dunnit" course which has never been satisfactorily solved.

The genuine scientist on the other hand reacted sensibly by standardising and tightening identification and dating procedures to prevent a repetition of this hoax. There are many unanswered problems at the present stage of our knowledge of human life and we should encourage all genuine research. It is quite a natural and healthy attitude if we find evidence to support a concept to look for further evidence but one must always be prepared to accept facts as they come to hand even if they contradict or modify our initial hypothesis. Also it is imperative to make sure our evidence is sufficiently weighty to justify a theory.

There are two mathematical laws which the fundamentalist evolutionist seems to ignore. The first is the famous Second Law of Thermo-dynamics. As Erwin Schrödinger points out in his book *What is Life? Mind and Matter* (C.U.P., 1944), "Life seems to be orderly and lawful behaviour of matter not based exclusively on its tendency to go over from order to disorder, but based partly on existing order that is kept up." From the second Law of Thermodynamics we deduce the tendency for matter to resolve into a state of disorder unless energy is expended to prevent this happening or to move it into a different determined order. Whence the order? Whence the energy?

The second principle which appears to be overlooked is the Square Root of n Rule. In any physical law the accuracy of an assessment is gauged by setting an expected error equal to the square root of the number of specimens under observation. For example, if during an experiment one might expect 100 molecules of a certain gas to be present under controlled conditions, then according to our rule we would expect an error in the order of 10%; if we were dealing with a million molecules it would be likely that we would find an error of about ·1%. Now from time to time we are asked by palaeontologists and fundamentalist evolutionists to accept a single specimen as evidence of a certain development. Now the square root of one is one; in other words a single specimen is meaningless. It may be a freak. Its only value in reality is a stimulus to find and examine more and more specimens until the expected error diminishes to a point where an hypothesis can be accepted as reasonable. While single samples or sparsity of samples may not mean much in themselves the palaeontologist can nevertheless seek support from currently existing creatures. Here anthropology, zoology, biology and biochemistry may possibly combine to give added credence to the conclusions proposed or alternatively to make them suspect.

– The palaeontologist's enthusiasm for single samples has good support from the unique character of the DNA molecule, *viz* its ability to reproduce itself. If a desired fossil or preserved specimen is found there is always the strong probability that the sample found has influenced genetic history by passing on its unique DNA characteristics by procreation. This neutralises to some extent the application of the Square Root of n Rule. When we come to variations in species, however, we must remember that there is a cut off point where differences make procreation between like species unlikely or discontinuous. The obvious example is cross-mating horses and donkeys resulting in the birth of mules or hinnies. These creatures do not reproduce their species. This raises the problem that in a new species we require the almost simultaneous availability of compatible male and female elements. The different species found on our Earth today are in the main genetically incompatible. It is hard for anyone familiar with demographic mathematics to share the palaeontologist's excitement over single or sparse sampling.

So far our developmental pyramid has produced for us by direct creation, chance evolution, or directed evolution, mankind and an ecosystem which supports him. In other words we have dealt at some length with the *"soma"* aspect of *homo sapiens*. Let us now give some thought to the psychic potencies of this remarkable creature.

Man's Psychic Aspect

For a start we have an animal with a relatively large brain hypostatically united with an immortal element we call the soul. Man consists of body/soul not body AND soul. You cannot extract the soul from a human body and experiment with it or relate to it, nor for that matter can you deal with a man as apart from his soul. The whole idea of a disembodied soul stems from the acceptance of time as a universal constant. Einstein effectively laid this error to rest. That is why it is so important to understand the concept of eternity as a *higher level of existence* as explained in chapter 2. Again let us emphasise that when we are using human language we are limited by time/space boundaries. Fortunately the Bible and the Church teach consistently in this language but as the scriptural references used in chapter 2 indicate, the concept of eternity is clearly inferred. No difficulty whatever is experienced in reconciling biblical and dogmatic language with the picture given in this book, as long as we accept the limitations of our language in describing situations transcendent in relation to the limits of mortal experience. This soul of ours possesses potencies above and beyond anything found in the animal kingdom. It is capable of producing acts of imagination, affection, will and reason and it controls our unique gift of speech. It possesses a remarkable degree of freedom of choice which it exercises to produce the acts and attitudes carried out and adopted by each individual.

This gift of freedom is the key both to the most sublime acts of which man is capable and also to the problem of evil. The Christian thesis is that man was given freedom by his Creator so that he could *love* both God and his fellowman. Love is a freely determined act of self-giving by the lover to the object of his affection. A human person cannot be coerced into loving. He must be free to love in the *agape* degree. Remember that love in this dimension always involves the will, at least to some extent, in its act of giving.

God, the Almighty, the Omnipotent, the Creator and Sustainer of the universe is "Love", all giving, all act. In this context love implies a notion of tremendous *power*; the power to create from nothing, the power to sustain both substance and movement throughout the universe.

Believing this we observe all created things tending to develop towards their planned destiny. The healing of a wound is a wonder. The wound itself is indicative of the presence and power of evil. The healing process is a grace, an intervention of God to keep alive and to stimulate our faculties of faith and hope.

By giving mankind the gift of freedom his Creator invited him to share in the Divine power of "love". He invited mankind to be pro-creators, builders, sustainers, givers, both in his relations with God himself and with his fellowmen. In other words he gave his masterpiece in the material creation the ability to use the Divine power (*agape*). It was specifically to enable this potency to be activated that God gave mankind this gift of freedom of choice; an act which Fr. Bernard Bassett S.J. describes as "God's calculated risk". The Book of Genesis describes in a sensitive allegorical manner how this worked out. From all the luxury and profusion of the Garden of Eden, God forbade man access to one fruit only. This was essential if mankind was to have freedom of choice. Tragically the woman and the man, instead of *GIVING* their minds and selves completely to their most generous Creator, *TOOK* the forbidden fruit. They comitted an act containing the exact opposite of the idea of *agape*. In doing so they unleashed the full creative power of love as a destructive power of rebellion and selfishness. The opportunity presented to become co-creators was distorted and reversed producing the effect the Greeks call *hamartia*, the divine power preceeded by a negative index, an infinite power of destruction, disease, confusion and misery. Mankind passed from life to death, from light to darkness, and his choice of evil instead of good affected everything on the face of the Earth and, who knows, — perhaps the universe! *Hamartia* is like an evil disease, a poison gas. It is the epitome of disorder. Mankind continues by his nature to create, to build, to construct, to move towards the sublime, but is constantly thwarted without rhyme or reason by the intrusion of *hamartia*. It is this inherent tendency to disorder which we call "original sin". Man and his Earth were placed in a hopeless condition. However God's power (his *agape*) is infinite so that he gave mankind another opportunity to use the gift of freedom of choice positively.

Mary

A little over two thousand years ago a Jewish girl was born in a little town called Nazareth and she was chosen by God to give us a second chance. The girl's name was Mary. When she was about sixteen years old she was betrothed to a carpenter named Joseph. Betrothal in Jewish law at that time was a serious and definite committal to marriage. Before the marriage ceremony she had an extraordinary experience described in detail in the first chapter of St. Luke's Gospel. She was challenged by God to accept his offer to generate in her virgin womb a male child without normal copulation with a man. Fortunately for us all Mary's love of God was in the *agape* dimension. She accepted the challenge, fully aware that under Jewish Law (see Deuteronomy 22: 13-21) she took the risk of being stoned to death. In doing so she demonstrated love in the *agape* sense to its highest degree. As her Divine Son later said, "There is no greater love than this; than that a man should lay down his life for his friend". In Mary's act and later by the life, death, and resurrection and ascension of her God/man Son, the *agape* relationship offered by the Creator to the first man and woman in Eden was more than fully restored. This picture will be expanded in later chapters.

CHAPTER 4

REVELATION

EARLY in this book the principle of belief in God, the Creator of all that is, seen and unseen was proposed unequivocally. We have also dealt with mankind, a spirit/ flesh creature intelligent and free. He is part of all that is, seen and unseen. He has the gift of speech by which is included all means of interpersonal rational communication such as writing, signs, art forms, music and so on. Granting these facts is it reasonable to assume that, having created a creature capable of communicating intelligently, God would stand aloof from all communication with his masterpiece of creation in the material world and allow him to flounder in ignorance of the Divine will and all that can contribute to his fulfilment and happiness? The answer to this question on the premises proposed must be "no", and the corollary must be that there is only one source of revelation and that is God.

Natural Revelation

Revelation, that is enlightenment initiated by God for the benefit of mankind, can be examined at different levels.

St. Paul tells us God wills all men to be saved and to come to the full knowledge of the truth (1 Tim. 2:4). The Second Vatican Council in its Dogmatic Constitution on the Church states, "Nor does divine Providence deny the help necessary for salvation to those who without blame on their part have not yet arrived at an explicit knowledge of God, but who strive to lead a good life thanks to his grace" (*Lumen Gentium*, chap. 1 para. 16). In this sentence the reference to grace is significant. The question immediately arises as to how this "grace" operates.

Man has no explicit knowledge of God let alone of Christ. When he deals with revelation Cardinal Newman makes the point that it must be a revealing of *religious* knowledge. Let us create a character "Bill the bus driver". He has no religious education whatever but is a good husband, a loving father and a conscientious workman. There are many Bills and they are the salt of the earth. To provide for his family he is always available for overtime and finds his chosen lifestyle consumes all his energy. He is far too busy to think of "abstract" ideas like God. From his earliest days he has of necessity worked unceasingly and consequently is illiterate and has no formal education. Once a year he struggles to take his equally hardworking wife and the children for a week's holiday at the seaside or in the country. His soul literally soaks up the beauty of the sea, the sky, the wooded hills and at night-time the wonder of the star-filled sky. He takes his missus down to the "local" when the kiddies are asleep and revels in, and returns, the cheerful banter of the other people in the bar; he partners his wife at darts and enjoys both victory and defeat. What is Bill's source of "revelation"? The Second Vatican Council answers this question superbly in its document *Dei Verbum* in chapter 1, para. 3. "God who through the Word creates all things and keeps them in existence gives men an enduring witness to himself in created realities."

Going right to the other extreme of the human spectrum we find a dedicated pathologist, son of a father famous in the same field. At a different social level the pathologist is basically of the same mould as Bill. His whole time and energy is divided between his family and his profession. He is completely dedicated to the cure and prevention of human suffering. His "revelation" doubtless comes to him through his microscope and the parallel dedication of his assistants, and the patience of those he tends.

In both cases God has given these men enduring witness to himself in created realities and confirmed his revelation by endowing each man with the grace to lead a good life. These people are in what may be described as a "pre-evangelisation" stage. Given a final option in the process of dying there is little doubt they would opt for Christ.

This brings us to the point that scientific discovery has a right to be classified not only as a revelation but also as basically religious, i.e. revealed by God to mankind as Newman insists. It tells of God through the wonder of his works. We are also brought face to face again with the problem of evil (*hamartia*), for example when scientists having discovered the ultimate source of power and energy in atomic fusion, use that knowledge to produce a horrifying weapon like the hydrogen bomb. So much for revelation at the basic or natural level. Created realities reveal the nature and wonder of God even if the message is not explicitly recognised.

Theistic Revelation

Let us move up a step to those millions of human beings probably the vast majority of the human race whom we will designate for want of a better term as "theists". In this group concepts of the nature of the *Theos* vary from culture to culture significantly. The common factor is that they all subscribe to the existence of a Prime Cause of all things. Generally even polytheists have their Jupiter or Zeus the chief of all the gods. To these people revelation is available through the "created realities" already referred to. Also, in so far as they have created in their minds a picture of the Creator, to the extent that that picture corresponds with the ultimate "Reality", it is possible for God to communicate with them. As must be obvious from what has been written so far, it is beyond human comprehension to achieve unaided a full and correct notion of God. God is the ultimate theological mystery. We can see the need for his existence as clearly as we recognise our inability to comprehend him fully. The result has been throughout mankind's history to conceive a picture of God in human terms and characteristics (anthropomorphism). The limitations of these conceptions form a bar to the understanding of divine revelation.

A belief in God has one immediate effect on human beings. The sincere belief in a Creator who also sustains us, usually generates a comprehension to some degree of the immortal element in mankind. As soon as this stage is reached (which is itself a revelation) there is a logical tendency for the believer to order his conduct to conform as far as possible to that of his God or gods or at least to placate them. Thus a moral code evolves. Now a moral code will work only in a like minded community. Hence in any civilised society we find the introduction of sanctions and penalties coercing the members to comply with fixed standards of behaviour. Here immediately we perceive a result of revelation. We see in the behaviour of the believers an acted-out concept of their idea of God. Generally the rule is, the greater degree of anthropomorphism the lower and baser are the standards of morality flowing from that particular caricature of God. There is too much "man" mixed with God. A further principle has been achieved and that is that revelation becomes a force only when accepted by a like-minded community.

It is not possible in a book of this size to detail the multitude of theistic cults that exist in the world today. They are in the main distinguished by two opposing principles which we will call transcendentalism and pantheism.

Those people who worship a transcendent God are faced with the problem of identifying and describing their deity and normally introduce many human characteristics into the nature of their God and as already stated their moral codes, their laws and life styles reflect the extent to which they have humanised the deity.

Pantheism is a view of reality that tends to identify the world with God or God with the world. Naturally it emphasises the immanence of God in the world and ignores or greatly reduces the idea of his transcendence. Any religion that teaches that God created material things out of himself is basically pantheistic. The outstanding example is Buddhism. The natural corollary is that to describe Buddhism it is necessary to define it in each country in which it is practised as it naturally takes the shape of the philosophical and cultural standards of each race. Although it teaches high and altruistic standards these tend to constant degeneration as there is no fixed definition of the words used to describe its cults and beliefs. Thus the same words can be used in different cultures with basically different meanings. In fact Buddhism is implicitly atheistic. Pantheism of any kind tends to choke the reality of revelation as does any false idea of God.

Pre Christian Revelation

The Old Testament of the Bible is a fascinating library of books stemming from traditions many thousands of years old. Doubtless much material comes from a pre-literary stage of human development and has been passed on orally from generation to generation until finally an edition, doubtless freely edited time and time again in its transmission, was committed to writing. Most of the Pentateuch (the first five books of the Bible) has come to us this way. The Pentateuch is accepted as inspired by Christians, Jews and Muslims, in all, a formidable proportion of the human race. Amongst religious sagas it is distinguished immediately by its insistence on the existence of one God, Creator out of nothing of all that is, seen and useen. Remember that it was generated in an era of human history when as far as we are able to ascertain, most people believed in a plurality of gods. The monotheistic principle, doubtless a revelation in itself, opened up the whole idea of revelation in that men identified God as a person, omnipotent, eternal amd immutable. It made revelation available in two ways which we will call respectively the "objective" way and the "interpersonal" way. Objective revelation includes knowledge, principles, laws of nature and life, and guides to social mores and religious beliefs and activities. Interpersonal revelation is a relationship between an individual man or woman and the person of God. The idea of God as immutable has another important effect in that it provides an opportunity for the "wisdom"

GEOLOGICAL NAMES AND TIMES

The Earth (Geological Names & Times)				Years from Present	Life on Earth	Time Column Compressed to 1 year
Aeon	Era	Period	Epoch			
Phanerozoic	Cenozoic	Quaternary	Holocene (recent)	10,000	Homo Sapiens Modern Man	31 Dec. 11.50 p.m.
			Pleistocene	2,000,000	Early Man	31 Dec. 11 p.m.
		Tertiary	Pleiocene	10,000,000	Hominids	31 Dec. 6 p.m.
			Miocene	25,000,000		
			Oligocene	40,000,000		
			Eocene	55,000,000		
			Paleocene	65,000,000	Primates	24 Dec.
	Mesozoic	Cretaceous		135,000,000		
		Jurassic		190,000,000	Birds	16 Dec.
		Triassic		225,000,000	Mammals	13 Dec.
	Paleozoic	Permian		280,000,000		
		Carboniferous	Pennsylvanian	315,000,000	Reptiles	5 Dec.
			Mississippian	345,000,000		
		Devonian		400,000,000	Amphibians	30 Nov.
		Silurian		440,000,000	Land plants	
		Ordovician		500,000,000	Fishes	Late November
		Cambrian		520,000,000		
Cryptozoic	Proterozoic	Precambrian			Sea weeds and Invertebrates	Early October
	Archeozoic (Archeon)				Living cells	June
Azoic				4,550,000,000	The Earth stabilised	1st January

of the human race to accumulate. Objective or personal experiences of communication with God can be recorded; they need not be rediscovered by each succeeding generation but they certainly can be added to, opened up, modified and refined as men try to discover more and more the truth about God. God's response to this constant seeking becomes obvious as we study the Old Testament. It is a far cry from the manlike avenging God of the early books to the God revealed by the prophets: from the wholesale slaughter and intrigue of the Kings and Judges to the God of Isaiah (42:3ff) who "does not break the bruised reed nor quench the wavering flame" or of Micah (7:8) who says "what is good has been explained to you, man; only this, to act justly, to love tenderly and to walk humbly with your God". The Old Testament period produced the ten commandments which constitute a remarkable, brief and essentially practical set of rules for personal and social conduct. Codes of law and social *mores* even to this day are based to a considerable extent on the decalogue and an interesting observation might be that those areas of personal and social behaviour which are producing trouble in western civilisation are to a considerable extent those in which we have drifted away from the standards of the commandments.

The Book of Genesis is a very interesting human document. The reader is referred to two modern studies of the work by Bruce Vawter. The first entitled *A Path Through Genesis* was published in 1957, while the second, published in 1977, is called *On Genesis*. The study of these two works, while being rewarding for it's intense interest demonstrates the advances made in biblical scholarship during the past twenty years. Genesis portrays ingeniously:

1. God as the first cause of all material creation.
2. the development of an ecosystem in which human life could flourish and procreate.
3. the dominance of man over all created things.
4. the complementarity of human sexual relationships.
5. the emergence of a human "soul" and the consequent

ability for this amazing creature to "walk and talk with God".

6. man's freedom of choice.

7. the devastating effect of using this freedom "out of phase" with the will of God.

8. in the deluge story, the deadly destructive consequences of sin.

9. hope as a part of man's psyche.

10. man's utter dependence on God for sustenance and survival.

11. the phenomenon of physical death as a result of the loss of perfection, the *sine qua non* of eternal existence.

12. the readiness of God to provide a remedy for sin.

13. in the Tower of Babel story, the futility of man's efforts to save himself and his utter dependence on God's help (grace).

14. in the Abraham story, the vital importance of man's faith and confidence in God.

15. the evolution of a tribe of people whose sole trust and hope rested in God.

All these revelations come through a saga in which human virtues and vices are recorded with equal frankness. The portrayal of God is distinctly anthropomorphic but emphasis is laid on both the unapproachable, incomprehensible (transcendent) nature of God, as well as his close interest in human affairs and his availability to those who call on him (immanence).

Exodus tells us of the nation of Israel escaping from Egypt after four hundred years of enslavement. It is hard for us to envisage what enslavement meant. A slave had few more rights than an animal; sometimes less rights than most animals have today, where in the more civilised countries cruelty to animals is a criminal offence. The master of a slave could torture, mutilate or kill a slave as he willed. He could buy or sell individuals as he wished. Slaves often bred like animals with no family or communal life. They were simply labourers or in some circumstances objects of sensual pleasure which at times reached the depths of depravity.

The escape from Egypt described in Exodus tells the story of some hundreds of thousands of these illiterate, oppressed people being forced into community life with restricted experience for generations of family or tribal communities. Out of this chaotic situation Moses and Aaron developed a close knit nation in the space of forty years. The only rallying point was the common belief in the one God. Viewed against this background one can only describe the ten commandments (decalogue) as an astonishing revelation, setting a simple but highly effective set of rules for interpersonal and community relationship. Notice how the first four commandments root all that follows in faith in the one God and in reverence for him. Thus it was that obedience to these laws rose above politics and the daily problems and concerns. In the later chapters of Exodus there is much embellishment and detailed extension of the simple decalogue which portrays what appears to be an inbuilt tendency in human society, namely to multiply and complicate laws, sometimes to the point where they become too oppressive, so that "revolutions" follow and a fresh start is made. Inevitably history records that the same tendency recurs. This is of course the result of *hamartia* (original sin). We can't make a nation of saints by acts of parliament or edicts of dictators although we never cease trying to effect the impossible by regulation. In Exodus we have examples of treaties or covenants being made with God, based always on the principle, "You shall be my people and I will be your God".

The third book of the Pentateuch, Leviticus extends the later chapters of Exodus by recording all sorts of rules and regulations for personal and community life and for ritualistic worship. In this book we see the evolution of the ministerial priesthood and the idea of men consecrating their lives to the service of God in presenting the prayers and sacrifices of their fellowmen. We also see the custom of religious feasts and fasts introduced, as for example the Day of Atonement and the Feast of Tabernacles. The Books of Numbers and Deuteronomy complete the Pentateuch. They again consist in enlargements and modifications of existing laws to meet new situations.

The five books overall give a fascinating account of the evolution of a horde of ignorant, ill organised slaves into a highly organised nation. We see the growth of laws governing personal behaviour, family life, society and religion all based on the principle of God's omnipotence and transcendence yet asserting at every point his concern that his masterpiece of creation, mankind, should enjoy happiness by tuning his will to resonance with the will of the Creator.

To the modern mind many of the incidents recorded seem cruel and many of the rules harsh; nevertheless one can trace quite clearly a marked and upward tending development towards integrity, fairness and mutual respect. These five books are as stated a common heritage of Christians, Jews and Mohammedans. At this point in scripture revelation, Jews and Christians part company with the Muslims.

Common Judaeo-Christian Revelation

Both Christians and Israel commonly subscribe to at least another thirty-four books which together with the Pentateuch are called by Christians the "Old Testament". Most Christians include still another seven books in this compendium making a total library of forty six books. The difference in the two collections is due to the fact that there are two widely used "source-texts" of the Old Testament. The longer of the two versions is called the Septuagint and originated in Alexandria approximately between 200 and 100 B.C. where it was published in Greek. The shorter version is called the Masoretic Text and was published in Hebrew around about 100 A.D. Both texts have been subjected to centuries of revision. The Roman Catholic and Orthodox churches use the Septuagint version while most Protestants use translations of the Masoretic edition. Many Protestant bibles include the additional seven books in a section of their bibles called the Apocrypha.

These books, historically later than the Pentateuch,

indicate a steady development both in the content, nature and experience of revelation. They are classified by most scholars into three categories, namely the Historical books, the Wisdom books and the Prophets.

Each of these classes gives evidence of the fact and method of Divine Revelation in different circumstances. It must always be remembered that these ancient writings relate to nations, peoples and circumstances far removed from Western civilisation as we know it today. The discerning reader can however always find particular relevance to our times and society if he extracts the timeless messages they contain and reframes those messages in the historical and social circumstances in which we are living out our lives.

We saw how the effect of the ten commandments was to transform a horde of ignorant oppressed people into a civilised nation with a practical, working moral and social code of behaviour and how with experience those fundamental rules, based as they were on a treaty or covenant with the Creator, developed a strong individual and community sense of religious affinity with God which exists amongst the Jews to this day. Broadly the historical books reveal the development of relationships between nations. Disagreements and wars occur incessantly and then we see the emergence of negotiating skills and the restoration of normal relationships on an inter-tribal or international basis. All the strengths and weaknesses of autocratic forms of government are clearly outlined. The emphatic message of the historical books is the yearning of all men for peace based on justice, and that forms of government and international power, based on any other principle than justice, contain within themselves the germ of their own destruction and lead to war and turmoil rather than peace. Further, that those nations striving to live out their national destiny in resonance with the revealed will of God will ultimately prevail. Again we see the ever threatening power of evil thwarting all purely human effort to achieve perfection. The misuse of man's freedom to grab and enrich himself at the expense of others instead of

giving himself in the service of his fellow men is emphasised as the root of all evil.

The Wisdom Books are a unique collection of the works
of poets and philosophers, meditating principally on the
stories of the Pentateuch and the Historical Books, and
endeavouring to detect and emphasise the types of individual and community behaviour that seem to be in
resonance with the divine will. They do not hesitate to
offer advice to rulers and people as to how they should
regulate their thinking and action to avoid evil and do
good. An important development in these books is the
emergence of a conviction that it is a human duty and
obligation to praise and thank the Creator for his goodness
and mercy. They demonstrate an ever increasing consciousness of the power of evil and the need for men to
express sorrow to God for wrong doing both before God
and to their fellow men. The revelation comes through that
all sin is ultimately an offence against the Creator. Also
from experience and reflection they detect how easy it is for
men to obtain forgiveness of their sins by contrition,
confession and where possible restitution. A superb and
beautiful example of this revelation is Psalm 31 in translations of the Catholic and Orthodox bibles (numbered 32 in
Protestant editions).

In the Prophetical Books we encounter a further development in the purpose of God's self-revelation to men.
Usually dealing with the political and social situation in
which he finds himself the prophet speaks as inspired by
God whose will is revealed to him. He rarely if ever speaks
to individuals except to kings and rulers as representatives
of the people they govern. Quite often the prophet speaks
to tribes or nations. Since the prophet is an instrument of
God his message often transcends his own historical period
and even his own understanding. Sometimes his meaning
remains veiled until it becomes obvious in some future
figure or incident. Revelation reaches a peak in the
prophets of Israel. They obviously had experience of direct
communication with God and constantly remind men of
their duty to God and exhort them to repent, to obey and to

love. Prophecy in this sense is a gift peculiar to Israel and became the recognised means of guidance and encouragement of God's chosen people. The prophetical books taken as revelation emphasise some great principles:

1. there is one God and only one God.
2. he offers a saving relationship to mankind as a solemn covenant or contract.
3. in consideration for this relationship God requires an effective effort from mankind to live a religious, personal and social life which is in resonance with the known will of God already revealed.
4. God in his own time will send and appoint a perfect ruler who will reign over all mankind with absolute justice and integrity (the Messiah). He will be the Saviour of the world which, until his coming, is despoiled by sin (*hamartia*).

The story of God's revealing of himself up to the time of Christ parallels closely the progress of scientific discovery up to that time. Let us remember that one or two thousand years are an insignificant period in geological time. (See chart p. 81.) We have traced briefly the *crescendo* in religious revelation in the *millenia* immediately before Christ. In the same period we see a development in the depth of human thinking; for instance, in the Chinese, Indian, Egyptian and Greek philosophers. Also in this time the Egyptians and the Chinese in particular gave us the genesis of mathematics, astronomy, medicine, mechanics and principles of civil engineering construction. These sciences were developed successfully by the Greeks and Romans. In the social sphere we passed from the "might is right" principle of despotism, to the city/state system of the Greeks and then to the highly organised empire of the Romans. In retrospect it is not hard to see in the first Christmas Day the dawn of a new era.

Christian Revelation

The birth of Jesus Christ marks a turning point in our consideration of revelation. The whole notion of the word itself is changed radically, for in Christ, God reveals himself in himself. At the end of this book there is a summary of Christian belief known as the Nicene Creed. Excepting one variation in the Orthodox version of the creed over ninety five per cent of Christians assent to this definition of belief. As the exception noted deals with the Holy Spirit one could truthfully affirm a near complete consensus of opinion as to the nature and person of Jesus Christ amongst orthodox Christians. Jesus Christ is an historical figure. Modern scholarship dates his birth in Bethlehem in Palestine as between 6 and 4 B.C. and his death and resurrection at about 30 or 31 A.D.

All that follows is a revue of the notion of revelation developed from the conception of Jesus Christ in the womb of the Virgin Mary to the present through the eyes of a committed Christian.

Jesus Christ *is* God; the second Person of a Trinity of Persons each of whom is God and who together are God. All the absolute properties of God, eternal existence, knowing neither beginning nor end, omnipotence, perfection and majesty are possessed equally by each of the three Persons as they are also possessed by the Trinity; therefore no one Person is greater or less than another. As a result of this state of existence each Person and the triune God are beyond man's understanding; incomprehensible is the term normally used. We refer to the three Persons in human terms (because we have no other terms) as Father, Son and Holy Spirit. They are knit together by mutual love, utter and complete self-giving of one to the other. Therefore St. John tells us God is Love. From this we deduce that perfect "Love" is the power that creates and sustains the universe and everything that exists. Everything we know of the Trinity has been revealed to us. That revelation came to us in Jesus Christ, born as a man like us in all things but sin, in the historical era already described. His mother was a Jewish girl of Nazareth named Mary. The circumstances of his birth are described beautifully and in detail in the first and second chapters of St. Luke's Gospel. Mary was in every respect human, *perfectly* human. When Gabriel, God's messenger, informed Mary she was to give birth to a son he saluted her with the words "full of grace". Grace is a free gift of God to one of his creatures. She was informed that her child would be the Son of the Most High God. As any girl would, she asked how this could be as she was a virgin. The messenger told her no human father would sire the child who would consequently be called "Son of God". Reference has already been made in chapter 3 to the fact that in freely accepting this proposition Mary placed her life in jeopardy as she was already betrothed to a carpenter named Joseph. Here we have the extraordinary spectacle of a human girl whose confidence and trust in God was absolute and who was prepared to demonstrate her love in the *agape* sense by placing her life in God's hands. In the encounter between God and Mary we have perfect love meeting perfect love. On God's part the perfect love was intrinsic while on Mary's part the love was also perfect but a gift from God, grace in its plenitude. We have said God *is* Love. Hence in the incarnation of Jesus we have the beginning of the process of assuming fallen mankind into God, into Love! Here we have the power of love repairing the problem of sin, *hamartia*. A spiritual anti-toxin became available to mankind. We must never forget Mary was perfectly free. She had the right to refuse the messenger's proposition out of consideration for her own life and reputation. But love prevailed as a force superior to self-interest and hope and joy once more became human characteristics.

In the self-revelation of God to mankind in the incarnation of Jesus Christ we had the intrusion of the eternal into the time/space confines of normal human existence. The whole concept of revelation changed. First of all, all that had gone before, which we have discussed under various headings such as natural revelation, theistic revelation, pre-Christian revelation and so on, became relevant to the present. To the Christian all revelation given before Christ became part of an ever present "now" manifested in Christ. As Christ rose from the dead and lives now, that same corpus of revealed truth remains a present experience to men today as it did to the disciples of Christ two thousand years ago. So also, the second coming of Christ and the life of the world to come are brought into the category of immediate experience as the substance of Hope. Even the abiding presence of God in our midst became a fact the Church treasures in the Eucharist. We can now read the lovely poems in the book of Isaiah called the Suffering Servant Songs and recognise the face of Christ in their lyrics; so with all the prophets, the psalms and the literature of the Old Testament. Christ himself alerted us to this when he said, "Study the scriptures . . . these same scriptures testify to me" (Jn. 5:39). The scriptures to which our Lord referred were, of course, the Old Testament. Right from the beginning of the Christian Church both the Old and New Testaments have been revered as inspired.

Modern writers on the subject of revelation, emphasise another view of revelation and that is that it has a dynamic characteristic whereby objective, revealed truths defined at some period of history undergo a continuous process of development within a community by study, discussion, meditation and prayer. John Henry Newman gave birth to this idea in his famous *Essay on the Development of Christian doctrine*. It was also handled very well by Emile Mersch in his book *The Theology of the Mystical Body*.

Once the subject of the development of Christian doctrine is raised, any Christian who claims to be a member of Christ's Church quite rightly feels sad and often perplexed. Faced with Christ's words recorded in John's Gospel "There shall be only one flock and one shepherd" (10:16) and his prayer, "Holy Father, keep those you have given me true to your name, so that they may be one like us" (17:11), how do we account for the hundreds of Christian sects each claiming to teach the Christian faith as Christ wished it to be taught? There is only one answer. Sin, *hamartia*, is the cause and all Christians sin. People who are not Christians also sin. The problem of disagreement exists wherever mankind lives. In the political sphere we have opposing parties and within the parties we have factions constantly fighting each other. Strangely, each party in any country will claim that it's sole objective is the welfare of the state and it's citizens. Even in communist countries and other dictatorships we find dissidents and there is ample evidence that in the "party" itself there is intrigue, dissent, deceit and treachery. Similar ugliness exists without doubt in the business world and in sporting bodies.

From this position we may well ask; has the Church any characteristics which distinguish it from a political party or a multi-national business corporation? The answer is yes! Despite its divisions the two thousand year old Church is very much like an antique china plate. There are many visible, superficial cracks but underneath there is an obvious and identifiable unity. Collectors would point out that the cracks are merely the result of the plate's age and a proof of its authenticity as a genuine antique. No one would deny that the plate would be more beautiful if the cracks were not there.

If this be the case with the Church, how does it claim an "obvious and identifiable unity"? There are at least five factors which create a basic unity between the vast majority of Christians. They are:

1. A common faith that Jesus is the Lord and that he has risen from the dead.

2. Baptism, whereby every Christian becomes a child of God.

3. Acceptance of the Bible as the inspired Word of God.

4. A yearning for a complete unity among themselves, that they might be seen as one flock under one shepherd.

5. Acceptance of the tenets of the Nicene Creed, either explicitly or implicitly.

A person who is not a Christian might well ask: With this formidable area of agreement why are Christians divided? Again there is only one answer — sin! Certainly the sin can be identified in most cases as pride, prejudice or obstinacy.

Our questioner might, quite logically, persist and ask: You have said the vast majority of Christians would give assent to the five points listed above, what about the others?

Here we must face the problem of heresy. When Christians accept and give assent to some tenet of the faith with a majority approaching unanimity that particular belief can be classed as orthodox. it becomes part of a corpus of revealed truth known as the *sensus fidelium*. Those who oppose the particular belief are classed as heretics. These are people who are simply out of step with the regiment. It does not imply that they are individually good, bad or indifferent nor that they have no hope of salvation. It does, however, put them for the time being outside the visible structure of the Church. They are seen as a divisive influence.

An observation must be made at this point that the *sensus fidelium* in 1984 may be different from that of 1684. As an example let us examine the phenomenon of witchcraft. One of the earliest references to witchcraft can be found in the Bible in the book of Exodus (22:17). "You shall not allow a sorceress to live." The source of this reference could be dated in the order of 3,500 years ago. St. Paul names sorcery or witchcraft as a product of self-indulgence (Gal. 5:20). Obviously it was a concern in his day. Witchcraft was recognised as a problem in most parts of the world. In Western Europe it was classified as a crime, both in civil and ecclesiastical jurisdictions, up till the late seventeenth century. There appeared to be substantial agreement between Catholic and Protestant Christians in this matter. Witchcraft or devil possession is still considered a real problem in parts of Africa, Asia, the Indies and the Pacific Islands. In contrast, the Christian Church appears to have handed the problem to the psychiatrist. Despite this fact, obsession with the occult is still noticeably present in Christian countries. In 1623 Pope Gregory XV commanded that people like witches should, if they were convicted in an ecclesiastical court, be surrendered to secular jurisdiction and be given the death penalty. At that time the majority of Protestants would have agreed with this principle.

Is this an instance of a change taking place in Christian doctrine? No! It is a development. The underlying dogma is the same now as it was in the seventeenth century. The fact that witchcraft was considered evil in the middle ages and that in the twentieth century we laugh at the idea does not prove *anything* logically.

Development of the understanding of Christian doctrine is strong evidence that the Church is alive! It is basically not an organisation but an organism. It develops by the force of the life that is in it and that life is the active principle of the Creator, the Person of the Holy Spirit.

If Christians were not prone to sin, there is no doubt the *sensus fidelium* could be used as the final reference in matters of doctrine and morals. As we are all sadly aware, sin is still very much a fact in Christian experience, although individually the remedy for it is always available. Our Lord foresaw this problem and to counter it instituted two correctives.

He gave his apostles enormous powers. In Mt. 9:19 Christ told them "Whatever you bind on Earth shall be considered bound in heaven; whatever you have loosed on Earth shall be considered loosed in heaven". There are several other similar texts supporting and enlarging this idea.

To reinforce the apostles, in case they tended in their human weakness to rely on their personal judgement, Our Lord made available to them an unfailing source of inspiration when in St. John's Gospel he said to them (14:26) "The Advocate, the Holy Spirit, whom the Father will send in my name, will teach you everything and remind you of all I have said to you". This text as in the previous case is supported by a number of other similar promises by the Saviour.

The power and authority delegated by Christ are accepted by Christians of the Roman Communion and have been operative through a form of hierarchical government (the apostolic succession) throughout the two thousand years of their history. It is still a major unifying factor. The

unique characteristics of this belief and its operation in
practice will be discussed in our final chapter.

In Christ's coming and his utterances it is possible to
detect the idea of "relativity".

His references to the scriptures as testifying of him (not
testified of him), his promise to return at the "end of time"
all suggest the removal of time as a constant. Before
Pontius Pilate at his trial, the use of the phrase "I am" to so
describe himself infuriated the Jews because that was the
name God gave himself. This name no Jew would ever
pronounce, so holy did he consider it to be. In the book of
Exodus when Moses asked God what name he was to give
Pharoah to define the Deity who sent him, the reply was;
tell him "I am" has sent you. This name implies eternity, a
perpetual *now*.

Christians have imported this idea implicitly in the
Creed when they affirm as the *present* corpus of their belief
"the resurrection of the body and the life of the *world to
come*". Eternity is implied in all Christian dogma. The last
few verses of St. Matthew's Gospel contain Christ's
promise to his Church: *I am* with you to the end of time.
Life for the Christian in the time/space situation is only
one episode in his total experience.

This assertion could, with some justice be classed as
"being wise after the event" but at least there is nothing in
the Christ event in the least inimical to the "relativity"
notion.

Stranger still, however, in the language of relativity in
Christ's reference to himself as the *Light of the World*. The
results of modern scientific research into light present us
with an outstanding instance in which the theologian can
use scientific knowledge recently discovered to enable him
to develop the theology of light. On the other hand, the
picture emerging from theology thus enhanced cannot fail
to interest and stimulate the open-minded scientist.

Any modern scientific text book would describe light
as electromagnetic radiation to which the human eye is
sensitive. This definition alone indicates the relatively
recent unification between optics and electromagnetic

radiation. Light becomes visible when radiation waves are generated at a frequency in the order of 10^{12} kilohertz. The relation of light waves to other classifications of electro-magnetic waves is shown in a table at the end of this book (p. 229).

At this point the reader is asked to recall the section on "Relativity" (pp. 20–30). A contemporary of Einstein, Max Planck, discovered that energy, like matter, is not infinitely subdivisible. He posited that the energy of a system vibrating with a frequency v could be calculated by multiplying v by a constant namely 6.626176×10^{-34} Js. This is a most interesting constant because if you look at it carefully you will notice it has the dimensions of action, that is the product of energy multiplied by time. As soon as we speak of energy we are alerted to recall Einstein's equation $E = mc^2$. (E = energy, m = mass, c = velocity of light). In this equation the constant is the velocity of light. Viewing Planck's constant together with Einstein's equation we perceive a determinable relationship between energy, time, mass and light. The logical deduction from this is that we need a particle, a mass to be associated with the transmission of light. Einstein called this particle the photon. A photon is unique as at rest it has no mass while when it moves at the velocity of light it assumes the characteristics of an elementary particle. The idea of the photon presents itself to the theologian as the point where physics and metaphysics meet. At rest it has no mass while in motion it is matter. As an analogy of the "Incarnation" light is remarkable.

Light itself is invisible. It can be seen only when some material substance comes into its beam. This matter in turn becomes illuminated and visible. The illuminated object then becomes a source of light as it reflects the light which is shining on it.

When we meditate on the wonder of light from a theological point of view it is necessary to distinguish immediately between the light which is the object of study by the physicist, as described above and the Light of God. The first we call created light. The second, which is the unlimited Light which God himself is, we call uncreated light.

The simplest way to perceive the difference is that created light moves at a measurable speed, thereby demonstrating a limitation, while uncreated light is infinite, i.e. beyond the scope of measurement. Uncreated light is everywhere simultaneously. It simply is!

The theme of light persists right through the corpus of biblical revelation. The separation of light from darkness was the first act of the Creator in the Genesis story (Gen. 1:3ff). At the end of the Bible we are told the new creation (Rev. 21:5) will have God himself as Light (21:23). It is interesting to note that as early as the middle of the first century B.C. the writer of *The Book of Wisdom* differentiated between created and uncreated light (Wis. 7:29ff).

Jesus Christ used light to describe himself when he said: "I am the Light of the World". If we accept this statement as an analogy with the word light referring to created light, we recognise in Christ a great teacher enlightening his disciples with his instruction and his example. No doubt Christ presented himself to his followers in this way, for Scripture tells us he set aside his Godhead while he lived among us as man.

If, however we understand the declaration "I am the Light of the World" as referring to uncreated light, it assumes a staggering meaning, namely God is with us (*Immanuel*). As this statement came from Our Lord's lips it also identifies the "Word" with the "Light".

There is still another way in which we can read this text and that is to understand the word "light" as having a dual reference, first to created light and secondly to uncreated light. Assuming Uncreated Light as a title suitable for God, we have the word light containing a meaning relative to the creature, light and simultaneously denoting the Creator of light. In this case Christ becomes the personification of the whole notion, two natures in one Person, as the two ideas are fused together in one Word, "Light".

As an exercise in meditation boundless possibilities open up as we dwell on the statement: "I am the Light of the

World". A few examples might include the following ideas:

CONSTANCY: The speed of light approaching any beholder is constant. It is not affected by the motion of its source.

In Hebrews we read "Jesus Christ is the same today as he was yesterday and as he will be forever". (Heb. 13:8) In the letter of James: "All that is good, everything that is perfect comes down from the Father of all light; with him there is no such thing as alteration, no shadow of a change". (Jas. 1:17)

UNIVERSAL AVAILABILITY. Light illuminates all objects in its path. Those who move into its beam become illuminated. Their radiation is visible to those in darkness. (Tim. 2:4; Jn. 12:46)

TRANSCENDENCE AND IMMANENCE. It is impossible to "catch" light. No one can travel at the speed of light. The converse applies; there is no escaping the beam that is directed on to an individual. It is available to all who will move into its ray. (Tim. 2:4; Jn. 12:46, Mt. 26:18)

THE ENLIGHTENED RADIATE LIGHT. (Mt. 5:16)

In John's Gospel alone there are some fifteen different references to the word light used either in a descriptive sense or as analogy. The meaning of all these passages is deepened by a knowledge of the physics of light.

Under the heading "Light and Dark" there is a useful compendium in the *Dictionary of Biblical Theology* by Xavier Leon-Dufour (Geoffrey Chapman).

For the reader interested in developing his knowledge of the theology of light there is an excellent chapter in a book entitled *Christian Theology and Scientific Culture* by Thomas F. Torrance (Marshall Pickering).

We now begin to see what Einstein and his disciples have done for us. Copernicus, Gallileo, Newton and those who followed them gave us the notion that space and time were absolutes and based their physics on this axiom. By doing so they gave us only two alternatives,

1. To lock ourselves in a box with God outside, consequently making him utterly unknowable, or

2. To lock God in the box with ourselves and to create an absolute pantheism.

Einstein saw that these ideas had to be completely dismantled and demonstrated that our concepts of time/space had to be revised and re-expressed as dynamic, not static, and entirely contingent upon the propagation of light. Einstein in his four dimensional mathematics put a "window" in each side of our time/space box and enabled us to see what is going on "outside". We can now see and are beginning to understand the majesty of God and his nature as "Creator", as we view the universe expanding at near the velocity of light. We can also say with the psalmist "What is man that you are mindful of him?" and in case this gives us a feeling of despair we can turn to Genesis and learn that we are made in "the image and likeness of God". Our minds, our souls can now, in the twentieth century comprehend more than ever the awe inspiring mystery of the universe.

The effect of being able to see "outside our box" has resulted in a change in the philosophical attitude of our leading scientists. Newton, as already noted quite rationally kept science and religion apart. Religion was outside the box and science dealt with objects and phenomena inside the box. The attitude that science and religion should be entirely separate activities of the mind produced two disastrous attitudes. The first of these was militant atheism, reaching its peak in Marx and his disciples. The second was agnosticism, which produced a state of mind where the scientist using empirical methods established his findings with satisfying and logical accuracy, and, as he could not establish a relationship with God by empirical means he became disinterested. It will be hard for many to realise that these days are over.

Einstein, born in the Jewish tradition, believed in a God, though of a nature radical to the Judaeo-Christian understanding. In this century we have great scientists, men of the stature of Max Planck, Erwin Schrödinger, Sir John

Eccles and many others who have found no difficulty in accepting the compatibility of religion with natural science.

The effects of this revolution in human thinking could be shattering. Marxism is based on Darwinistic evolution theories and absolute atheism. If these two foundation stones of the iron curtain crumble who knows what will follow? Light, which at rest is metaphysical and in movement physical, could also be used as a prophetical analogy of the reunion of science and religion. We live in exciting times!

Field Theories

There is evidence recently of the growth in the number of curious minds who baulk at the acceptance of facile terminology, the use of "trade words". Fashionable stock words to explain the inexplicable, such as reaction, fission, fusion, compound, atomic energy, molecular activity, chemical action, planetary motion, mutation, gravity, morpho-genesis are often used glibly to cover mysteries as vast as the universe. They can become stock in trade weapons to deflect attention from vital questions such as how or why. Pseudo-scientific or Pseudo-religious explanations of the nature just indicated can never be classed as "revelation". The true theologian, the true scientist and the true philosopher are of one mind in seeking the ultimate root origin of things. Whether it is acceptable or not, it must be realised that there is only one answer, and a common one at that, for the root and origin of all being, the reality exhibited by created things, and that is God. Revelation therefore cannot be anything else but religious. Revelation as already stated is a self-revealing of God to mankind for his uplifting and good, and that revelation became an actuality in the Incarnation of Jesus Christ. After his Resurrection and before the event we call the Ascension, Christ told us "the Holy Spirit whom the Father will send in my name will teach you everything" (Jn. 14:26). Let us look dispassionately at this promise. We

have indisputable evidence of the existence of men of
tremendous intelligence before Christ's birth. The remains of Egyptian and Chinese architecture and civil
engineering works, the emergence of thinkers of the calibre
of Parmenides, Socrates, Plato, Aristotle are surely sufficient proof; yet at the time of Christ the Earth was
generally thought to be flat; the sun and moon were lights
revolving round it, while mechanically the greatest
achievement was possibly the wheel. By today's standards
the knowledge of physics, chemistry, medicine, surgery
and mechanics was elementary indeed. In the short time of
2000 years since Christ's promise of the teaching of the
Holy Spirit (2000 years is a flick of the fingers in geological
time) knowledge has advanced to the extremes of sophis-
tication we accept today. The acceleration of physical
knowledge is obviously in the nature of a geometric
progression. Christ foretold this evolutionary process
when he said "I still have many things to say to you, but
they would be too much for you now. But when the Spirit
of Truth comes he will *lead* you to the complete truth."
(Jn. 16:12ff) Here is Christ himself confirming the necessity for gradual development in human knowledge and
thinking. Intruding into these two great promises is the
inalienable gift of human freedom of choice.

The poet James Montgomery wrote:
    "Prayer is the soul's extreme desire
    Uttered or unexpressed."
One cannot help but wonder what heights we may have
reached if humanity's "extreme desire" had been that the
Holy Spirit would "lead" us:
    "To act justly
    To love tenderly
    And to walk humbly with our God."
    (Mic. 6:8)
Regretably and obviously, our "soul's extreme desire"
has been to acquire knowledge of physical things and this
we have received and are receiving. Not that this
knowledge is to be despised, but concurrently with its
revelation, selfishness and greed (*hamartia*) have distorted

our use of it towards the acquisition of material possessions and the deadly weapons needed to guard our "treasure" and to plunder the same wealth from others. We have used what has been revealed to us as a means to lead a soft life, not necessarily a good one.

Critical minds looking for the ultimate how and why of existence are leaning towards what could be called in general terms "field theories". Most of us will recall from school days what happens when we place a piece of waxed paper on top of a bar magnet lying on a table and then gently sprinkle iron filings onto our paper. The filings fall into lines coincident with the lines of force radiating from the magnet. Over the past century enormous and productive research has been done on radiation, fields and resonance. A common little transistor radio set tells us a lot. We switch it on and we can hear it come alive. Nothing intelligible, however can be detected until we tune it so that it operates at the frequency of a transmitting station. When that happens we have a resonance with the field of the transmitter and we hear music from say, station 4QR. If then we move our tuning control so that our set oscillates at the frequency of station 4QG we perceive the phenomenon of our *same* little receiver making audible an entirely different programme. What is being suggested now is that "fields" may be the answer to the questions "What is life?" and also "What is the origin of the various species of life on Earth?". The DNA molecule is basically a chemical combination of carbon, oxygen, nitrogen and hydrogen. Do the almost infinite number of permutations and combinations possible create a resonance with different existing "fields"? Does the fact that my DNA molecule is different from that of a kangaroo indicate that each of us is in resonance with fields operating at different "frequencies"? Are new species generated by life's building blocks becoming resonant with different fields?. The whole hypothesis is fascinating. It could supply the answer to human phenomena like hypnosis, extra-sensory perception, insights and so on. The creation of a "field" requires energy measurable in terms of Planck's constant. Where does the energy come from? The simplest answer is from both created and uncreated light which ultimately means God. Einstein was obviously interested in "field theories" and since his time other scientists have pursued the subject. One book, *A New Science of Life* by Dr. Rupert Sheldrake, is reviewed in a later chapter. A different approach is taken by Dr. H. S. Burr in his work, *Blue Print for Immortality*. It is in this area that we may see the next development from Scientists or Theologians.

A few paragraphs back we mentioned that the only inexhaustible "power house" for the design and creation of fields is God. As is obvious from our previous discussions we arrived by several routes at the conclusion that God is unknowable by human endeavour. We may well go on to ask; "Are all our scientific and theological researches an exercise in futility?" The Christian can answer "No!" All revelation, all development or evolution of human thought, are merely a preparation for still another manifestation of Jesus Christ for as we say in our creed:

He will come again in glory
To judge the living and the dead,
And his kingdom will have no end.

It is at this point, the end of time that we can look forward to eternal answers.

In the meantime the field theories are attractive in various areas of research. Let us reconsider life and death. Let us postulate the idea of God as a power-house of inexhaustible and unlimited output who radiates his power at an infinite number of frequencies. We could classify the frequencies into the human band, the plant life band, the bird life band, the fish life band and so on. When a baby is conceived we could assume that its particular cell structure resonates to a frequency in the human life band and that this phenomenon is the "breath of life". Referring back to our analogy of the radio receiver we know that if some vital part of the set wears out or is damaged it ceases to function. Using our field hypothesis could this be what causes human death? A defective radio set becomes a useless mass of metal and plastic. A dead human is simply an inert mass of protein, bone and water. There is an intermediate state where some minor defect occurs in either radio set or human existence. In each case resonance is detected, each is alive but output is inhibited or distorted until the defect is either repaired or becomes "fatal". All of us with experience of radio sets have experienced the frustration of interference, when some unwanted source of radiation intrudes on our frequency either from an undesired station or from a thunder storm. Analogously this experience could be equated with *hamartia*. Communication, between man and God is effective when man's "extreme desire" is in tune with the operating frequency the Creator has planned for *that person's life*. Again when we consider the Christian doctrine that grace works on nature, the field theory would cover the fact that different people possess different abilities. As already suggested field theories could possibly bring up answers in matters like extra-sensory perception, human relationships, team work, learning abilities and possibly useful answers in the disciplines of psychology and psychiatry. After all, the human brain and nervous systems are operated by electro/chemical stimulations which must result in the generation of fields. Modern development in this area will be discussed in a later chapter.

CHAPTER 5

SCIENCE AND MAN IN THE TWENTIETH CENTURY

NEVER in human history has the self-estimation of man descended to a more disastrous and humiliating level than was current at the end of the nineteenth century. Strangely enough, intelligent men at the turn of the century would condemn this opening sentence as outrageous. They would point out that the century had produced a plethora of great men in every department of living. It was the century of great artists, Courbet, Seurat, Cezanne, Gauguin, Millais, Turner; of the engineers of the Steam Engine, Watt, Stephenson and their successors; of immense civil engineering works; literature of the standard of Dickens, Thackeray, Pope, Byron; poets like Wordsworth, Keble, Keats, Emerson, Longfellow, Poe, Browning, Arnold, Patmore, Rossetti and Stevenson; philosophers of the order of Hegel, Feuerbach, Kierkegaard, Bergson, Gilson, Nietzsche, Mill, Spencer, Bradley, Marx, Bosanquet. Among the theologians were Newman, Mohler, Sheeben, Bonnetty, Bautain, Noldin, Fénélon, Blondel, Schleiermacher, Coleridge, Lightfoot: all outstanding men. In every branch of knowledge, medicine, surgery, anaesthetics, chemistry, biology, electronics and so on, one could produce long lists of greats. The tragedy of the loss of true human values lay in the fact that the century's scientists, most philosophers and many theologians, living as they were in the age of rigid mechanical empiricism and mathematics, in the age when Darwin had produced the idea of man as ultimately a machine, a freak of nature, fell under the influence of that climate. Thank God not all of them did. This age of paradox needed no God because it had all the answers to everything. Things were stated to be right or wrong, black or white with a degree of certitude which, on a moment's reflection, is simply not within human competence. Truly great minds locked themselves in the time/space box as if all reality, all truth were to be found there. God could not be found in the box, no surgeon could excise a human soul and send it to the laboratory for analysis, so these two ultimate realities were simply ignored. Man himself became man's God. The most disastrous product of this age was the emergence of the dialectic materialism of the Marx, Hegel, Leninist state which by force either of persuasion, indoctrination or physical violence eliminates or at least attempts to eliminate mankind's distinguishing characteristic of freedom of choice. Although this lived-out disaster still affects about half of the world's population the fact is that, with Einstein's opening the windows of our "box" and letting us see not time or space as absolutes but rather *light*, plus the general questioning of crude Darwinism by microbiologists and others, the very foundations of the Marxist ideology are seen to have no basis in truth.

There is a discernible movement amongst the elite of our scientists back towards theism (a belief in God), and this is based on the principle of the balance of probabilities. This means for us, for the ordinary man or woman of the world, that there is nothing to be ashamed of in our faith in God and that our faith is certainly reasonable.

Four Challenging Books

As a brief study of the way things are moving in the twentieth century it is proposed to submit a review of four notable books by eminent scientists published between 1940 and 1981. The books are:

Man on His Nature by Sir Charles Sherrington (1940, C.U.P.)

What is Life (1944) and *Mind and Matter* (1958) by Professor Erwin Schrödinger (combined reprint 1967 by C.U.P.)

The Self and Its Brain by Sir Karl Popper and Sir John Eccles (1977, Springer International).
A New Science of Life by Dr. Rupert Sheldrake (1981, Blond and Briggs).

Man On His Nature

This book was written by one of the most famous scientists of the twentieth century, Sir Charles Sherrington, one time Waynflete Professor of Physiology at the University of Oxford. He died in 1952. The book, which was published in 1940, contains the material used in the Gifford Lectures delivered at the University of Edinburgh in 1937–8. In his preface to the second edition, Sir Charles states his intention as follows: "The book stresses the view that man is a product, like so much else, of the play of natural forces acting on the material and under the conditions past and present obtaining on the surface of our planet". My copy of this lovely book, to which reference will be made from time to time, is a paper-back reprint published by the Cambridge University Press in 1975. The book was written before Einstein's work had made the impact on thinking which is now becoming evident. Sir Charles obtained his M.A. degree before his M.D. and D.Sc. The breadth and deepness of his reading reveals the great wisdom of training in the humanities before qualifying in science. Sherrington (obviously and intrinsically), in his studies for his M.A., learned *how* to think, before his scientific studies gave him *something to think about*. As a result his writing has a richness and maturity about it which in itself is fascinating. His style invites serious study by educationalists to deal with a pressing contemporary problem, which is growing more pressing day by day; by this is meant the "laser beam" effect of intense specialisation and the need for communication between disciplines at top level, with the object of broadening the outlook of specialist students so that they can talk with each other. Above all something must be done to curtail or retard the accelerating development of what has already been re-

ferred to as "trade languages". Giants of the order of
Sherrington and Schrödinger are always readable. If they
are obliged to use words peculiar to some discipline they
are gracious enough to define them in simple terms. There
is an urgent need today for the teaching of logic, epistemology and ontology as a prelude to the first year of
science courses, and throughout all courses an insistence
on the ability of the student to express himself simply in
the vernacular.

A subtlety is obvious in the opening pages of Sherrington's book where his use of the initial capital letter when
writing the words Nature, Truth and Science gives the
God-like inference these terms deserve. He is not ashamed
to demonstrate awe. Our author immediately raises issues
already touched upon in previous chapters such as revelation of God by the study of created things. Tracing
sixteenth century renaissance thought through the writings of the Parisian physician, Jean Fernel, he gives some
fascinating material on the gradual emergence of the
empirical approach to scientific discovery. Interestingly,
Fernel had studied philosophy before he tackled medicine.
The thrust of the first chapter is, however, to get *behind* the
clearly defined steps of empiricism to the ultimate "why"
and "how". Fernel is shown to regard Nature as God's
active agent. He obviously saw things as being more than
the sum of their parts. He detected the inbuilt dynamism
that material things possess apart from their physical
composition. For Fernel it was necessary that his "Natural
Religion" and his Christian Faith should be a unity. There
could be no dichotomy between Science and Religion.
Fernel would never accept that the world was simply a
material thing, "by chance, out of chaos". Despite
evidence of Platonic thought, Fernel insisted on the unity
of the human person. Although he introduced "soul" into
his monumental work on physiology he was quite firm in
his concept of "mind" as not being material. In Sherrington's words "He considered the action of the mind as part
of physiology" in the same way as Thomas Aquinas
following Aristotle defined the soul as the "form" of the

material body. Fernel insists "that man is man all through". He would agree with our definition of a man as body/soul rather than body *and* soul. Fernel used, as we do, the thesis that the soul is simple (it has no parts), and therefore it cannot disintegrate, as proof of its immortality. The opening chapter of the book is fascinating because, in a way, Fernel is nearer to modern thinking than the genius who wrote the book we are reviewing. From his place in eternal existence may Sir Charles guide my faltering pen as we try to show him as the pioneer of the reunion now in process between "science" and "religion". Fernel was before Galileo and Newton and would be more at home with Einstein than with either of them. In his summing up of his brilliant opening chapter Sir Charles says, *inter alia*, "We, in our time, are therefore differently placed for inference from the natural to the divine than were our ancestors some short dozen generations back". And again, "Yet not for us to forget is our escape from a long nightmare — the exchange for a monstrous world of one relatively sane." The final sentence of the chapter reads: "The position for reading from Nature's lips what she may have to say of Godhead, never yet in the past, was what it is for us today." In the index to this powerful work there is not a single reference to Einstein although many of the great unifying effects of the philosophy of the Master of Relativity have been foreshadowed with inspired accuracy.

Sir Charles Sherrington's philosophy of science origin- ates, as one would expect, from the mind of a physiologist par excellence. Today, thirty-odd years after his death, many of his propositions could be especially well de- veloped from micro-physics, macro-physics or any other well-developed discipline.

One of the latest theories concerning the nature of life, namely the "Field Theory", has been dealt with briefly in preceding pages. Back in 1940 Sherrington wrote in his third chapter, "Life as an energy system is so woven into the fabric of Earth's surface, that to suppose a life isolated from the rest of that terrestrial world even briefly, gives an image too distorted to resemble life. All is dovetailed together." Further down on the same page (79) he says "We remember . . . the almost inconceivably small and the almost inconceivably great . . . yet in doing so they have left no gap between their extremes." He gives reassuring support of our suggestion that the Earth, as a planet, could be unique when he says (same page): "Life as we know it is . . . specific in time and place. . . . All of life as we know it could exist probably nowhere else than on this planet's surface, where it is." Proposing as he does that life is an energy system we are faced with the necessity to find a power house to supply that energy. As his vision extends from "the almost inconceivably small" to "the almost inconceivably great" our "Power-house" must be larger than all created reality. It leaves us no option than to propose it as "God". As all "creatures great and small" are in motion and, as Einstein has shown us how these moving entities all "relate" and as all motion presupposes initial energy, we can immediately see at least one reason for Einstein's famous remark, "Science without religion is lame, religion without science is blind". There must be a God.

In chapter four, Sherrington, writing from his immense competence in physiology, describes what he calls the wisdom of the body. It is fascinating reading but an omission, when on page 97 he is discussing how sometimes in the formation of a human baby things go wrong, is justification for the idea of *hamartia*. If our body/mind, our radio receiver, gets out of resonance with the life-giving fields, or another field (evil) intrudes into its frequency, distortion will result.

A paragraph on page 98, describing the emergence of the baby as a being physically independent of its mother, raises an interesting philosophical point. Sir Charles writes: "In the foetus a short channel joins the root of the lung-artery with that of the main artery of the baby. Immediately following birth the lung enters activity, and this side tracking of its blood-supply would be disadvantageous. A little before the foetus is actually born this channel is shut by a special small muscle. This muscle, so far as is known never used in the foetus, springs into action at birth and shuts the channel. Having performed its function it degenerates and disappears; the channel in due course becomes obliterated under disuse." Quoting from Sir Joseph Bankcroft (*The Brain and its Environment*, Yale University Press), he adds "it would seem very difficult to claim that the muscle which closes the ductus at birth has been differentiated as the result of any specific conditions to which it has been subjected — much less any specific use which it has subserved". Sir Charles then concludes "It is an instance of a final cause". From the point of view of a physiologist this appears to be indisputable but looked at by a philosopher who has been trained in the mathematics of "combinations, permutations and probabilities" it is necessary to go further. The probability of this amazing and complex series of "combinations and permutations" occurring by accident or chance or blind evolution can be dismissed as impossible. (If it *is* claimed to be by blind evolution, one might ask what the casualty rate would be during the evolution process?) No! There is overwhelming evidence of design here, and one would never classify a *design* as a final cause. Surely the "final" cause is the Designer! In fairness to the author it must be said that he finishes his reference with a quotation from R. C. Punnett's work, *Forty years of Evolution Theory*, where Punnett sums up "we can only understand an organism if we regard it as though produced under the guidance of thought for an end", as a final cause at work.

If the reader of this book is not familiar with Sherrington's work it is suggested that he read pages 105 to 116 of the edition quoted, where the author describes the physiology and functioning of the eye. The argument for design and Designer is overwhelming. These twelve pages are mind-boggling. Having read them one can only exclaim with the Psalmist "We are fearfully and wonderfully made" (Psalm 138/9).

Chapter five is a description of the methodology of evolution and establishes a powerful argument for its acceptance. The difficulties and gaps in the evidence already referred to are well covered. It is, however, a chapter dealing with some subjects in which science has made marked advances since the author's time. His last sentence summing up his résumé of the evolutionary process and referring to life's reproduction says "if our materialist . . . today submits that he holds the key to it, he can, we *may* think, go into court with a good case". His use of the word "may" (italics mine) demonstrates the subtle mind of the author. What he has demonstrated with remarkable skill is the "engineering" of evolution and the "how" in terms of the biology of 1938 of the reproduction of life and its characteristics, but every example quoted of continuity or of a characteristic of a species, relies for the "life" factor on an already living bud in some form or other.

The author's next chapter, called "A Whole presupposed of its Parts", handles brilliantly a mystery of living creatures where observably all the parts which go up to make the organism tend to work consistently towards preserving the character, unity and efficiency of the whole of which they are components. The more complicated the organism, the more remarkable and efficient this co-operation becomes. In the human it reaches a peak. I decide to do some writing. The decision having been made my legs carry me to my study, without any conscious command to "get up and walk", I turn on the light, adjust the radiator, open the shutters, move my chair back and sit in it, scan my manuscript, check my references, pick up my pen, move my pad to a suitable position, stare into space for a while till I "collect my thoughts"; then and only then do I commence to write. My *will* to write has produced all these actions more or less subconsciously. If during the evening a friend were to ask me "How did you spend your afternoon?" my sole reply would be "I did some writing". None of the countless preliminary moves would enter my consciousness, let alone my speech. Moreover my friend would be perfectly aware of the preparatory moves, in general, implied by the fact that "I did some writing". If a mutual acquaintance were to say to him, "I think I saw

Ralph Mitchell walking down this passage this afternoon", our friend would probably reply: "Yes, it would be Ralph, he told me he spent the afternoon writing". Every part of my highly complex self co-operates in the effect we call "doing one thing at a time". This inherent characteristic is capable of quite remarkable activity in the situation we call "self-survival". One jumps from the path of an undetected car long before the fleeting vision transmitted to the brain produces a calculated order from the mind requiring my body to jump backwards half a metre. Our involuntary acts, such as breathing and sleeping all take place unconsciously for the benefit of the whole body. There is an interesting observation on page 163 which has bearing on our evolving hypothesis of fields where our author says, "To attach mind to energy would have been thought at one time to make all human behaviour perforce part of a necessitarian scheme of things: part of a Laplace universe". Human nature is diametrically opposed to any idea of determinism. Each of us is aware of his faculty of freedom of choice. If we persist with our field analogy we must allow our free soul the option of varying the frequency at which we resonate. It can tune out "God" and tune in "evil". Again the last words of this chapter which is a quotation from Lloyd Morgan, the biologist, affirms "the primary aim, object and purpose of consciousness is control". To which the author adds "Dame Nature seems to have taken the like view". If the capitals used for Dame Nature indicate a bias towards Theism one could scarcely quarrel with this view.

Chapters seven, eight and nine are reviewed as a whole as they deal with the material covered by another book also to be reviewed, namely *The Mind and its Brain* by Sir Karl Popper F.R.S. and Sir John Eccles F.R.S., a book written nearly forty years later than Sir Charles Sherrington's work.

Chapter seven deals with the central nervous system of the brain. Immediately we find a differentiation between "mind" and "brain". For brain the term "finite mind" is used and it is immediately proposed that the integration of the body and its ability to concentrate on "one thing at a time" is beyond the control of that organ we call the brain. There is, of course, a remarkable degree of integration, particularly of the so called "involuntary acts" by the nervous system and the brain.

In discussing the predatory nature of living things the author raises some interesting points. If we are looking for the ultimate answer to what is "life" *per se*, we must pause to consider whether "life" itself is sacred and again whether life exists in a hierarchy of values. The human population of the Earth is growing at an ever increasing rate and humans eat nothing but living things be they vegetable or animal in origin. When we eat flesh we must realise that our meat is the result of protein synthesis in the animal produced by its metabolism working on living food.

Purely from observation, human life appears to be different in the fact that (with rare exceptions) no predator relies for its existence on the hunting and consumption of the human animal. It seems to be obvious that a phase in history is rapidly approaching when "all life on the planet shall be subordinated to one life. That one life, human life, seems on its way to something, natural truly, but nevertheless super-human" (p. 172).

Christianity proposed this two thousand years ago when the writer of the second letter of Peter said "What we are waiting for is what is promised: the new heavens and the new earth where righteousness will be at home". There is a frighteningly prophetic ring about the tenth verse of this chapter of Peter's letter for us who live in these days of massive nuclear armament. (Sir Charles Sherrington was spared knowledge of this spectre when he wrote his book.) The verse I refer to reads: "The Day of the Lord will come like a thief, and then with a roar the sky will vanish, the elements will catch fire and fall apart, the earth and all that it contains will be burnt up". It is after this that Peter refers to the new heavens and the new earth. Our creed also refers to this in its final tenet "We believe in the life of the world to come".

A Catholic priest must differ from Sir Charles' summing

up in the middle of page 173 where he concludes "For us, man's mind is a recent product of our planet's side, produced from mind already there long previously, yielding man's mind by gradual change of previous mind". The Roman Catholic Church's ruling that each man's soul is directly and personally "infused" by God at the person's conception is much easier to live with. Using again our analogy of God as a transmitter radiating infinite power on an infinite number of frequencies and that our mortal life and individuality depends primarily on our being able to "resonate" in tune with the transmitter, we are able to account logically for most of the problems our author raises. One of the functions of our soul or mind is, in the allegory, to act as a "receiver". One would hesitate to express an opinion at variance with such a distinguished author, except for the fact that in this conclusion he has stepped out of the limits of his empirical specialisation into the area of metaphysics.

Chapter eight establishes with the competence of this great physiologist that the brain is the organ of liaison with the "mind". Immediately the point is made, concurring with Aristotle in the "oneness" of the individual mind and body. The Platonic notion of the body and soul is laid to rest. An interesting observation is that philosophers as far apart as Aristotle and Freud both study the phenomenon of mind as wholly separate from the anatomy of the brain.

In the chapter nine Sherrington raises an issue later pursued by Pierre Teilhard de Chardin, the Jesuit Palaeontologist. They both tend to agree that there is evidence of mind (Sherrington) or soul (Teilhard) in things we might class as non-living. This is an interesting area. What gives some miniscule primitive existences a "blind urge towards food"? Both agree and are as one with Aristotle in the conclusion that life at its lower limit defies demarcation. Sherrington's view in his own words is expressed, that at the lowest level, "Mind with nothing left but the potential germ of what in evolution's hands has budded into recognizable mind" (p. 209). This sounds like a plausible hypothesis but note that our author obviously gives "evolution" the power to organise and "hands" to do its work. Surely his "evolution" must have "mind" to effect the astonishing mutations "its" craftman's hands have produced say between the "mind" that governs the motor action of single cell life and the tremendous mind of the author who produced the book we are studying. In fairness it must be added that our author does pose an unanswered question, "What has evolution had to evolve mind from?" (p. 209). On the next page Sherrington discusses the evolution of mind in the human foetus and its disappearance or devolution at death. As this book is an attempt to construct an apologia for orthodox Christianity it must be posited at this stage, that all the problems Sherrington has raised do not exist for the Christian, who is prepared to admit an intelligently organised evolution-ary process as at least a part of God's method of creation. If in the preceding discussion we substitute "God" for "evolution's hands" and the infusion of the human soul as a direct act of God we have little to concern ourselves with, except the excitement of further research into the meta-physical development culminating in the evolution of the sub-human souls of the lower orders of living things.

Further if we refer back to chapter 2 of this book under the sub-heading "Eternity", we see how our author's problem of the devolution of the soul (at least the super-soul: the human soul) ceases to exist. There is no devolu-tion but an elevation of the whole person into the eternal mode of existence. That remarkable gift of God to mankind we call "faith" produces an intellectual climate of "peace on Earth to men of goodwill" simply unattainable from scientific studies. As must be expected every scien-tific discovery raises more questions than it solves. Faith deals with concepts like "existence" and "act". It poses the "answers" to which all discoveries from natural revelation tend. In no way does faith imply some static frame of understanding, rather it carries with it the exciting pros-pect of endless development of knowledge, natural and supernatural. The wonder of this gift is its equalising force. It possesses a soul in peace irrespective of power, wealth, learning or any human attainment. It transcends mortal problems by creating a very real relationship with the transcendent God, immanent in the Incarnation of God in the man Jesus Christ.

Our writer goes on to give some graphic descriptions of the working of the brain and nervous system which all support the idea expressed in the naming of the chapter "Brain collaborates with Psyche".

The tenth chapter of our book introduces the idea of a telephone exchange as a useful analogy of the working of the human brain. Forty-five years later it is more than possible that Sherrington would have thought of our brain, perhaps as a telephone exchange, computer controlled, with the computer itself sensitive to a controlling radio system working on numerous frequencies all again dominated by a master frequency which enables us to resonate in tune with God. The chapter, one of the most fascinating in the book, goes on to describe in considerable detail how the nervous system and the brain work. Remembering that this book was written before computers were invented it is interesting to read, when discussing the cognitive power of the brain (p. 226) that our author refers to it as "An automatic card-index on an enormous scale". Today one would automatically think of a computer with a very large memory bank.

Summarising as a physiologist Sir Charles concludes that there is no connection between the brain and the mind. Here he is speaking as a disciplined empirical scientist who, having completed his measurements then admits the existence of the immeasurable, in our language the eternal and infinite soul.

He comes to our aid versus the materialist on page 229 where he accuses materialism of running rough-shod over the mind. As he points out the materialist uses the term matter without scientifically defining the limits of the concept.

On the next page our author makes the important distinction that the scientist defines life as an affair of chemistry and physics while mind "escapes chemistry and physics". We would add to that the observation that defining "life" in terms of chemistry and physics ultimately boils down to describing the physical conditions under which life can be present. What "it" is that is present slips over the edge of the boundaries of scientific research because "it", life, is also something that cannot be measured or analysed. It is interesting to note that in Hebrew literature, e.g. the Old Testament, the "soul" is not identical with the "Spirit". To the Hebrew the soul is the sign of life but God, the Spirit, is the *source* of life. In Greek (Platonic) thought the soul is thought of as emanating from the Spirit and is therefore identified with it. The modern view of man goes a long way towards recommending a return to the usage of the early Christian Fathers who described man as body, soul (his spiritual identity) and spirit (the principle of life emanating from God and returning to him at death). (Augustine: *On Faith and Creed*, ch 10:23). Here we have a reference to life *per se*, which the body/soul of man does not provide. "Body, Soul and Spirit" fits in well with the emerging "field theories" of life.

The remainder of the chapter was certainly visionary in 1939 and is devoted to the now strongly held and developing view of the "unity of things". This is based, of course, on the current scientific view that all things may, in the ultimate, be expressed in terms of energy ($E = mc^2$: Einstein). Energy, used to effect any change, must come from some other thing, therefore any "change" in one thing can theoretically at least effect a change in everything else. The important point for Christian theologians and philosophers is that today's energy concept transcends the existing Aristotelian concepts of matter and form.

Right at the beginning of chapter XII, which is entitled "Altruism", our author coins a word "anthropise" which he then uses in the sense that to anthropise is to use word and thought patterns limited by human experience.

Almost immediately, in his second paragraph of this chapter Sir Charles pin-points the limitations of physics and chemistry and in truth all strictly empirical scientific

disciplines. This is a superb paragraph of crucial importance. Let us use the author's own words: "When physics
and chemistry have entered on their description of the
perceptible, life disappears from the scene and consequently death. Both are anthropisms. Absolute beginnings
and absolute endings there are none. Change from one
phase to another is not in fact ending or beginning. There
are no beginnings *de novo*. Absolute time disappears and so
too absolute space." This is, to a large degree, a philo-
sophic summary of our Chapter 2. The Christian theologian cannot help but be stimulated by the inference that
having disposed of time and space as absolute we are left
with only one tangible absolute. That absolute is LIGHT.

Pages 262 and 263 touch on the immense problem of
evil. Most of these problems can be understood if we
accept the Christian thesis which rests on revelation and
observation. The axioms underlying the Christian view
have been stated in chapter 2 under the headings "eternity" and "love" and in chapter 3 under the heading
"Man's Psychic Aspect". Human sin results from a misuse
of man's freedom. Man's freedom was given him to
empower him to love; that is to "give" to the object of his
affection. God is love, therefore love is an almighty power.
The use of freedom to take and grab for selfish ends
releases a power of destruction and chaos beyond
measurement. This is the cause of the mystery of evil. In
Christ, his teaching, his sacrifice and his work we find the
only way of escape from the destructive power of evil. Our
author under review comes close to agreeing with us on
page 279 when talking about man he arrives at the
conclusion: "There is nothing good nor bad except himself", and again on page 281 when he says: "A positive
charity is wanted; passive negation is not enough. In effect
it needs a soul-growth which shall open out a higher self."
Here in the reasoning of a brilliant empiricist we have an
introduction to the Christian theology of baptism and
grace. These lead him to the conclusion, "The great religions bringing their altruism are evidence of a new tide.
Man must lead or go" (p. 288). Then soliloquising on

"Nature" which he personalises, he concludes "Bethink you too that perhaps in knowing me you do but know the instrument of a Purpose, the tool of a Hand too large for your sight as now to compass. Try then to teach your sight to grow." Here is pure drama in this conclusion reached through a strictly scientific approach. Only one step further is necessary when we reach this point through "natural revelation" and that is the prayer of the blind man "Lord let me see" (Mk. 10:51).

To summarise: Sherrington, arguing from Fernel, makes as his first important point: All matter, from small things to large things, is in motion. The maintenance of this state demands an enormous and continuous source of energy which we propose comes from God.

In chapter four our physiologist gives examples varying from the birth of a baby to the mechanism of the eye, which to this author, trained in civil engineering construction, constitute overwhelming evidence of "design". Design is an exercise of intelligence. Intelligence is a function of the "designer" not the design. Again we have evidence to support the existence of a superlative intelligence which we name as God.

Other principles established by our writer, *all from a strictly empirical methodology*, include:

Mankind's freedom of choice, the concept of brain and mind (soul) as separate interacting entities, progression towards what the author calls "super-human life" (in our terms eternal life), materialism is logically untenable, the unity of all created things, that an action in one thing produces reactions in all others. Here we have support for the idea of design and Designer, the existence of moral principles, the problem of evil.

Christianity, basing it teaching on *the natural law and revelation*, concurs in all these findings, and as already pointed out has logical and reasonable answers to questions honestly left unanswered by the empiricist who wrote this remarkable book.

CHAPTER 6

SCHRÖDINGER

A Physicist's View

HAVING worked through a famous physiologist's study of man and his nature, we are now to consider many of the same problems from the point of view of one of the physicists of the twentieth century, Professor Erwin Schrödinger, taking as our references a series of Lectures delivered at Trinity College, Dublin in 1943 entitled "What is Life?" and the Tarner Lectures given at Cambridge in 1956 entitled "Mind and Matter". The Cambridge University Press has helpfully published both series in a single volume, of which mine is the paperback reprint dated 1977 and entitled: *What is Life? Mind and Matter.*

It is interesting to note that Schrödinger's early education included humanities at which at an early age, he did quite well although never at the level achieved by Sir Charles Sherrington. To the discerning reader, this fact is evident, from the author's lucidity of expression (even when writing in English), his faultless logic and his impish sense of humour. The works we propose to review give the average reader, who would be unable to comprehend our author in his advanced mathematics, a chance to brush with the scintillating mind of a great scientist. To any person anxious to study the vital material proposed by the titles, the reading of these works is a stimulating delight.

In the preface to *What is Life?* the problem is raised of the difficulty (already referred to) in an age of enforced and intense specialisation, of bringing together the findings of our rapidly expanding knowledge in various disciplines in some cohesive and universal philosophy of science. He suggests the very term "University" suggests a unifying intention rather than merely being a central administration from which the various disciplines radiate in a laser-beam fashion, having no cohesion at the limits of their exploratory fields. His summarising of this situation is well worth quoting in full:

"We clearly feel that we are only now beginning to acquire reliable material for welding together the sum total of all that is known into a whole; but, on the other hand, it has become next to impossible for a single mind fully to command more than a small specialised portion of it.

"I can see no other escape from this dilemma (lest our true aim be lost forever) than that some of us should venture to embark on a synthesis of facts and theories, albeit with second-hand and incomplete knowledge of some of them — and at the risk of making fools of ourselves."

The pious hope of the author of this book is, that if the above quotation forms an umbrella large enough to shield a giant like Schrödinger, there may be a little room under it for me too. Some aspects of the problem have disappeared since Schrödinger's day with the advent of computers with vast memory storage capacities. Against this there runs the current tendency to programme computers to extend and intensify the "laser-beam" effects of intense specialisation. Some day, doubtless, a genius will turn up with ability to programme a computer on a more or less universal base; somebody like a Leonardo da Vinci, artist, poet, anatomist, engineer, architect, scientist and inventor. Then and only then can we hope to get answers which will assist us in coming to terms with the unanswered and perennial: What does all this knowledge signify?

Physics is, of course, the science of measurement. Naturally our author immediately interests himself in the vast variations in size between atoms and molecules and we humans who occupy ourselves with measuring them. We have already touched on this concept in chapter 3. However, in the ultimate the importance of all things to us is the effect they have on ourselves, that is on what we sense, what we think about, that which our senses record and what we perceive as the result. This raises a question in our physicist's mind. He expresses it thus:

"Why should an organ like our brain, with the sensorial system attached to it, of necessity consist of an enormous number of atoms, in order that its physically changing state should be in close and intimate correspondence with a highly developed thought?" (p. 9).

Schrödinger's term "highly developed thought" seems to correspond with Sherrington's term "mind". He is concerning himself at this stage with why our sense perceptions are too coarse to register impacts of single atoms or small clusters of atoms.

His response is important. He gives two reasons which have two consequences. His first is that "thought" (the occupation of the "mind") is perforce orderly, and the second is that it deals with material things detected by the senses which, too, have a degree of orderliness.

The consequences of these answers to his question are also proposed as twofold; again in his own words:

"First a physical organisation to be in close correspondence with thought (as my brain is with my thought) must be a very well ordered organisation, and that means that the events that happen within it must obey strict physical laws, *at least to a very high degree of accuracy*" (italics mine).

"Secondly, the physical impressions made upon that physically well ordered system by other bodies from outside obviously correspond to the perception and experience of the corresponding thought, forming its material, as I have called it."

These observations based on the human necessity to work within a reasonably ordered existence demand that within our time/space experience things need to work within physical laws which are, with minor variations, consistent, accurate and orderly.

Newtonian mathematics and classical physics provide us with this essential framework and our earth-bound technology simply cannot operate without them.

However, once we get below the size of a molecule in the "small things" area of twentieth-century knowledge, or for that matter beyond the limits of our solar system in the "big things" area, reality takes on different characteristics as our diagram no. 3 attempts to demonstrate.

For instance, we know atoms always involve a completely disorderly heat motion and this alone works against our being able to formulate any law governing what will happen between a small number of atoms. It is only when we are dealing with very large numbers of atoms that statistical laws of reasonable accuracy begin to emerge. In many ways human beings are very like atoms in their behaviour.

Life assurance offices base their premium rates on statistical evidence referred to as Mortality Tables. Many well known tables are based on an assumption of the simultaneous birth of 100,000 babies. By deducting from this figure the number of deaths that can be expected in the first year of life, calculated from records of actual deaths occurring say in statistics relating to a known population, they arrive at the number they expect to survive and commence the second year of life. This process is continued until, say at age 95, either all have perished or the number surviving is insignificant. If these raw data, duly graduated, are plotted as a graph in which the vertical axis represents the number living and the horizontal axis the age of the survivors from year to year, a nice regular curve emerges rising somewhat steeply during early childhood, then flattening out from adolescence to middle age, from which point it becomes steeper year by year to the cut-off point. In dealing with statistics, mathematicians, particularly physicists, have developed a simple calculation by which they can gauge the extent of the error their crude data are likely to yield. Obviously, the larger the number of samples involved in an experiment the greater should be the accuracy of the findings. Just as the behaviour of one atom or a small cluster of atoms is unpredictable so it is with human statistics. If a life assurance company insures the lives of 100,000 babies born simultaneously it could expect its actual experience to coincide with the results predicted by its mortality table with about 99.7% accuracy. The physicist's gauge of the extent of error likely to be experienced in statistical mathematics is known as the $\sqrt{n}$ rule. For instance in our life table based on the 100,000 lives the square root is 316.2 giving an expected divergence of 0·3 of one percent. If our mortality table were based on the experience of 1,000,000 lives we could expect 99.9% accuracy, while on the other hand if we compiled a table relating only to 100 lives the inaccuracy could be gauged as 10%. Carrying this idea to a single life we find that, as the square root of 1 is 1, the experience of a single life is unpredictable. Watching television programmes and "opinion polls", where predictions are made on three or four figure samples a degree of scepticism is certainly justified.

These last observations are to some extent a diversion from the thrust of Schrödinger's book, where this section is devoted to demonstrating how our senses, our brains and our minds are tuned to size limits within which our intelligence can formulate laws which operate with great precision. In our daily work when we deal with atoms we deal simultaneously with enormous numbers of them, so many in fact, that our $\sqrt{n}$ rule predicts such miniscule deviations from our certainty that we disregard it. In all this we are again presented with an immensely powerful argument for our Designer as against random chance, for being what we are where we are.

In the next chapter our author points out that as and when *we* are dealing with atoms, we require huge numbers of them so we can formulate "exact" laws of physics to allow us to go about our business in an orderly way; on the other hand, when *atoms* are dealing with us they become very effective operating in incredibly small groups and also that their effect on us is very orderly indeed. Here of course he is referring to chromosomes and the nucleic acid molecules. We have already dealt with this phenomenon in Chapter 3. Our physicist continues his chapter with a lucid explanation of the functions (and sizes) of chromosomes, genes and hereditary mechanisms generally. He concludes by describing the whole reproductive process of life as a marvel but dramatically posits a mind boggling "second marvel" which he speculates may be beyond human understanding and that is that we humans possess the power of investigating and acquiring real knowledge of the mechanisms governing the reproduction of life. This process is not completed by the brain. It requires essentially the co-operation of the mind. The brain records all that the senses of the research scientist feed to it, but acceptance, rejection, judgment and correlation are exercises esssentially of the mind.

As one of the purposes of this book is to draw attention to the convergence of thinking between scientists of different disciplines, chapters 3 and 4 of Schrödinger's book are dramatic in that in them he discusses hereditary mechanics, mutations and other biological wonders in terms of Quantum and Wave Mechanics!

A few points have considerable bearing on our objective. Darwin's proposition that the small variations obvious in large numbers of individuals of the one species are the material on which natural selection works is proved to be mistaken. Schrödinger (following de Vries) considers that mutations "occur" rather than "develop" in the nature of quantum jumps in the gene molecule. However, these changes are then inherited according to Mendel's laws. Our author raises another very interesting point resulting from his reflection on the tragedy of two great world wars. Whereas in times past, martial combat seemed to favour the survival of the fittest, the mass slaughter of healthy youth in World War I and World War II could have the opposite effect. Only fit and healthy young men were conscripted into the opposing armies leaving the sick and not so fit at home to do the breeding. If ever nuclear warfare breaks out, still another element will be introduced, in the effect of radiation as a mutation agent in the survivors (if any).

Available as an argument for a God (and also for our analogy of God as a transmitting station of infinite power

radiating on an infinite number of frequencies) is
Schrödinger's insistence that changes are in fact "jumps"
(quantum jumps). If the jump is to species having greater
energy, or as he puts it (p. 53) "a higher level", then some
outside source of energy is required by the new species. If
the change, however, be to a lower level, the surplus energy
is dissipated by radiation. Of course the greatest "mutation" a Christian hopes for is the change from mortal to the
eternal mode of existence. The exemplum is the resurrection of Jesus Christ by the power of God. Our change is by
his "grace" (p. 53).

Chapter 5 is a model of lucid argument using theories
(Delbruk's Model), in discussion relating to the
probability of the structure of a gene remaining stable in
face of the heat motion in which they exist. By using
arguments and examples accepted in chemistry and
physics we are led to his conclusion that basically a
molecule is a solid of crystalline nature. Non-crystalline
substances (amorphous) emerge from the author's reasoning as liquids of very high viscosity. By similar chemico/
physics formulae and telling analogy, Schrödinger concludes that a "gene or perhaps the whole chromosome
fibre" is an aperiodic solid.

This title is conferred because the chromosome fibre
does not grow by simple repetition like a periodic crystal
but on the other hand develops as we have already seen as a
chain having no limiting factor to its length and where,
instead of constant formal repetition as in a periodic
crystal, each group of atoms has a unique function not
necessarily resembling that of any other similar groups.
The results of these groupings are obvious in the various
forms of life on Earth. Our author sees clearly that the
genetic codes produced by this ingenious grouping of
atoms in the chromosome and genes not only indicates a
"plan" but contains within itself whatever it needs to put
the plan into operation. In other words your "genes" and
mine were planned to produce you and me.

The preceding two sentences would seem to indicate
that our author has gone as far as our present knowledge of

physics will allow us to go in this study of the relevance of the laws of physics to living matter. However, early in chapter 6 while admitting this, he proposes that other laws of physics will emerge which will account, not only for the "plan", but also "whatever is needed to put the plan into operation". There is a well known law of physics to which we have already referred and that is the Second Law of Thermodynamics which is based on the inherent tendency of matter to go into disorder. This is also referred to as the Entropy principle. The way the man in the street would express this is that things tend to get untidy unless energy is expended to tidy them up. No housewife would quarrel with this. Normal human life tends to be quite stable statistically. We have already referred to this in our discussion of the Mortality Tables used by Life Assurance Offices. If we base our statistical mathematics on large numbers of human beings we can produce very reliable and regular tables and curves. You will also remember when we discussed the $\sqrt{n}$ rule that the accuracy of our statistical calculations rested on the number of "lives" we considered in our tables. The experience of any one particular life can never be predicted by reference to a mortality table. Schrödinger raises the question of the relative stability of organisms and puts forward a theory to account for their avoidance of rapid decay. We have agreed that nature tends to disorder or decay if you like. Where then do we get the energy to maintain the stable order of our bodies? The biologist tells us through metabolism, that is our ability to eat food, turn it into energy and rid ourselves of waste in a nice balance which provides the necessary energy to maintain order and avoid the resolution into the ultimate disorder which we call death (which the physicist would call thermodynamical equilibrium). In order to relate the biological term with statistical mathematics, the term negative entropy is introduced which is really a measure of order. An ingenious mathematical approach is proposed to measure this "order".

Schrödinger's theory has met with some opposition from physicists. From the theological point of view statistical approaches to the riddle of life are not yet satisfying. If we can measure life in terms of entropy versus negative entropy and neatly balance our opposing forces we are confronted with the problems of "Why death?" "Why the vast differences in the life spans of individuals of the same species?"

The final chapter of this compendium of lectures was written in 1944 and its essential charm lies in revealing the humility, honesty and open-mindedness of a truly great mind. All through these lectures, pointers have been given as to possible developments which could assist us in formulating ideas of life based on statistical mathematics, and it is obviously the author's hope that progress will be made along the lines he suggests. However, right at the outset of chapter seven, Schrödinger states "From all we have learnt about the structure of living matter we must be prepared to find it working in a matter that cannot be reduced to the ordinary laws of physics". Our author then contrasts the utterly disorderly and unpredictable behaviour of an individual atom with the phenomenal order and planning obvious in the DNA and RNA molecules, which we have already discussed. Living things are obviously guided by a "mechanism entirely different from the probability mechanism of physics". Life cells and their component molecules behave in a way completely different from non-living matter, and quite beyond the competence of chemists and physicists to explain. The empiricist deals with producing order from disorder by a "mechanical" process (p. 85). On the contrary, the phenomenon of life produces order from order. Schrödinger suggests that we must be prepared to find a new type of physical law or in his own words a "non physical" or "super physical law". (A theologian would probably prefer the word "meta-physical".)

It is in the conclusion to this chapter when discussing the relation between clockwork and organism, that Schrödinger makes his historic statement already quoted that the single cog (allegorically present in an organism as a chromosome fibre) "is the finest masterpiece ever achieved along the lines of the Lord's quantum mechanics" (p. 91).

The epilogue to this magnificent discussion underlines the imperative that the scientist needs the theologian and vice versa. Schrödinger's thinking at this stage leads him to the conclusion that the closest a *biologist* can get to proving God and his own immortality at one stroke is the assertion "Hence I am God Almighty". The author is not proposing blasphemy, but in reality is saying that without revelation this is the ultimate conclusion possible without help from God (grace). The definition is the limit beyond which empiricism cannot go. Read in this light, the statement "Hence I am God Almighty" is of enormous importance in so far as the author affirms that his science and mathematics have led him to the inescapable conclusion that we cannot account for "life" without a "God Almighty". This sort of conclusion epitomises the swing of modern scientific thought away from the absolute a-theism of the late nineteenth and early twentieth centuries. It shows the infiltration of Einstein's work (and of his great disciples) blossoming into a new and exciting concept of reality. Having made his case for the existence of an Almighty God, Schrödinger in the final three sentences of this work states unequivocally his assertion of human immortality (p. 96).

In our closing chapters, we will attempt to show our analogy of eternity, our premise that the difference between persons is largely the difference in the sum total of their individual experiences, the Christian revelation of the Mystical Body of Christ and other beliefs, on the one hand, provide highly logical and relevant solutions which could be read parallel to Schrödinger's essays, and on the other hand how our author's contributions based on strict empirical science can stimulate the development and deepening of Christian doctrine.

We now come to part two of the paper-back edition previously referred to. It contains the substance of the Tarner lectures delivered at Trinity College, Cambridge in October 1956 and is entitled "Mind and Matter". It is important when reading this material to remember the passing of thirteen years between the Trinity College (Dublin) and the Cambridge lectures. This part of the book consists of six chapters. While it is obvious that Schrödinger intends to develop all his thinking as a physicist, he consistently moves across into areas which fifty years ago would have been branded as metaphysics and therefore "taboo" in a scientific work. He opens his chapter with a question framed empirically about a metaphysical problem! The question is "What kind of material process is directly associated with consciousness?" (p. 99). After thoroughly destroying the rationalist objection that the question is a non-issue, he deals with Spinoza's thesis that every particular thing or being is a modification of the infinite substance (God) and its inevitable conclusion of "universal animation". These lectures were delivered, of course, before Père Teilhard de Chardin's book *The Phenomenon of Man* in which Spinoza's theme is developed factually and speculatively to a remarkable degree. One could in hindsight wish Teilhard, the visionary, and Schrödinger, the scientist, could have exchanged ideas. They were comtemporaries! There is much in Schrödinger's work that would complement Teilhard's idea of the movement from the geosphere, to the biosphere, to the noosphere. Our author considers consciousness as an evolutionary force associated with the faculty of learning of a living being. He considers the "knowing how" a faculty of the unconscious functions, a reflex activity of the brain. He supports this idea from every day experience, an idea he summarises in the sentence "any succession of events in which we take part with sensations, perceptions and possibly with actions gradually drops out of the domain of consciousness when the same string of events repeats itself in the same way very often" (p. 102). When we are quite used to performing some action we do not consciously think about the detailed sequence of acts necessary to produce the result, unless some unusual factor intrudes. We then become conscious of the intrusion and our method of overcoming it. If the intrusion occurs a number of times its impact on our consciousness lessens proportionately. We become "used to it".

Interestingly enough our responses to a problem become increasingly efficient as the problem itself passes from the conscious to the unconscious category of actions. Courageously and logically, our author immediately applies his thesis to the question of ethics. With obvious exercise of self discipline, he posits the basis of all ethical codes as self-denial. A Christian theologian would prefer the word "love" used in the *agape* sense which is but a positive way of expressing the same basic idea. Schrödinger consistently takes his stand as a scientist. However, without actually saying so, he gives a useful analysis of *hamartia* (original sin) when he says "our conscious life . . . is necessarily a continued fight against our primitive ego" (p. 106). He goes on to say, "For our natural self our primitive will with its innate desires is obviously the mental correlate of the material bequest received from our ancestors". Here one must ask, and I think our author would like us to ask, does not this statement immediately propose a complete break between "homo sapiens" and every other living creature? Schrödinger gives some support to this idea when he admits "consciousness is a *phenomenon* in the zone of evolution" (p. 107 italics mine). This of course fits in nicely to the Christian dogma that each individual's soul is infused at or near conception. Our analogy of field, frequencies, the "All Powerful Multi-Frequency Transmitter" and "individually tuned-in receivers" covers all that our author proposes. Using the word "infused" in relation to the soul is important. The human soul is an important essential component of every person. Every person is immortal in his or her *completeness*. If this statement causes problems please refer back to the material on eternity in Chapter 2. It is essential to comprehend our existence moving without a break in our self-consciousness from the temporal level to the eternal level.

On page 146 our author quotes Sherrington's statement

from his book we have already dealt with (p. 218): "Man's mind is a recent product of our planet's side" and our author then goes on to comment, "I agree, naturally. If the first word (man's) were left out, I would not."

This mind is quite outside the limitations of the science which deals exclusively with material things. It always operates in a situation we call "now" and we have already arrived at the conclusion that eternity is a constant "now". Against this, one may posit that I can recall events that happened years ago or I can foresee an event which is yet to happen. This merely confirms the eternal character of the mind because what I remember is brought into the "now" of my consciousness or alternatively I can "see" now an event which has not yet happened.

There is a tremendous lesson to be learned if we accept a directed evolutionary process as the methodology of the creation of the human body with which a soul or mind is fused, and also accept as a corollary the emergence of ethical systems based on self-denial. If utter selfishness replaces self-denial (or *agape*), if we allow mass destruction of our fittest and bravest young men, if we interfere on a huge and unprecedented scale with the natural reproductive mechanism by contraception, abortion and voluntary sterilisation, could it be that by so doing we may activate a reversionary mechanism of de-volution to the point where the resultant brain is no longer capable of inter-action with a human immortal soul? Widespread increases in radiation activity, a hazard which might occur at any minute in a nuclear war, could also affect the destiny of our race. It is becoming increasingly obvious even to the most militant atheist that high ethical and moral standards are as essential to our survival as food and drink. Atheistic humanism will never sustain a high ethical code. Human beings are obviously not perfect so there is little sense in aiming to become "imperfect". Humanism as a standard is like water. It cannot rise unaided above its source but it is always capable of flowing to a lower level. Much more and of a positive nature will be said of this problem when we come to deal with the phenomenon of Jesus Christ, God/

man. All scientific thinking, indeed the whole philosophy of science produces nothing but questions and riddles. It is not until our immortal souls (or minds) meet the mortal/ eternal Person of Christ that our writhing, striving consciousness can meet real peace. As Schrödinger says, "We know when God is experienced, this is an event as real as an immediate sense perception or as one's own personality" (p. 150). Most of the other ideas our author brings forward have been touched upon in previous chapters.

Points of immense interest to the Christian philosopher reading Schrödinger's work include his:

1. Immediate perception of order and design in microphysics.

2. The relation of the atomic zone of existence to mankind.

3. Argument for the validity of the balance of probabilities as a method of dealing with research both in micro-physics and demographic mathematics.

4. Insistence on the importance of the uncertainty principle.

5. Support for definite individuality and uniqueness of brain and mind (soul) and their ability to interact.

6. Proposition that mutations in species and forms of life appear to occur suddenly in the nature of quantum jumps, not gradually as proposed by Darwin and his disciples.

7. Pointing out the need for essential availability of outside energy to overcome entropy and the problems posed by the second law of thermodynamics as applied to evolution. (The Christian would say that there must be a God to supply the exact amount of energy at exactly the right time to enable orderly evolution to occur.)

8. Argument for the existence of an overall "plan" in the development of life.

9. Establishment of limits for physics and empiricism.

10. Assertion that immense realities exist beyond the limitations of Newtonian classical mathematics.

11. Plea for a "new physics" to extend into the area we now call metaphysical. (Systematic Theology should

provide this in substance if it be continually revised and expressed in modern terms.)

Thirteen years later at Cambridge our physico/philosopher goes further, supporting his theses set out above by raising such questions as "What kind of material process is directly associated with consciousness?" In his reply he demonstrates the weakness of Teilhard de Chardin who baulks at sin and ethics. Once we establish the fact and validity of ethics we are faced as a matter of "common knowledge" with the existence and power of *hamartia*. *Every principle enumerated above is in complete harmony with Christian theology.*

One can only conclude a review of a book of this importance with an earnest plea that it be read or, if this has been the privilege of the reader, perhaps it might be well worth while to read it again.

CHAPTER 7

POPPER/ECCLES

THE book we now propose to study will, in all probability, be designated as a milestone, by generations yet unborn in the history of man's perpetual and compulsive search for truth. It bears the title *The Self and its Brain* (Springer International, 1977). Its purpose is to propose that the relationship between the human mind and the brain is an interaction between two distinct and separate things. This view is supported against those who consider mind and brain to be identical (that is, two aspects of the one thing) and another view called parallelism. Sir Karl Popper F.R.S. is a world famous philosopher who describes himself as an agnostic, while Sir John Eccles F.R.S. is a brain scientist and a believer in God. Both men in the best tradition of profound scholarship have a deep respect and sympathy for each other's views. Both are evolutionists and while Sir John Eccles would in our language defend the thesis of the "immortality of the human soul", Sir Karl would, I imagine, leave that as an open question but tend, at the stage arrived at in the book under review, to doubt it. Both would support the concept of man as a unique creature, but Sir Karl would see the gulf between animal and human consciousness as far less significant than would Sir John.

In the interests of brevity, the authors will be referred to from this point onward as Popper and Eccles. No disrespect would be possible from the pen of one whose admiration and respect for both men is so high and sincere.

As emphasised in the Introduction a strong tendency is developing for leading academics in many disciplines to become more and more interested in the philosophy of science; how in particular their own studies are moving towards the unity of things and thought. Hence they are tending to talk to each other and that is exactly what has happened in the book under review. The format of the book is unusual. The first section is written by Popper dealing with the thesis from a philosopher's point of view; the second section is the work of Eccles writing as a neurologist; but the third section is unique and most exciting. After having read and digested each other's work they engaged in a series of walks and talks which they recorded on tape. These conversations form the third section of the book. As a result of the intellectual stimulation these debates fostered in the great minds concerned, modifications, deletions and additions were made by the respective authors to part I and II of the book.

The resultant format may well set the pattern for serious text books of the third millenium. The method provided a fertile ground for the generation of insights, for modification and rounding off of ideas and clear identification of still unresolved differences of opinion. This system is ideal as our experience and thinking move from the black and white, right and wrong atmosphere, which in the last 150 years so often divided scientists and thinkers into camps of "goodies" and "baddies" or "baddies" and "goodies" depending on the reader's preformed rigid preferences. It harmonises beautifully with the blooming thought patterns proceeding from the theory of relativity and the re-discovery of the importance of the "subjective" in philosophy, psychology and even science.

Popper

Popper's first chapter is entitled "Materialism Transcends Itself". Quoting from Kant's *Critique of Pure Reason* the author brings out two points we have already covered, first that as our knowledge and viewing of the Universe indicates its enormity and complexity to us, we tend to feel miniscule and unimportant; secondly that the more we consider the consciousness of mankind, human personality, freedom and intelligence, our self-esteem is expanded significantly. As we saw from both Sherrington's and Schrödinger's works, awe-inspiring as our expanding view of reality is, even more impressive is the ability of our minds to view, measure, and evaluate the ultimate scales of astronomy and macro-physics and the minutiae of microphysics. Wonderful as this is, the mystery is compounded by the fact that every human being is different. As we have established already, the materialist doctrine that men are machines simply does not fit the facts. Mankind has every right to be viewed as an amazing phenomenon. The author, while obviously disagreeing with the idea of man as a machine, has great respect for materialist philosophers, particularly when their thinking leads them to humanist ethics. Here speaks the honest agnostic. Ethics that are humane are doubtless admirable but we have already outlined the perils of humanism as a base for any ethical system and the inbuilt weakness of such a system, tending to let it slide down hill.

Before proceeding further, let it be said that all that follows is intended as a stimulus and encouragement to read in full Popper's section of the remarkable book we are studying.

What is written here is merely an overview of the work. The method used will be to take the summary our author has graciously provided, setting out the main results of his contribution which is written as a sort of epilogue (p. 209) and then refer back to the text for the arguments supporting his conclusions. Popper does not hesitate to point up some difficulties arising from his thesis. As this book is an essay at Christian apologetics, where we feel that the Christian faith can contribute to easing the pressure of problems and uncertainties an attempt will be made to put our case.

We have already outlined our author's criticism of materialism. He develops this further by re-presenting J. B. S. Haldane's "Refutation of Materialism" in a new form, which clearly demonstrates that materialism is self-defeating and that it cannot be supported by rational argument. He presents his "Haldane Revised" in the form of a dialogue between an "Interactionist" (obviously himself) and a "Physicalist". The dialogue occupies some five pages of the book and demonstrates the value of argument by dialogue, which regrettably is so little used in contemporary debate. It would not be right or proper to attempt to precis such a masterpiece. It should be read. Popper himself, however, summarises when he says "I do not claim that I have *refuted*. But I think that I have shown that *materialism has no right to claim that it can be supported by rational argument*; argument that is rational by logical principles . . . for these standards appear from the materialist's point of view as an illusion or at least an ideology" (italics mine).

The Identity Theory

The next step in his argument is a case against the so called parallelism and identity theories concerning the mind/brain relationship. Before proceeding further, however, it is absolutely necessary to become familiar with two ingenious and time-saving devices Popper uses to define first of all what he calls cosmic evolutionary stages, and secondly a similar table relating to the programme of reductionism; that is, the "systems" in which matter is presented to the mind as it develops from infinitely small "particles" (?), to the ecosystems with which we are all familiar. Our author elects to classify Cosmic Evolutionary stages in the following form. He refers to these stages under the titles of World 1, World 2 and World 3. As Christianity, using this system, would require a World 4, this has been added to the author's diagram but is distinguished by being enclosed in dotted lines as against the continuous lines enclosing the original box (Table 1).

This table is not regarded as complete but is a great aid in following the author's arguments. It is a tidy device. The author admits an intuitive prejudice against this over-view of the creative evolutionary process; so he supplements his Table 1 with Table 2 setting out what has been called "the

Table 7: Some Cosmic Evolutionary Stages

World 4 Eternity (the everlasting now)	(7) Full Realisation of Self — Universal Communication Knowledge supersedes Theories — Participation in never ending Creation — *Hamartia* vanishes
World 3 (the products of the human mind)	(6) Works of Art and of Science (including Technology) (5) Human Language — Theories of Self and of Death
World 2 (the world of subjective experiences)	(4) Consciousness of Self and of Death (3) Sentience (Animal Consciousness)
World 1 (the world of physical objects)	(2) Living Organisms (1) The Heaviest Elements; Liquid and Crystals (0) Hydrogen and Helium

programme of reductionism''. This table conforms to the generally accepted picture from the biologist's standpoint. Consistent with the dotted box added to Table 7, an addition has been made both below and above the original box which it is hoped will be of use later in this book as our defence of orthodox Christianity develops. These additions are in no way intended to modify the thrust of Popper's argument and should be disregarded by the reader until specifically referred to in later chapters.

In fairness it must be stated that our author states explicitly that his tables are oversimplified and incomplete. They are obviously designed to present a comprehensible picture from which much detail has been omitted in the interests of clarity. It is a consolation to us, as we have tried to present difficult complex notions in the form of diagrams and analogies in other contexts, to know that Popper has had similar difficulties. The same limitations apply to the dotted boxes we have added to the original tables. The author admits the problem of disorder (*hamar-*

tia) and acknowledges that it does not show up in his tables. The identity theory of mind/brain, has many supporters who describe it from various viewpoints. It is fully dealt with in Sections 16, 20, 23 and 24 of the book being reviewed. Its various proponents describe it in different terms and nuances, but in essence it boils down to acceptance of the fact that our senses transmit information to the brain, which, stimulated by the chemical and electrical activity that the messages generate, dictates a reaction appropriate to the situation. This being so, what we call mind or soul or self is part of and identical with our physiological make up.

The paragraph just written is revealing. It represents an attempt to reduce the concept of the identity theory to a basically simple statement. In so doing the obvious deficiencies of the theory become apparent.

Let us deal with one example for a start; that of human language. If, as an experiment, a carefully contrived

Table 8: Biological Systems and their Parts

(13) Eternal level of existence achieved making ecosystems, metabolic systems and reproductive systems redundant, disorder eliminated
(12) Level of ecosystems (11) Level of populations of metazoa and plants (10) Level of metazoa and multicellular plants (9) Level of tissues and organs (and of sponges?) (8) Level of populations of unicellular organisms (7) Level of cells and of unicellular organisms (6) Level of organelles (and perhaps of viruses) (5) Liquids and solids (crystals) (4) Molecules (3) Atoms (2) Elementary particles (1) Sub-elementary particles (0) Unknown: sub-sub-elementary particles
(X) God — a Spirit — pure Act — immaterial — eternal — limitless energy — Creator *ex nihilo* + Love (*Agape*)

situation were presented to a number of people, one at a time and if each person were asked to respond verbally to the situation, to describe or comment upon it, we could be certain that we would receive as many different verbalisations as we had persons. If we recorded each person's reply under the three headings of observation, judgement and reaction, it is virtually certain that highly significant differences would be detected. This is a problem highlighted every day in a law court of minor jurisdiction where say three witnesses of a traffic accident might be asked to tell the magistrate what they saw at a certain time in a certain place.

Any person having experience of adjudicating in such a situation would confirm the fact that from normal, honest people vastly different accounts will be told. This is hard to reconcile with the identity theory, for each person received more or less the same input from the senses.

Physiologically nerves and brains of healthy persons are very much alike; yet descriptions vary! This seems far apart from our experience in chemical and electrical experiments. In these, if the input is similar and conditions are the same, variations in reaction will be very small indeed.

This brief and incomplete picture omits the phenomena of the deliberate lie or an omission known to the witness to be important.

Obviously, after the brain has indicated a suitable response to the situation based on the evidence received from the senses, some other power intervenes and either confirms and dictates a course of action based on the response put forward by the brain, or modifies or rejects it consciously.

Remembering that the purpose of my book is to draw attention to the movement towards theism which is developing in this century among scientists of various disciplines, the change from antagonism to mutual interest between philosophers of science and modern theologians, and most importantly how orthodox Christian beliefs harmonise with modern thinking and even challenge it to step into the "faith" climate; bearing all this in mind, we are now examining the work of an agnostic philosopher and a brain scientist who is a theist. As already stated, the method employed is to review the four books chosen from the many written and being written, each one of which contributes to the subject in a different way. It is of course necessary to be absolutely fair and impartial. Popper's logic and reasoning are both brilliant and original and are based on very wide reading covering more than twenty centuries of human thought. It will be necessary to refer to his two tables, already reproduced, especially Table No. 1. Here then is his description:

"The identity theory (or the 'central state' theory) can be formulated thus. Let us call 'World 1' the class process in the physical world. Then let World 1 (or the class of objects belonging to it) be divided (as in section 16) into two exclusive subworlds or subclasses, in such a manner that World 1 (m for mental) consists of the description in physical terms of the class of all the mental or psychological processes that will ever be known by acquaintance, while the vastly larger class, World 1 (p for purely physical) consists of all those physical processes (description in physical terms) which are not mental as well. In other words, we have

1. World 1 = World 1_p + World 1_m.
2. World 1_p. World 1_m = 0 that is, the two classes are exclusive of each other).
3. World 1_m = World 2.

The identity theory stresses the following points:

4. Since World 1_p and World 1_m are parts of the same World 1, there is no problem raised by their interacting. *They can clearly interact according to the laws of physics.*

5. Since World 1_m = World 2, mental processes are real. They interact with World 1_p processes, exactly as interactionism asserts. So we have interactionism (without tears).

6. Accordingly, World 2 is not epiphenomenal but real (also in the sense of section 4, above). Therefore the clash between Darwinian point of view and the epiphen-

omenal view of world 2, described in section 20, does not occur (or so it might seem — but see the next section).

7. The 'identity' of World I_m and World 2 can be made intuitively acceptable by considering a cloud. It consists, physically speaking, of an accumulation of water vapour, that is, a region of physical space in which water drops of certain average size are distributed with a certain density. This is a physical structure. It looks from the outside like a white reflecting surface; it is experienced, from the inside, as a dull, only partially translucent, fog. The thing as experienced is, in theoretical or physical description, identical with a structure of water drops.

According to U. T. Place (1956), we can compare the inside view and the outside view of the cloud with the inside or subjective experience of a brain process and the outside observation of the brain.

Moreover, the theoretical description in terms of water vapour, or a structure of water drops, can be compared to the not yet fully known theoretical physical description of the relevant physico-chemical brain processes involved.

8. If we say that fog was the cause of a car accident, then this can be analysed, in physical terms, by pointing out how the water drops absorbed light, so that light quanta which otherwise would have stimulated the driver's retina never reached the retina.

9. The upholders of the central state theory or identity theory point out that the fate of the theory will depend on empirical corroboration which can be expected to come from the progress of brain research.''

Parallelism

Popper, with keen analytical discernment, posits the idea that the theory of Parallelism relating to the brain/mind relationship actually includes the Identity Theory as a special instance, which could be included under the general umbrella term "parallelism". Again, there is tight reasoning as the author concludes that, while his argument does not negate the idea of parallelism, he refutes the claim that this theory is based on a legitimate empirical basis.

As the Identity Theory and the Parallelism Theory are "stock in trade" of materialists, and as materialists accept, in general, only what can be proved by the empirical method, Popper has dealt materialism a devastating reverse by demonstrating that the explanation of the mind/brain relationship is denied empirical support. How necessary it is that Christian theologians should study the author's work.

Some Remarks on the Self

As a Christian it is necessary to comment on chapter 4 of Popper's section of the book. The first reaction of a Christian theologian is one of gratitude for the clear unreserved outline of the inevitable conclusions at which an agnostic must arrive if he thinks through logically. So many agnostics refuse to think about the problem of self, soul, consciousness or, self-awareness, probably because such thinking would tend towards the same conclusions at which Popper arrives with disarming courage and frankness; namely self-annihilation at death. Our author's degree of courage is enhanced by the fact that he supports the brain/mind problem in favour of interaction and also that he refuses to allow materialism the support of empirical science. He affirms a close belief in a statement attributed to John Beloff: "I have no craving for personal immortality; indeed I would think the poorer of a world in which my ego was to be a permanent fixture". Yet having made this assertion goes on to say "I wish to state clearly, unambiguously that I am convinced that selves exist". As he believes that mind or self exists independently of his physical brain, we appear to be faced with a paradox, for as we have already established a spiritual entity is imperishable and therefore eternal.

Christianity has much to contribute here. Its first comment would be on the statement "*I* have no craving for personal immortality". As a Christian believes that he is a creature of God and that his soul (mind, self or personal consciousness or whatever one likes to call it) is spiritual in nature and is infused at his conception, it does not matter what *his* "craving" might be, since his eternal existence is an inevitable result of his nature. The next statement "Indeed I would think the poorer of a world in which my ego was to be a permanent fixture", demonstrates a laudable humility and could also be uttered in sincerity by any Christian, with the exception that, through Christ's great redemptive act, his eternal existence can be completely fulfilled, free of all blemishes and defects, active in utter unselfishness, an essential part of the Mysical Body of Christ, co-operator and eternal co-creator in union with God who is Creator of all that is, seen and unseen. What a difference in outlook! Christianity possesses another treasure in its doctine of the Mystical Body of Christ. In this each "self" is seen as a cell in the continuously growing body of all Christians including all those now alive in the mortal sense and those who have entered the eternal state. Of this body Christ himself is the head. Those members living on Earth are cells in process of development. As in a human body every cell needs every other cell, and every cell tends to support and complement every other cell, so it is in the Mystical Body. If one cell says "I have no craving for personal immortality", the contiguous cells will answer, "We crave the pleasure and stimulus of your personality forever". Certainly in our mortal state we developing cells are prone to sickness from the poison of sin, but we have a sure antitoxin in the salvific power of Christ. All this and more will be opened up when we deal in a later chapter with the Church.

In this section of his book Popper raises the idea of self as "the ghost in a machine". The author rightly supports those who will have nothing to do with dualism. The Christian view of man, as outlined in our chapter 2 under the heading "Eternity", in which St. Paul's assertion taken from the Good News translation of the second letter to the Corinthians (5:2) "we shall not be without a body" sums the matter up and seems to satisfy the perennial wrestling between supporters of monism as against dualism.

In section 33 of Popper's fourth chapter he arrives at certain conclusions important to our thesis. He admits that an analogy between the brain and a computer may be valid but stresses that a computer is useless without a programmer, and of course in our context the programmer is the mind or self. The liaison between the mind and brain is intimate. The mind, in Plato's words, is the pilot of the ship.

Should the reader of this book be persuaded to read Popper, and hopefully he has or will do so, we must at least comment on argument proceeding from a conjecture of a brain transplant! (pages 117 and 118). After reading part 2 of the book by Eccles, which gives an idea of the immense complexity of the brain and the neuro-sytem complementing it, it is hard not to consider the possibility of a brain transplant, as an hypothesis too complex to be considered seriously and it might be pertinent from a theist to suggest that this is by design to ensure the survival of the individual personality with brain to "match" or "resonate" with the infused soul (mind) and with God (Transmitter) who energises it. To the Christian, God, soul (or mind) and brain are in union, in tune separately and uniquely as far as each individual is concerned.

Popper himself gives support to this criticism when on page 120 he suggests "that the brain is owned by the self — the self is always active". St. Thomas Aquinas considers the soul the "form" of the person. Dealing with the biological approach to human knowledge our author (p. 121) gives one of his distinctions of various forms of knowledge, claiming that knowledge in the subjective sense is World 2 and knowledge in the objective sense is World 3 knowledge (please refer back to Table 1) and that this distinction arises only on a human level. This to the Christian theologian is important, as it marks clearly the distinction between the souls of sub-human creatures, which may have reached their potential by an evolutionary process, and the unique human soul infused by the

Creator. This difference is essential if we accept mankind as the link in the chain of life joining the material and eternal levels of animation, and if in all creation there is a divine plan. The author concludes his discussion of this point with an italicised assertion: "*Fully conscious intelligent work largely depends upon this interaction between World 2 and World 3*". This is undisputable if, as Popper states, "there are two great sources of our information: that which is aquired through genetic inheritance and that which is acquired throughout life". The Christian would add a third, namely "revelation". The "two only" theory would keep us earthbound, but the soul even during our life on Earth, likes to soar above World 3 towards World 4, as our great musicians, poets, artists and above all our ethereal Christian liturgies give powerful evidence. If the soul (or mind) is immortal, then room must be given for it to manifest its yearning for freedom from its time/space confines. It constantly yearns to look out of Einstein's windows in the time/space capsule towards the "light", and light comes only from World 4.

In his consistently interesting way, our author on page 132 deals with learning from experience and the effect this learning may have in changing our aims and preferences. He makes the point that these changes are rare and slow, with one remarkable exception, that of "conversion". Conversion to the dialectical materialism of Marx, to Buddhism, to Christianity or to any ideology is a remarkable phenomenon, as any convert will testify. What happens? Probably the "field of resonance" analogy is the most apt. Imagine tuning a radio set when suddenly it comes into resonance with a transmitting station, and a piece of music or an address is heard which goes straight to the heart of the listener. We really find then three identities operating on the one frequency; the transmitter, the receiver and the listener. The impact on the listener can be overwhelming to the extent that he, as it were, locks himself to this frequency. That which he hears becomes so much part of himself that his whole hierarchy of preferences must perforce be re-ordered to accommodate his new insight. His personality, soul, or self, can from that moment be modified. He never loses his sense of continuity with all he was before, but the experience of his conversion becomes an event as important to him as his birth. He can become a new man for better or for worse.

Popper's summing up of this chapter is fascinating. An acknowledged agnostic, he says:

"If I should be asked to expose the bare bones of this chapter, I should say that there seems to me no reason to believe in an immortal soul, or in a physical substance which can exist independently of the body. (I leave open the possibility, which I regard as far-fetched, that the results of physical research may change my judgement on this point.) Yet it has been recognised that the talk about a substantial self is far from being a bad metaphor; especially if we remember that 'substances' are, it seems to be replaced, or to be explained, by processes, as was foreseen by Heraclitus. We certainly experience ourselves as an 'essence': the very idea of an essence seems to be derived from this experience, which explains why it is so closely akin to the idea of a spirit. Perhaps the worst of this metaphor is that it does not stress the intensely active character of the self. If one rejects essentialism, one may still describe the self as a 'quasi essence', as that which seems essential to the unity and continuity of the responsible person.

"What characterizes the self (as opposed to the electro-chemical process of the brain on which the self largely depends — a dependence which seems far from one-sided) is that our experiences are closely related and integrated; not only with past experiences but also with our changing programmes for action. Our expectation, and our theories — with our models of the physical and cultural environment, past, present and future including the problems which they raise for our evaluations, and for our programmes for action. But all these belong, at least in part, to World 3.

"This relational idea of the self is not quite suffic-ient because of the essentially active and integrative character of the self. Even so far as sense perception and memory is concerned, the model of 'inflow' (and perhaps 'output') is quite insufficient, since everything depends upon a constantly changing programme: there is active selection, and partially active digestion, and active assimilation; and all these depend upon evaluations" (p. 146).

That is why I have had the temerity to add World 4 to his Table 1. If our author could go along with the idea expressed in our Chapter 2, that we shall always know ourselves as men and women, one could say of him in Christ's own words: "You are not far from the Kingdom of God". The crux of the argument could be expressed thus: looked at from our point of view in the time/space continuum, human death viewed by an agnostic gives us a choice of accepting only two options: either that the body decays and a disembodied soul survives, or alternatively the whole person body/mind is extinguished. If we accept the second alternative it becomes a powerful argument for the body/mind identity theory which Popper rightly rejects. If however we view human death in the thought patterns of relativity the thesis put forward in Chapter 2 is not only tenable but likely. It certainly has strong biblical support. It is simply a question of viewing the same sequence of events from relatively different levels of existence.

Christian theologians and philosophers have wrestled with this problem from St. Paul's day, as did the Greeks before them. It is only now that we have been released from the concept of time and space as universal absolutes that a rational solution seems possible.

If the thesis put forward in Chapter 2 is acceptable, it means that we can quite legitimately go on describing human death and its consequences in conventional time/space language as long as we understand that the difficulties which arise are only those of semantics and not of realities.

May we claim that our hypothesis put forward in Chapter 2 seems to comply with the conditions put forward by our author for the validity of a new hypothesis which he sets out on pages 148 and 149 of his book? The Very Reverend Professor Thomas Torrance of Edinburgh has written splendidly in this area with his outstanding competence as a theologian. Three of his books, *Space, Time and Incarnation, Space, Time and Resurrection* and *Christian Theology and Scientific Culture* make a great contribution to this debate, as does a book entitled *Creation and the World of Science* by Dr. Arthur Peacocke, Director, Ian Ramsey Centre, St. Cross College, Oxford, written from the point of view of a biologist.

Eccles

If this book does no more than to stimulate a wider reading of *The Self and its Brain,* in that alone it could find justification for its publication. The high quality of Popper's opening chapters is at least maintained by Sir John Eccles F.R.S. He is an Australian who graduated from the University of Melbourne, a Rhodes Scholar who studied at Magdalen College Oxford, where he later became a Fellow. His degrees include an M.A. and Ph.D. He was for four years President of the Australian Academy of Science and is an Honorary Member of the American Academy of Science. He held the chair of Physiology for seven years at the University of Otago, New Zealand. This is by no means a complete *curriculum vitae,* but will serve to give some idea of the academic brilliance of the author. Expectations one might build up from his profound scholarship are, if anything, enhanced by his eight chapters in the book we are reviewing.

The purpose of our book is clearly set out in the Introduction. So once again we must restrain our review to those parts of Eccles' work which either support or work against our thesis. Every encouragement is, however, given to those prepared to tackle the work in full. It is a deeply rewarding experience.

For our purpose Sir John has made the task of reviewing and commenting on his book very easy.

He starts each chapter with a resumé or precis of its contents which he then develops in the text which follows. Thus the overall picture of his work is easy to see. In chapter 7 we have the author's theory of mind/brain interaction clearly summarised. We propose to start from this summary and then attempt to show how the strictly scientific chapters support the author's theory, commenting on any detail particularly applicable to our thesis as we go.

Eccles holds uncompromisingly, that the self-conscious mind and the brain are separate entities. He has developed his theory of the interaction between the self-conscious mind of a human being and that person's brain with particular reference to the dominant hemisphere of the brain (normally the left). He makes the statement that "its role for animals and for the minor hemisphere is debatable". This is important. Christian theologians who follow the Thomistic tradition hold that the human soul as infused directly by the Creator is immortal. Minds of other living creatures are quite different from the human soul.

Interestingly, Eccles has developed his theory in chapter 7 from the three World hypotheses of Popper whose diagrams have been reproduced in this chapter. Being an evolutionist, he refers to Popper's thesis and diagrams as "a very interesting *development* of the self-conscious mind". We have held to the doctrine of the divine infusion of the human soul, but if one thinks about it there need be no conflict between the ideas of "development" and "infusion". It boils down to "how" and "what".

It would be only fair at this point to quote the author verbatim from page 355: "Briefly the self-conscious mind is an independent entity — that is actively engaged in reading out from the multitude of active centres in the modules of the liaison areas of the dominant cerebral hemisphere. The self-conscious mind selects from these centres in accord with its intention and its interests and integrates its selection to give the unity of conscious experience from moment to moment. . . . Thus it is proposed that the self-conscious mind exercises a superior

PRE WORLD 1	WORLD 1 PHYSICAL OBJECTS AND STATES	WORLD 2 STATES OF CONSCIOUSNESS	WORLD 3 KNOWLEDGE IN OBJECTIVE SENSE	WORLD 4 GRACE
THE CREATOR (ex nihilo) (Beyond worldly experience)	1. INORGANIC Matter & energy of cosmos 2. BIOLOGY Structure and actions of all living beings human brains 3. ARTEFACTS Material substrates of human creativity of tools of machines of books of works of art of music	Subjective knowledge Experience of perception thinking emotions dispositional intentions memories dreams creative imagination	Cultural heritage coded on material substrates philosophical theological scientific historical literary artistic technological Theoretical systems scientific problems critical arguments	Prayer Revelation Eternity — "Perfect possession of interminable life held wholly all at once"

Popper and Eccles (p. 359). Tabular representation
of the three worlds that comprise all existents and
and all experiences as defined by Popper/Eccles (modified)

Diagram 9

interpretive and controlling role upon the neural events by virtue of a two-way interaction across the interface between World 1 and World 2. It is proposed that the unity of conscious experience comes, not from an ultimate synthesis in the neural machinery, but in the integrating action of the self-conscious mind on what it reads out from the immense diversity of neural activities in the liaison brain."

To assist his readers Eccles has expanded Popper's diagrams to illustrate his summing up of chapter seven. The diagrams are reproduced on pages 153 and 155.

As Christian theologians we must complete the picture as we see it (and know it) by indicating in boxes outlined in broken lines the unique property and privileges of the human soul. By property we refer to its ability to communicate with its Creator (prayer) and by privileges we include the divine communication with a freely willing, loving soul (grace and revelation).

On page 357 Eccles states that at 18 years of age he had an overwhelming experience as a result of which "his life was changed". We have also quoted Schrödinger when he said "We know, when God is experienced, this is an event as real as an immediate sense perception or as one's own personality" (p. 150). The author of this book is also familiar with this phenomenon, as are millions of people alive today. This is the excuse I offer for expanding the table. In fairness it must be said that from an empirical point of view the tables as drawn in their original form are perfectly valid; indeed they should not be extended. They show clearly the boundary line beyond which empirical science cannot proceed. The great scholastic philosophers and theologians claimed that theology *is* a science, "the Queen of Sciences" was their term. A vast change has taken place in this century from the attitude that science will eventually provide answers to all questions, to the present view (and perhaps I oversimplify) that we can now *prove scientifically* that much knowledge must come from methods beyond those considered as legitimate in our laboratories or ideas expressible in the terms of pure mathematics. Schrödinger is explicit in this view when he

Diagram 10

BRAIN⇌MIND INTERACTION

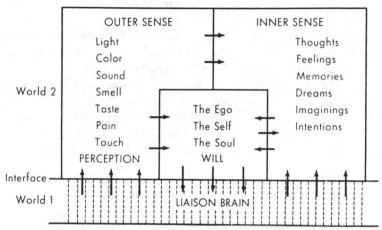

Popper and Eccles (p. 360). Information flow diagram for brain-mind interaction. The three components of World 2: outer sense, inner sense and the ego or self are diagrammed with their connectivities. Also shown are the lines of communication across the interface between World 1 and World 2, that is from the liaison brain to and from these World 2 components. The liaison brain has the columnar arrangement indicated. It must be imagined that the area of the liaison brain is enormous, with open modules numbering a hundred thousand or more, not just the two score here depicted.

says "I do not find God anywhere in time and space . . . God is spirit" (p. 150). However, let us stress that the work of our scientists is invaluable. Surely Sherrington, Schrödinger, Popper, Eccles and all true and single-minded scientists deepen our understanding of the words already quoted from the document *Dei Verbum* of the Second Vatican Council "God . . . gives men an enduring witness of Himself in created realities". To think any other way is to court despair and frustration. The mental state of the unbeliever is poignantly expressed by Pascal. Eccles quotes him from the translation by J. M. Cohen (1961):

> "When I consider the short extent of my life, swallowed up in the eternity before and after, the small space that I fill or even see, engulfed in the infinite immensity of

spaces unknown to me and which know me not, I am terrified, and astonished to find myself here, not there. For there is no reason why it should be here, not there, why now rather than at another time. Who put me here? By whose order and design have this place and time been allotted to me? . . . The eternal silence of those infinite spaces strikes me with terror" (p. 357).

As the whole thrust of our book is dependent on the co-existence and relationship between my "self" and Almighty God, the validity of the concept of my soul, self, mind or self-consciousness as immortal, and not a part of a physical organ called my brain, is of the utmost importance.

It is now proposed to examine a few of Eccles' contributions as a brain scientist to the theme of this book. He claims to have established (and this claim is generally supported by other neurologists/physiologists) the actual area of the brain where the interaction between mind and brain takes place. This is part of the left hemisphere, although he admits that the right hemisphere can under certain circumstances be involved in a limited way. As already mentioned, he designates the left hemisphere as the dominant hemisphere and the right as the minor hemisphere. It is interesting to note that amongst its many functions the left hemisphere controls speech. As an aid to the understanding of the specific performance of the two hemispheres, Eccles provides us with a diagram on page 352. He gives credits for this conception to Levy Agresti and Sperry (1968) and Levy (1973) and adds a note that he has added to the original lists. This diagram is reproduced on the following page.

The method of ascertaining this information is almost beyond question, as it was established by tests on patients who had undergone surgical operations, involving in one case the removal of a hemisphere of the brain, in another, called commissurotomy (which is a severing of the *corpus callosum,* the multi-channel cable connecting the two separate hemispheres) and other surgical procedures of equally drastic dimensions.

Of great importance to our thesis is Eccles' remark on page 353: "The hemispheric specialisation is unique to man". The author explains how this might have come about through evolution but it appears to us to be an important piece of evidence in our view of evolution as a *guided* methodology of the Creator. We would go further

Diagram 11

DOMINANT HEMISPHERE	MINOR HEMISPHERE
Liaison to consciousness	No such Liaison
Verbal	Almost non-verbal
Linguistic description	Musical
Ideational	Pictoral and Pattern sense
Conceptual similarities	Visual similarities
Analysis over time	Synthesis over time
Analysis of detail	Holistic-Images
Arithmetical and computer-like	Geometrical and Spatial

Popper/Eccles p. 352. Various specific performances of the dominant and minor hemispheres as suggested by the new conceptual developments of Levy-Agresti and Sperry (1968) and Levy (1973). There are some additions to their original list.

and assert that, in establishing and identifying that area of the brain where the interchange between soul and body takes place, our scientist has drawn yet another line indicating the limits of empirical investigations. This statement in no way inhibits the idea that much more can be discovered concerning the detail and mechanics of the interactive process or that this should be pursued.

On page 243 Eccles states "We can only dimly imagine what is happening in the human cortex (the outer layer or rind of the brain) or indeed in the cortices of the higher mammals, but it is at a level of complexity, of dynamic complexity, greater than anything else that has been discovered in the universe or created in computer technology".

To anyone who has had some training in the mathematics of probabilities, combinations and permutations, Eccles' presentation of brain physiology and brain functions makes it utterly impossible to hold to the theory that life itself and above all the human brain, could evolve by undirected random chance. If one has also been involved in civil engineering construction the evidence for "design" becomes overwhelming and we can't have a design without a Designer. If we accept the Christian thesis of man as the psychosomatic link in the overall creation process destined to move "mud" into an eternal level of existence, then the "plan" resulting in the realisation of the human brain fits into the overall design perfectly, like a Rolls-Royce piston into its cylinder. In our brain we have our "mud pie" developed to the stage where it can interact with "Spirit".

It is pertinent to remark at this stage on the strength of the "fundamentalist" attitude of so many scientists, who will work in their laboratories day by day with honesty, dedication, accuracy and acute logic, yet who will persist against all evidence to the contrary to adhere to the idea of evolution by random chance, ascribing unexplainable phenomena as due to "nature". What exactly do they mean by that word "nature"?

At this stage one must recommend a reading of Sherrington's chapter on the eye in *Man on his Nature* then Eccles' chapter 2 of the book under review. Believer or unbeliever reading these chapters with an open mind must at least be filled with a sense of awe and wonder, and awe and wonder are the first steps to God. Reading modern books like these, written by empirical scientists, we can foresee the immense revolution that must take place if truth prevails (as ultimately it must). Over half the world's population live under Marxist forms of government, giving at least outward consent to the "random chance" theory of life and above all of human life. Of the remaining people, the majority are locked into materialism which is as ugly as it is illogical. If these people think at all, they become fundamentalist Darwinians, not that they believe intelligently in Darwinism, but they do not want to believe in God. It would be most interesting to ascertain how many Marxists and Materialists have read either *Das Kapital* or *The Descent of Man*.

In the Epilogue to Chapter E2 the author quotes from Mountcastle (1975) who says, *inter alia*:

"At the level of sensation your images and my images are virtually the same and readily identified one to another by verbal description or common reaction. Beyond that each image is conjoined with genetic and stored experiment information that makes each of us uniquely private. From that complex integral, each of us constructs at a higher level of perceptual experience his own, very personal, view from within."

Here is another empiricist emphasising from the scientific point of view an important Christian belief; that is that we human beings are individually unique, not that that is of much importance in itself, but it is of immense significance when related to the concept of the Mystical Body of which Christ is the head and we are the cells; not only are we marvellously designed but we form part of that mosaic of which each living cell in a body is an essential part with a different function.

In chapter 3 of Eccles' work (p. 275) there is interesting evidence in support of our hypothesis of "fields". It emerges from the question "What happens when I will a certain action to take place?" I decide right now to slap my desk with the palm of my left hand. All my physical resources of which I am conscious (or in some aspects unconscious) are engaged in writing this paragraph. For no reason whatever and certainly not in reaction to any input from my sensory section I "will" to smack the desk and immediately I do just that!

Eccles quotes the results of some experiments of Kornhuber on human subjects. It was discovered that "willing" leads to the build up of a wide ranging potential "over the top" of the brain. This phenomenon results in a complex series of reactions described in fascinating detail by the author (pp. 275/6). Here we are presented with empirical evidence but the great problem still stands. What *caused* the rise of the negative potential spread? There can be only one answer and that is the mind, soul or self, interacting with the physical brain. Here is a simply understood example of interaction. The results described above cannot be accounted for by any "identity" or "parallel" theory, but an interaction based on resonance between two fields is quite tenable. *My* soul is tuned to *my* brain. You could *will* my brain to set in motion processes which would result in my slapping the table but the event will never happen unless you first communicate your willing to me and then only if I *will* to comply with your will. Your personality or soul is obviously operating on a different frequency from mine. An intervention is justified here. The writer has had this experience and it has been confirmed in discussion with happily married people, usually in a marriage of long duration, that from time to time one partner can effectively will the other partner to do something or take some attitude without exchanging words. One wonders whether sub-consciously these two people can "will" themselves to "tune in" to the other partner's field! Having played for years in a symphony orchestra one becomes conscious of some over-riding and compelling power, much more effective than the conductor's baton, which produces a degree of co-ordination and *sympatia* between seventy or eighty entirely different personalities playing different instruments, many of which involve the use of distinctly separate techniques to produce a musical note. There are numerous recorded incidents of large orchestras success-fully playing involved symphonic music without the aid of a conductor. One is tempted to ask (from experience) "Is not some field active here? How can one account for the superbly co-ordinated result, remembering that with every player it is necessary for his mind to will and activate the complicated muscle movements necessary to produce a note and that that note should be soft, loud, swelling, diminishing, in flowing or staccato mode, strictly in time, or retarding or accelerating in rhythm?"

All this is interesting but can be distracting as it verges on the area of para-psychology and the purpose of this exercise is to use the conclusions of empirical science to establish the reasonableness of Christian orthodoxy.

As a final reference to chapter 4, after giving a fascinating account of the physiology and functions of the language centres of the human brain, Eccles concludes, "In the evolution of man there must have been most remarkable developments in the neuronal structure of the cerebral cortex that has made possible the evolution of speech". We cheerfully appropriate this sentence and add it to our evidence for our belief that evolution is a *guided methodology* directed to the emergence of an animal body developed, particularly by its unique brain, to the point where it can interact not only with its own soul, but also by speech with other souls.

The Dialogue

This section of the book under review consists of twelve discussions between Popper and Eccles covering issues arising from their reactions to each other's writings in parts I and II respectively. The discussions range over points where clear base lines are required. An example is their opening search for a common understanding of epistemology, where further thought has stimulated deeper probing into areas of fundamental agreement, conclusions in which they are at variance with each other and attempts (highly successful) to enunciate clearly their common agreement on the interactionist theory of the mind/brain relationship *vis-à-vis* the identity theory and parallelism.

The dialogue is intensely interesting throughout. Its application to this book is limited to our attempt to show how modern scientific thought and the philosophical ponderings flowing from it are consistent with orthodox Christianity, and particularly in this section to show how Christian doctrine and thought can complement empiricism and its philosophies by offering solutions in areas where science and the philosophy of science are by their very nature constrained to give up in their search for final answers.

We will consequently restrict this essay by quoting questions or answers offered by both authors which are of particular interest to us and then offering a commentary on them from the Christian point of view. We must always remember both authors are deliberately restraining their contributions, as far as possible, to a strictly scientific approach. However, it must be remembered that Popper classes himself as an agnostic (albeit a remarkably open and unbiased one) and Eccles is a believer in God. It is inevitable that in this dialogue these divergent attitudes should colour the views of each party to the debate.

Dialogue 1 (p. 425), Popper. Wisely this discussion opens with an attempt to define the nature, theory and validity of knowledge. Generally speaking it conforms with the military principle of starting from a secure base. Popper takes the usual view that knowledge is built up from observations.

Comment: The Christian from teaching, or better, from experience would add immediately a surer source, i.e. revelation. Its supreme importance will be emphasised again and again in this section. We can't get anywhere without it. Both writers have agreed that modern scientific methods can go so far and no further. This view is backed by our physiologist Sherrington and our physicist Schrödinger. In our final chapters we will endeavour to show that an orthodox Christian scientist can be stimulated in his scientific work by a correct understanding of the place of revelation in the search for knowledge.

Dialogue 1 (p. 428), Eccles. Discussing knowledge in relation to a new born baby, he describes its sensory structure as "built in the most designed manner".

Comment: Eccles is an evolutionist but obviously is in some sympathy with our definition of evolution as a "methodology of creation". He explicitly believes in God.

Dialogue II (p. 438), P. "The question of how consciousness came into life is of course an incredibly difficult one because the evidence is almost nil. Just as is the evidence of how life came into the world."

Comment: Research may throw more light on these vital questions in time. Further knowledge could of course come from developments in research into light or from work in the area described by Rupert Sheldrake as morphogenetic fields. The doctrine of direct infusion of the immortal soul by God in every human life is really the only satisfactory answer as far as mankind is concerned. As for life itself, there can only be one Author, for all life we know comes at least from a bud or spore of an already living organism. Consciousness in sub-human living forms is certainly different from human consciousness and may have developed on evolutionary lines. Even if it did, the Originator of the phenomenon must logically be God.

Dialogue II (p. 439) P. "I do think that the evolutionary hypothesis more or less *forces* us to attribute lower degrees of consciousness to animals. My conjecture has what one may call a partly evidential and partly intuitive basis." (italics mine).

Comment: The discussion concerning the possible existence of consciousness in the sub-human animals is a magnificent contribution. The word *forces* (emphasised above) worries me. Surely an hypothesis should never "force". The evidence for, and the logic supporting an hypothesis might be strong but the moment these elements "force", surely the hypothesis ceases to exist and we have a "law" or at least a "theory". Eccles, the brain scientist, is excellent here. If I summarise him correctly, the nearest he can approach the idea of consciousness in animals is to admit the possibility of its existence in some degree, but in his reasoning, between the so-called consciousness of an animal and that of a human being "there is a great gulf fixed". This is good support for the Christian thesis of the "infused" human soul.

Dialogue II (p. 442) P. "It seems to me that self-consciousness or the self-conscious mind has a definite biological function namely to build up World 3, to understand World 3, and to anchor ourselves in World 3."

Comment. To concentrate on World 3 and to live there would be ideal except for the fact that as in World 1 and World 2, World 3 is also permeated by the deadly "poison gas" of *hamartia*. The Christian looks for the "new heavens and the new earth", hence the presumption of adding World 4 to Popper's Table 1.

Dialogue II (p. 448), E. "When we go on to the question of self-consciousness, we have to take an important sign or test of this, *how consciousness came not to man as a whole but to each individual man in his own lifetime from babyhood up.*" (italics mine)

Comment: Here Eccles puts the case for the direct infusion of an immortal soul (in Christian terminology) in a nutshell. Popper's reply admits this with characteristic honesty: "I do not think we have reached full agreement".

Dialogue III (p. 449), E. Karl, could you start our discussion by saying a little about World 3.

Comment: Popper commences his reply: "World 3 is the world of the products of the human mind." His definition of his World 3 concept is lucid and remarkable. In itself it is a powerful argument for the "mind" as a separate entity from the brain. His use of the symphony as an example is convincing and moving. From the Christian angle, he paints a picture of the potency of the human mind completely consistent with its destiny as the link capable of joining and elevating the material to the eternal level of existence.

Dialogue III (p. 455), E. "It is certain that the growth of the brain came on amazingly fast in the million or two years of the Paleolithic Age, developing in Neanderthal man a brain as big as ours and which, as I already mentioned, was associated with some cognizance of primitive spirituality."

Comment: A Christian reading this, immediately connects the idea with the Genesis story. Suddenly we have a man with a brain large enough to interact with an infused soul and simultaneously evidence of "primitive spirituality". To the fundamentalist Christian, we would warn that while a "million or two years" means something to a mortal, to bind God by time is anthropomorphism extended to a point close to blasphemy.

Dialogue III (p. 455), P. Summarising a long paragraph contributed by Popper it would appear fair to state that *inter alia* he introduces the phenomenon of the lie and in discussing lies, myths, stories and so on states "I don't think there is anything comparable to this on the animal level at all".

Comment: What tremendous support this gives to the Christian view; not only of the Divine infusion of the soul but also of the misuse of the intellectual freedom with which man is endowed. We have already referred to sin as the infinite power of love in a negative or destructive sense. As God is by definition omnipotent, the power of evil can never be a threat to God, but in human experience it can have frightening potency. The union of mankind with God through the mediation of Christ (God/man) is the only hope we have. Knowledge and education in themselves are no answer to *hamartia* because simultaneously with the developement of antibiotics, social services, health-care for the masses, we have the perfection and proliferation of nuclear weapons, guided missiles, chemical and bio-chemical poisons, starvation and exploitation. The call to repentance, to return to Christ and his Church is no longer some relic of early superstitions, persisting in unenlight-ened sections of the world's population, but an urgent matter requiring an immediate positive response. The alternative is annihilation of the human race in its mortal state. The free choice is entirely ours. God will not destroy us; he has given us our most prized gift, freedom. We can use this freedom to create, to build up, to love, to turn to him or we can use it to grab, to take, to destroy all we have and are. At this point of time the second alternative stares us in the face.

Dialogue III (p. 457/8), E. Following his finely de-veloped concept of evolution, Eccles proposes World 3 as having an anatomy, a physiology and a history. He proposes it as the story of the cultural evolution of man. This great man, however, seems to be trapped in the unreal world of academia which is very much a part of World 3. He is excited, and rightly so, with human achievements in art, literature, and so on. Here he finds an interesting distinction between biological evolution and cultural evolution.

Comment: It is here that the academic world appears

unreal. Great scientists are by their very nature positive thinkers. Few of them have much experience of the rough and tumble of the market place, let alone the morality or immorality of international politics. This problem was emphasised in the last comment. It is the problem of the obvious evolution of a more exciting, lovelier world, but simultaneously and parallel with it and developing at the same rate, we have a hideous, cruel, vicious and self-destructive world all in together in the World 3 box. Surely this must be seen as mankind's most urgent problem. As we hope to show, Christianity alone has the answer to this, how essential it is to use the "upper layer of the mind" which can be tuned to God; further to use this mind, this soul, to speak to God asking for a deeper understanding of the revelation of himself in Jesus Christ. We simply must have a World 4 and academics and scientists must look up from their microscopes to the Creator who fashioned the object they are studying on the microscopic slide. Only thus can full understanding come. Science and religion NEED each other. There should be no division between searchers for the truth.

Chapter IV of the Dialogue is devoted to Abstract Ideas and the Self.

Dialogue IV (p. 464), E and P. Both writers appear to agree explicitly in regard to the existence and function of the "ghost in the machine".

Comment: We, naturally, from our point of view prefer the word "soul", and we would say soul *of* the machine and not soul *in* the machine.

Dialogue IV (p. 467), E. "I have a feeling of the tension in my mind. I have read a great deal now on the neurological side and much on the anthropological side and on the philosophical side and we have had all these discussions and all the time I have a feeling that something may break. I mean that some little light at the end of the tunnel may be sensed or some flash of insight may come: I, of course, know very well that there's no guarantee it will come."

Comment: The fact of revelation is the answer. One can

picture the mind as the middle layer of a skull cap consisting of three layers of material. The inner lining (the liaison brain) correlates all reactions registered by the physiological brain together with the proposed reactions appropriate to the situation and feeds this material to the middle lining of the cap which represents the mind or soul. The outer fabric of the cap represents the liaison function between the person and God, the Light of the World. It is in constant communication with the middle lining and when finely tuned can pick up signals from God and feed them to the middle lining, the soul.

We then have a picture where the soul is fed information and suggested reaction from the brain and if in tune with God, simultaneous inspiration from God. The soul which possesses the God-given gift of freedom of choice then makes its judgment and transmits its preferences through the inner layer, the liaison brain, back to the physical brain for active response.

This picture satisfies most observable reactions of human beings to the problems of daily living. It also allows us to account for the fact that, in similar circumstances, different persons may react in different, unpredictable ways. The phenomena of inspiration, insight and evil can also be comprehended in this way.

Dialogue V (p. 472), P. In a fascinating discussion on the extent to which sensory perceived information registered by the brain reacts on the mind and how the mind simultaneously selects, rejects, criticises and feeds back messages to the neuronal system Popper makes a vitally important statement: "I would also like to make another point, namely, that in a way the self-conscious mind has a personality".

Comment: This coincides exactly with the orthodox Christian idea of the soul as the "form" of the person concerned. Coming from a prominent agnostic philosopher this represents a high point in the noticeable convergence of thought taking place in the last years of this millennium.

Dialogue V (pp. 478/9), E. After a brief reference to the

micro-field theory of Pibram, Eccles says "If we were to stretch the analogy very far, we could liken the module to a radio transmitter-receiver so that it functions not only for transmitting to the mind, the self-conscious mind, but also for receiving from it. I think this concept is valuable. . . ."

Comment: This idea has already been expressed in an enlarged form. It is important to note Eccles' remarks as they form a tenuous link with the next book we propose to review. Sheldrake's *A New Science of Life*.

Dialogue VI (p. 495), E. "As a challenge, I will present a very brief summary or outline of the theory as I see it. Here it is. The self-conscious mind is actively engaged in reading out from the multitude of active centres at the highest level of brain activity, namely in the liaison brain. The self-conscious mind selects from these centres according to attention and interest and from moment to moment integrates its selection to give unity even to the most transient conscious experience. Furthermore the self-conscious mind acts upon these neural centres, modifying the dynamic spatio-temporal patterns of the neural events. Thus in agreement with Sperry, it is postulated that the self-conscious mind exercises a superior interpretative and controlling role upon the neural events." To this Popper added, ". . . We could make it stronger by making clear that the liaison brain is, as it were, almost an object of choice of the self-conscious mind. That is to say, if a certain part of the brain is not available, the self-conscious mind will seek another part as its substitute."

Comment: Here is the summary we have been looking for. It is vitally important coming from men of the calibre and competence of Popper and Eccles, remembering that they have both reached their conclusions as scientists. Once again we have now a philosopher and a brain scientist reaching this vital position. Again it reaches a boundary as far as science is concerned. As far as it goes, it is orthodox Christianity, and invites the Christian theologian to add to it to complete the picture. It seems obvious at this stage that the more science can tell us of the workings of our remarkable brain and "mind" the deeper the theologian will be able to develop his theology of the "soul". A good reference is the article on "soul" in the *Encyclopedia of Theology* (ed. Karl Rahner, Burns and Oates, 1977). The Second Vatican Council provided substantial matter on this subject. From the many references two quotations are particularly useful in our context: "Man, though made of body and soul, is a unity" and "So when he recognises in himself a spiritual and immortal soul, he is not being led astray by false imaginings that are due to merely physical or social causes. On the contrary, he grasps what is profoundly true in this matter" (translations by Austin Flannery O.P. from *Gaudium et Spes,* #14).

Dialogue X (p. 543), P. "I myself hope for a revolution in physics because I feel that the present state of physics is unsatisfactory . . . the present physics will have to be valid as a first approximation because our present physics is extremely well corroborated."

Comment: Schrödinger makes the same plea and it is also implicit in Sherrington. It would appear that the revolution is under way. If we trace the work of Faraday, Clark Maxwell, Hertz, Michelson, Morley and other giants preceding Einstein, Einstein himself and his shattering insights, the Lorentz Transformation equations, four dimensional geometry, the uncertainty principle, the tensor calculus, quantum mechanics, Sommerfeld and his Theory of Atomic Orbits, Fitzeau's work on Addition of Velocities — the list could go on and on — we certainly find a new concept of physics evolving. At a guess we could finish up with two complementary schools, the Newtonian time/space approximation physics, and the Einstein School of Macro/Micro physics — the probability school. Until we start discussing atomic fusion and fission, the Newton School is immensely useful, in fact indispensable, to Earth bound mortals. However, the philosophy of science must move constantly with the Einstein School. Sharp dividing lines, black and white definitions, are simply not real, no matter how useful they are as guides.

Dialogue XI (pp. 552ff), E and P. Preliminary Comment.

History could easily and logically classify pages 553 to 561 inclusive of *The Self and its Brain* as amongst the most important contributions literature has given us in the twentieth century. To readers of this book, may I make a plea that if you have not already read this material you should go straight to your library and do so. While it would be unfair to quote it and comment on it in every detail, we have picked out a few salient points in which it is hoped some modest contribution may be made to the debate. It is inspiring to read how these two great scholars stand in awe before the wonder of the human phenomenon, as revealed by their studies and discussions. Their humility, honesty and courage immediately stamp them as great, and above all their open-mindedness sets the ideal attitude for scholars in any discipline in these amazing years, in which electronic technology has made the advancement of knowledge and co-ordination of ideas so swift and relatively so easy. Having reached the stage where we have taught grains of sand to do a lot of our thinking for us (and that is really what a computer amounts to), how vitally important philosophical minds are in the constant struggle for us to comprehend the deep underlying significance of our day by day discoveries. If we neglect our philosophical meditations, we face catastrophe. We immediately dehumanise ourselves and become mere slaves of our machines. We will now proceed to pick the eyes out of the debate recorded on pages 552–561 and endeavour to show where Christianity, a revealed religion, can indicate spiritual attitudes in which solutions to some of the problems raised may be found; for basically some of the questions are *spiritual*.

Both authors appear to agree on the spiritual nature of the "mind". It is interesting to note in this great summing up, that the words "spirit" and "soul" appear more frequently than they do anywhere else in the book.

Dialogue XI (p. 552), E. "We have developed and clarified the concepts of the self-conscious mind. . . . It comes in much more now into the total human performance than I had ever dared to think. The self-conscious mind is responsible for the act of attention, selecting from

all the immense activities of our brains . . . from moment
to moment. . . . Conscious experience is also there in
memory, . . . The self-conscious mind is not just there
receiving . . . it is actively engaged in modifying the brain
. . . we have returned to the views of past philosophies that
the mental phenomena are now ascendent again over the
material phenomena. . . . Now I raise the question: What is
the self-conscious mind? How does it come to exist? How
is it attached to the brain? . . . How does it come to be? . . .
What is its ultimate fate, when in due course, the brain
disintegrates?"

Comment: The above extract is incomplete. In attempt-
ing to be brief, we have perhaps committed the crime of
quoting out of context. A conscientious effort has been
made to avoid this. The full text of couse has a richness not
fully revealed by the abbreviation.

The positive assertions one greets with joy, justifying
our view that there need be no dichotomy between the
scientist and the Christian in our views of the phenomenon
of man. The final questions are both highly pertinent and
universal. Christianity proposes satisfying answers to all of
them. We will attempt brief answers here. These will be
enlarged and collated in our final chapters. We would
answer the first question, "What is the self-conscious
mind? How does it come to exist?" by identifying it with
the spiritual, yet individual "soul" *infused* by God, as
Creator, into every human being *ab initio*. Both our authors
have identified the "mind" as unique and peculiar to man,
both have agreed that its origin cannot be ascribed to any
source known to science. The next question is, "How is it
attached to the brain in all its intimate relationships of give
and take?" No satisfactory answer has been proposed by
our authors. The solution may be found in the idea that the
soul is "infused". It becomes as much part of us as our
brain — the two are inseparable and always will be, as we
attempted to explain in Chapter 2 under the heading
"Eternity". Our personal resurrection becomes a necessary fact of our being. "You will always be a man."

Dialogue XI (p. 553) P. "I think that these 'What is'

questions are not in general very important, and that they are really not very good questions to ask. They are of a form that no really enlightening answers can be given to them."

Comment: At this point, young students of philosophy at seminaries and universities who happen to be wading through the maze of conflicting "ontologies" would throw their text books in the air and call for "three cheers for Popper". These questions are, however, primary to human understanding, not simply chronologically but also analytically. It would not be rash to suggest that a child's perception is characterised by the question "What is that?" The mere asking of this question is in a way an indication of the spiritual nature of the "mind". It is looking for metaphysical reference points. It recognises even at this early age that an object consists of more than the sum of its parts. It has an *ens*, or identity — a name. Young children instinctively learn to pronounce nouns before any syntax, all as a result of "Wot dat?" Comment follows shortly after, in words like good, bad, nice, nasty. Having been a victim of the circumstances, the writer agrees heartily with Popper's criticisms and implied weariness with the seemingly endless and often profitless debates around the subject of "being" but the question will never go away. It is interesting (and rare) to find a confessed agnostic so explicit in the explanation of his agnosticism. To a believer like Eccles, the questions are instinctive and very important because they stem from his absolutely constant reference point which is of course, God — absolute being — from whom all other beings come into existence (contingent being). When Eccles asks, "What is the self-conscious mind?" he is asking the question in a relative sense, the underlying meaning unexpressed might be "In what way does the mind exist in relation to God?" If the questioner cannot put the question with the nuance of this underlying reference to God then certainly Popper is honest and right when he says "what is? . . . questions are really not very good questions to ask". The difficulty is that notwithstanding Popper's objections, these questions *are* asked universally and continually. The writer is not an ontologist but the universal and chronological primacy of "wot dat?" is certainly of theological significance.

Further in his reply to Eccles, Popper says of the self-conscious mind, "It is something utterly different from anything which, to our knowledge, has previously existed in the world. . . . It can be self-reflexive; that is to say, the ego can be conscious of itself." These are vitally important statements from an agnostic as they state in his words exactly what the Church has taught. The soul is infused by God. While a man must be thought of as body/soul, for he cannot be a man without either element, "the soul can be conscious of itself" as Popper states. As another writer has said, "Not only do we know but we know that we know". It is fascinating to see how a great agnostic scholar and a professed evolutionist are able to arrive at such fundamentally important conclusions.

Dialogue XI (p. 554), P. "I want to emphasize how little is said by saying the mind is an emergent product of the brain. It has practically no explanatory value and it hardly amounts to more than putting a question mark at a certain place in human evolution. Nevertheless, I think that *this is all which, from a Darwinian point of view, we can say about it* . . . it is extremely important to realise that explanation is never ultimate . . . so we find we have to stop somewhere . . . and evolution cannot be taken in any sense as an *ultimate* explanation" (italics mine).

Comment: At this point in history an orthodox Catholic Christian may accept evolution as the process by which man's body came to be in its present state of development. However, the acceptance and belief in an all-wise God having a perceived (revealed) purpose in the creation of man seems to require logically that human creation has been a planned and guided process. For instance, taking the superb description of the nature and function of the human brain presented by Eccles in this book it becomes close to impossible to imagine this material masterpiece coming to be without predetermined design. The creation of each individual soul and its infusion does not appear to have been formally defined by the Church. It seems to have been implied by the Fourth Lateran Council. However, it is doctrine obviously taught and held universally for so long, that it would doubtless be classified as part of the "deposit of faith" guarded by the Church. This doctrine appears to "fill the gaps" Popper explicitly discloses above. The important fact is that nothing he has discovered scientifically or concluded philosophically confronts the Christian doctrine explained above, but on the contrary gives it not inconsiderable support.

Dialogue XI (p. 555), P. "The origin of life may have happened only once, and it may be essentially improbable and if so would not be subject to what we normally call explanation; for explanation, that under given conditions, an event is highly probable."

Comment: This comment gives strong support to the stand taken on "the balance of probabilities" in our Chapter 3.

Dialogue XI (p. 555), E. "I believe that there is a fundamental mystery in my existence, transcending any biological account of the development of my *body* (including my brain). . . . And just as I can't give a scientific account of my personal origin — I woke up in life, as it were, to find myself existing as an embodied self with this body and brain — so *I cannot believe that this wonderful gift of a conscious existence has no further future, no possibility of another existence under some unimaginable conditions.*" (italics mine)

Comment: Here is the parting of the road between the scientist (believer in God) and the philosopher (agnostic). The believer sees a developing plan in which *he* personally is involved. As he ponders the wonder of his existence and the eco-system in which he lives, he develops a sense of wonder, of awe. In his scientific investigations he constantly uncovers miracles of ingenious design — from this natural stimulation he develops confidence in the Designer and a desire to know him. To these early yearnings the Creator responds and a miracle occurs, the phenomenon of faith, a one-to-one relationship with the Creator. This is an overwhelming experience, which can never be forgotten.

It, in turn, leads to the spiritual phenomenon of "hope" so clearly expressed in the quotation from Eccles above.
Dialogue XI (p. 556), P. "Where we may perhaps disagree is on another point which I will now put forward — with a certain hesitancy. It concerns the question of survival. First of all, I don't look forward to an eternity of survival. On the contrary, the idea of *going on for ever* seems to me utterly frightening. . . ." In his reply to Popper, Eccles says, . . . "I think that, Karl, you are put off by all the very crude attempts to describe life after death. I am put off by them too. . . . Thus there may be some central core, the inmost self, that survives the death of the brain to achieve some other existence that is quite beyond anything we can imagine, . . . Our coming to be is as mysterious as our ceasing to be at death. Can we therefore not derive hope because our ignorance about our origin matches our ignorance about our destiny? Cannot life be lived as a challenging and wonderful adventure that has meaning to be discovered?" (italics mine)

Comment: This is a wonderful exchange of ideas. To those readers who feel with Popper, I would suggest that much of the dilemma he exhibits is directly involved with two possible misunderstandings. When he says, "the idea of *going on forever* seems to me utterly frightening", he seems to disclose an inadequate appreciation of the meaning of eternity. The words "going on forever" imply *movement* through unlimited *time*. On reflection the phrase "unlimited time" could be described as a conflict of terms. Eternity by definition is *outside* the concept of time which by its very nature is limited. Einstein seems to make this clear. One could not agree more with Eccles when he talks about "the crude attempts to describe life after death". Some fine work has been done lately on this subject by modern theologians. Two books mentioned in our bibliography contribute some splendid material in this debate. They are *Je ne meurs pas* by Roger Troisfontaine and *Mysterium Mortis* by Ladislaus Boros. Both are available in excellent English translations under which titles they are listed in the Bibliography. Chapter 2 of this book might assist in the Eternity *vis-à-vis* Time problem. Again in a vital area the problem of evil has been overlooked by both authors.

On page 558 Sir John Eccles makes a fascinating disclosure about Sir Charles Sherrington whose masterpiece *Man on His Nature* we have reviewed in this volume. Sherrington, as we have already ascertained, was a strong advocate of dualism; body/soul, brain/mind, or whatever terms suit, but he wrote against immortality. Eccles goes on to say of him, in a conversation he had with that great man just before his death in 1952, "he gave me to understand that he had perhaps changed his mind on this, stating 'For me now the only reality is the human soul' ".

The dialogue we have just dealt with, quoted with extreme brevity above, should be read and re-read in its full form. It took place at 5 p.m. on 29th September 1974. It resumed at 10.30 a.m. the next morning.

Dialogue XI (p. 559), P. "Concerning the vastness of our ignorance . . ."

Comment: A lot is said in these six words. In the time/space continuum in which we spend our short mortal experience, our ignorance must be perennial! Our sciences open a box for us only to let us find another box inside. Einstein and his confrères certainly opened windows for us to look out towards the "light", but even they are not big enough to let us get out. Is it necessary then to spend our whole mortal existence in frenetic questioning? No, certainly not, for we are offered the peaceful consolation of Revelation, in Christ. In the Christian Revelation all our *ultimate* destinies are disclosed although not by any means are we given all the detail. It is for us to develop our understanding if we can, both in the fields of theology and natural science, by prayer and study in each; but certainly, in Christ, we can pursue our search in peace. As St. Augustine said, "You have made us for yourself, O Lord, and our hearts are restless until they find their rest in you".

Dialogue XI (p. 559), E. "My position is this. I believe that my personal uniqueness, that is my own experienced self-consciousness, is not accounted for by this emergent explanation of the coming to be of my own self. It is the experienced uniqueness that is not so explained. Genetic uniqueness will not do . . . my brain is built by the genetic instructions of a quite unique genetic code. . . . It has to be recognised that with 30,000 genes there is chance of $10^{10,000}$ against that uniqueness being achieved. . . . *So I am constrained to believe that there is what we might call a super-natural origin of my unique self-conscious mind or my unique selfhood or soul.*" (italics mine)

Comment: Mirabile dictu! Here, from a dialogue between two men, world famous in their disciplines and developing their arguments logically, comes this conviction from the least likely source, the scientist! It harmonises perfectly with the Church's doctrine of infusion of the individual soul.

When I was studying for the priesthood at St. Paul's Seminary for Late Vocations in Sydney in 1971, I did the probability exercise Eccles has just quoted. I cannot remember the exact figure I obtained, but it was of the same order as Sir John's. I was awe-struck by the revelation of my *absolute uniqueness.* In a talk to my fellow students, I quoted the figure I had calculated. I searched in vain for some expressions of awe on the faces of my audience. I could not detect any. On the contrary there were obvious signs of relief and consolation!

Dialogue XI (p. 560), P. "I would like to stress . . . that evolutionary theory never gives us a full explanation of anything *coming into being in the course of evolution.* . . . We don't know how birds developed from reptiles nor really why birds developed from reptiles. In a sense, evolutionary theory is terribly weak as an explanatory theory, and we should be conscious of this. . . . I think man, for all we know, developed from a *cousin* of an ape. This is a conjecture, but it is pretty well founded.

"I think that with respect to consciousness we have to assume that animal consciousness has developed out of non-consciousness . . . At some stage *this incredible invention was made.* . . . It is incredibly improbable that life ever emerged; . . . but it *did* emerge . . . we do not have . . . an explanation for the emergence of life, or for the emergence of the human brain." (italics mine)

Comment: In these paragraphs, Popper is so close to Eccles and indeed to Christian teaching that it is difficult to pinpoint what separates us.

Popper has already stated that evolutionary theory never gives us a full explanation of anything coming into being in the course of evolution (see above). This admission leaves him no option when talking about the appearance of consciousness but to frame the sentence, "this incredible *invention* was *made*". It is hard to conceive an invention without implying the existence of an inventor, or something being made without the pre-existence of a maker.

A Short Summary

In the introduction to this book we have stated that orthodox Christianity can be demonstrated to be entirely reasonable and that science and religion need each other. There should be no separation between them.

The book we have just reviewed, *The Self and its Brain,* gives valuable support to our thesis. From the large amount of material available let us summarise some of the conclusions which uphold the objects we set out to justify. It is reassuring to remember that Eccles and Popper arrived at their findings by methods generally acceptable to scientists.

In the first six chapters, *inter alia*, Sir Karl Popper makes the following points which support the Christian stand. They are:

1. Materialism has no right to claim it can be supported by rational argument.

2. It can be demonstrated by a mathematical type of reasoning that the brain cannot be identical with the mind.

3. The brain is owned by the self (mind or soul).

In chapters E1 to E8 Sir John Eccles makes an entirely different approach. His contribution is that of a brain scientist who is no mean philosopher, in contrast to Sir

Karl who is a philosopher widely read in science. The points made include:

1. By the physiological examination of its working and testing post-operative results on brain-surgery patients it is demonstrable that the mind and brain are separate entities which react with each other. He provides diagrams to demonstrate how this happens.

2. Minds of other living creatures are quite different from the human mind.

3. In his article on the evolution of speech there is support for Schrödinger's contention that major changes in the evolutionary process resemble quantum jumps rather than slow developments.

In the dialogue the authors present us with the following material useful in developing our thesis;

1. *Dialogue III, P.* Our philosopher brings up the problem of the lie or deceit as unique to human beings. This of course supports the Christian doctrine of original sin (*hamartia*). This trait is peculiar to God's creatures who have been given the gift of freedom so that they can, if they will to do so, exercise it to love in the full *agape* sense.

2. *Dialogue IV, E.* Sir John uses the expression "looking for light at the end of the tunnel". This is a striking metaphor if one assumes the end of the tunnel to represent the limit of research by the empirical method. Looked at this way the "light at the end of the tunnel" is an apt analogy for Christ, for revelation.

3. *Dialogue P.* The statement is made, "Self-conscious mind has a personality". This fits the Christian idea of the infusion of a unique soul for every human being.

4. Throughout the dialogue the field theory obviously presents itself to the authors.

5. *Dialogue X, P.* Our philosopher wants a "revolution" in physics, at the point where Christian philosophers see a bridge between the physical and metaphysical in the Incarnation of the Son of God in Jesus Christ.

6. *Dialogue XI, E.* The question is asked what happens to the self-conscious mind at death as its immortality appears to be proven. As already discussed there is an

equally urgent question about the appearance of the self-conscious mind at the beginning of human life.

7. *Dialogue XI, P.* Our philosopher is sure that the mind is not an emergent product of the brain.

8. *Dialogue XI, E.* Eccles makes an act of faith when he asserts there is mystery in his existence and that he cannot conceive the death of his mind.

Points 6, 7 and 8 taken together are answered by the infusion of the soul by God and the phenomenon of the eternal life discussed in Chapter 2.

CHAPTER 8

THE FIELD HYPOTHESES

ALL four of the great men whose books we have reviewed, Sir Charles Sherrington the physiologist,
Professor Erwin Schrödinger the physicist, Sir Karl
Popper the philosopher, and Sir John Eccles the brain
scientist, consider our present physics deficient or incomplete. They value physics as a useful, even an essential tool
in our daily work, be it that of a scientist, doctor, engineer
or indeed philosopher, but they all see that it falls short of
ultimate explanation. It needs another dimension to make
it satisfactory.

In a way, physics has reached a stage where it is
implicitly defining its own limitations, yet there is naturally a reluctance to abandon the remarkable system
of experiment and observation that has so dramatically
increased our knowledge over the past two or three
hundred years. In no way is it suggested that this system
should be abandoned. We have reached a stage where we
cannot do without it. Its value to the human race has been
and is immense.

In the great upsurge of materialism following Copernicus, Galileo, Newton and many other great minds,
culminating in Charles Darwin and persisting to this day
(though obviously weakening since Einstein), one essential
value of reality was lost. A mechanistic view of things
predominated, even up to and including mankind. The
view was that the whole consisted of its parts properly
assembled.

It was not until the late nineteenth and early twentieth
centuries that this view was criticised as deficient and
thinkers began to have another look at the Greeks.
Obviously when "parts" were assembled we had more

than a collection of parts; we had an entity with characteristics of its own transcending that of any of its parts. In other words the Aristotelian doctrine of "form" was again recognised. This renewed view of reality is reflected in the works of men like Jan Smuts and Alfred North Whitehead who both insisted that things consist of something more than their parts. A further stimulus to the Aristotelian doctrine of matter and *form* was given by Pope Leo XIII, when in the late nineteenth century he encouraged the teaching of Thomistic philosophy in Catholic seminaries.

All the authors we have studied so far have insisted on this view in their remarkable studies of the phenomenon of "mind" or "soul" as a reality in mankind — but a reality not amenable to analysis or dissection by physical means. It is ethereal — spiritual.

Sheldrake — The Hypothesis of Formative Creation

Here lies the problem. Modern physics and mathematics have developed during the materialist age and they serve materialism very well indeed. Now we have re-discovered realities that are not material, we have simultaneously realised that materialist physics and mathematics tend to define their own limitations. For instance, if we accept the Aristotelian principle that all natural or physical bodies are composed of matter and form as essential substantial principles, we find that our physics and mathematics can deal quite adequately with the principle of "matter" but are of little or no use in connection with "form".

How does "form" originate? What makes a particular thing identifiable in its own right? We can detail its properties and if our analysis is complete we can say, that is a rose, or that is a frog. But that is not how we identify things. A person may have no knowledge of botany or zoology whatever, but confronted by these objects he correctly identifies them as rose and frog respectively. He recognises their "form".

Further, why does a fertilised frog's egg always produce a frog and why does a rose tree always produce roses and not a daisy or two? We know how it happens but do we know why? These are childish examples but they lead up to the great questions "Whence this noticeable order in things? What force governs and controls order?"

Obviously arising from the limitations of conventional approaches to the greatest "What is" question of all, "What is life?", a book was published in 1981 entitled *A New Science of Life* (Blond and Briggs). The author is Dr. Rupert Sheldrake who holds a Ph.D. in biochemistry from Clare College, Cambridge. His other academic distinctions include a Frank Knox Fellowship at Harvard and his appointment as the Rosenheim Research Fellow of the Royal Society. The sub-title of his book is "The Hypothesis of Formative Causation".

In our effort to show the emerging convergence of thinking between theologians and scientists we have chosen to attempt a detailed review of this book for several reasons:

1. Because the author is highly qualified in still another science. We can now add a highly qualified biochemist as a witness, and attempt to show that from his point of view he supports the principles advocated by Sherrington, Schrödinger, Popper and Eccles.

2. Because his thesis is based on the idea of variant fields, which as already indicated seems to be the most likely area for future "prospecting".

3. It is a courageous and novel presentation thoroughly researched.

4. The writing is true to all scientific principles. Where questions raised remain open the author has indicated the areas where solutions may lie and all these are consistent with his strictly scientific approach. He has not expressed any personal preference.

5. He quotes from the book we have just reviewed in Chapter 7.

As with all the other books reviewed in this work, an earnest plea is made that Sheldrake's book should be read. The books of Sherrington, Schrödinger, Popper and Eccles have been presented to demonstrate, amongst other things, the development of thinking among outstanding scientists and a philosopher over the period between 1937 and 1977. The reviews have been presented in chronological order.

Dr. Sheldrake in his book addressed himself in 1981 to finding an hypothesis which might answer scientifically vital questions discussed in the books previously reviewed.

At the risk of being tedious, where it is considered that the definition of a term or an explanation of a special meaning of an ordinary word might help the general reader, the flow of this chapter will be interrupted to explain the particular concept. We will start with the subtitle, *The Hypothesis of Formative Causation*.

The Oxford Dictionary gives the meaning of the word "hypothesis" as "a supposition or conjecture put forward to account for certain facts and used as a basis for further investigation by which it may be proved or disproved". Sir Karl Popper on page 148 of *The Mind and its Brain* demands of a new hypothesis before allowing it to replace an earlier one:

1. It must solve the problems which its predecessor solved at least as well as did its predecessor.

2. It should allow the production of predictions which do not follow from the older theory; preferably predictions which contradict the old theory.

The meaning of the word "formative" is given in the Oxford Dictionary as "forming something". But Sheldrake uses the word in his book with a deeper significance, tying it to the philosophical notion of form already referred to briefly. The idea of "form" in this book is all that makes a thing in its totality of existence and which distinguishes it from everything else. In the case of the human being, we have already seen how our recent cracking of the genetic code emphasises strongly how different every individual is physically. When we accept also the individuality of the human soul as independent of, but reacting with, the individual brain, we have an immediate explanation of the unpredictable variation in manner and behaviour of each separate person. The classical presentation of the soul as endowed with the faculties of will, imagination, reason and affection plus the outstanding distinguishing characteristic of freedom of choice makes human behaviour under any given set of circumstances predictable only in terms of probabilities. The author of this book served as an officer in the Australian Imperial Forces throughout World War II and by sheer chance found himself in action most of the six years or so of that awful event. From experience gained there and in years of work in private enterprise he can claim to have been in charge of many thousands of men over long periods. To him the attempt to predict human behaviour by demographic mathematics based on observations of selected groups of people under controlled conditions tells us nothing more than that the group concerned exhibited certain characteristics. The extension of that finding to predict the behaviour of any other group, except in terms of vague probabilities, must be regarded as nonsensical and using such information to predict the behaviour of a particular individual is and must be a vain exercise. If it is successful, from the mathematical point of view it must be regarded as a fluke.

In Newtonian physics, energy is proposed as the cause of all movement and change. Standard scientific activity is concerned with the development and testing of mathematical models of selected and definable aspects of things in this world or its universe in accordance with the principle just enumerated. We can ask where the energy came from and be told it was supplied from the local electricity grid. If we are not satisfied with this we can be shown hydro, fuel fired or atomic fission power plants; if again we are not satisfied we will be told that really it all stems from the sun. All that has happened is that our question has been pushed away 93,000,000 miles; it has not been answered nor is it fair to ask Newtonian physics for the answer. Science as we know it is simply not competent to provide *ultimate* answers. Never let it be said we are underestimating the genius of Newton or the competence of scientists and the empirical method. Out of fairness these ultimate questions should not be asked of the scientist. Just as the Christian theologian must have access to the scientific knowledge if he is going to make sense and operate efficiently in the world of today, so the scientist must go to the Christian theologian if he wants ultimate answers. These have been *revealed*, not discovered. They appear to mesh beautifully with all modern science can tell us. Of course we will find difficult areas here and there at present and doubtless throughout the remainder of the Earth's existence or the survival of the human race in its mortal experience. We must realise we have no certainty whatever of the duration of the Earth's existence or the survival of humanity. This fact does not worry the Christian in any way. Either event is an exciting prospect.

The "New Science of Life" proposed by Sheldrake is based on the existence of what he calls "morphogenetic fields". Most readers will have a working notion of the concept of "fields". Among the best known would be gravitational and electromagnetic fields. The field itself denotes in the above cases the region in which a massive body exerts it influence or "pull" and in electronics the region in which an electrically charged body or magnetized body exerts its influence. While Newton's mathematics relating to gravity gives us accurate and workable models as far as our Earth and solar system are concerned, it must again be emphasised that no reason is available for the existence of this force itself. Similarly, electromagnetic fields are described as waves of energy emanating from the electric charge. Both these views have been modified by Einstein and his disciples to present the gravitational field as curved in the presence of matter. The difference in the two views is best illustrated by the example of the moon. Newton proposed that the moon moves around the Earth because it is pulled towards it. Einstein on the other hand has the moon moving around the Earth because the actual space in which it moves is curved. Again in electromagnetic fields the disturbances or waves are, in the relativity context, regarded as sub-atomic units called photons. Each represents an individual amount of energy (quantum) related to the matter from which it originates, so that each kind of particle has its own special type of field. The reason for this very brief and incomplete explanation is to demonstrate that if we are looking for the "truth, the whole truth, and nothing but the truth", we *must* escape from the constrictions of time/space thinking. So much for "fields"; let us now consider the rather formidable words morphogenesis and morphogenetic.

Morphogenesis in Sheldrake's book means the development of form or structure (in the sense already described) in the whole course of development in an individual's life history, or in other circumstances the restoration in a living body of tissues or organs that have been removed. Morphogenetic is then the adjective denoting a relationship to morphogenesis.

The following is an attempt to present in summary form Sheldrake's *Hypothesis of Formative Causation*. It is an abridged form of the summary he sets out on pp. 115ff of this book. The detailed arguments can only be had from the original work the reading of which is again recommended.

1. In addition to the causes proposed (and accepted) by modern scientists for the formation of distinguishable things from sub-atomic particles through atoms, molecules, crystals, cells, all things up to and inclusive of living things, a further distinct basic cause known as "formative causation" exists and imposes a spatial order (shape) on the changes effected by energy. It is not energetic nor can it be reduced to causes brought about by gravitational, electromagnetic or other physical fields.

2. This new cause depends on the existence and function of morphogenetic fields. Each distinguishable thing has its own morphogenetic field which operates to produce the thing with all its distinctive characteristics as the various parts come within its range of influence.

The morphogenetic field first becomes embedded in one of the characteristic parts of the thing from which its influence extends to the other parts as they become available to form the "whole".

3. Morphogenesis of inorganic matter is rapid, but

morphogenesis of living things is slow. A given type of morphogenesis usually follows a particular pathway like a canal. This is called a "chreode" (*sic*). In multicellular living things, development takes place by the operation of a succession of morphogenetic fields.

4. The fourth section of Sheldrake's summary is one of the most radical and interesting: the characteristic form of any particular thing is determined by the forms of previous similar systems which act upon it across time and space by a process of morphic resonance. (An analogy might be that the new thing by its very nature finds itself tuned in to the field of the previous thing and thus reproduces what is transmitted by the original.)

5. All similar past systems act upon a subsequent similar system by morphic resonance which once established persists unattenuated by space or time.

6. While the hypothesis claims to account for the repetition of form, *it does not attempt to explain how the first example of any form came into being.* Sheldrake in characteristic style enunciates the available choices as to the origin of the first "form" as chance, as a creativity inherent in matter, or as a creative intelligent agency.

The third alternative is the obvious choice of a Christian theologian. We would call this third creative factor, God. However, the second alternative put forward — "creativity inherent in matter" — instantly poses the question "Where did this power come from?", and the answer could again be God.

The summary already given is sufficient to give an overall picture of the hypothesis which is all we need. In a further six paragraphs, Dr. Sheldrake has given a tightly knit and ingeniously detailed view of the operation of his system and greatly strengthens his claim for the validity of his concept.

His final sentence is an exciting challenge, both to himself and others. He says, "The hypothesis . . . is capable of being tested experimentally".

Some of the most interesting parts of Sheldrake's book deal with early experiments conducted to test the assertions made in paragraphs 4 and 5 above. In brief, rats were selected and placed in the centre of a maze and the time they took to find the way out was recorded. They repeated the exercise several times and, as might be expected, they completed the exercise in less and less time. The experiment was repeated in other widely divergent locations after a considerable period of time and in these later exercises the performance of entirely different rats approximated the best times of the last of the initial experiments. In the last experiments, two groups of rats were used: some had been trained and the others undertook the exercise the first time. *Exactly the same tendencies were found in the untrained rats.* This of course could be explained in terms of the "morphic resonance" in which our author is so interested. Doubtless better and better controlled experiments are proceeding.

Phenomena of this sort raise interesting questions related to the constant shattering of records in athletic contests. Training methods doubtless have something to do with it, but the consistency with which world records are broken over identical distances and similar tracks could point to some "causation" factor on the lines of Sheldrake's hypothesis.

Sheldrake also raises the question of individual human behaviour. While genetic influences are admitted as significant, our author suggests that "specific" patterns of behaviour themselves depend on the inheritance of motor fields by morphic resonance.

In his final chapter, the author demonstrates how his Hypothesis of Formative Causation could harmonise with four widely accepted but different metaphysical theories.

The *first* is what he calls "Modified Materialism". Crude materialism is based on the assumption that only matter is real and therefore everything depends on matter for its existence. Einstein's famous equation $E = mc^2$, which expresses all matter in terms of energy, made it necessary to revise the tenets on which materialism is based. The revised definition of materialism is that the universe is composed of matter *and* energy and all forms we know have evolved from this source. "Human life has no purpose beyond the satisfaction of biological and social needs. Neither life itself, the evolution of life nor the universe as a whole has any purpose or direction" (p. 201). It is interesting to note that this is also held by Marx. As morphogenetic fields impinge on and influence material things, they can if desired in this sense be considered an element of materialism. It will of course be recognised that materialism would insist on the identity theory of mind/ brain interaction which Popper and Eccles seem to have refuted successfully in their book.

The *second* metaphysical concept which Sheldrake claims to be compatible with his hypothesis he calls "The Conscious Self". This section is important to us because it reinforces Popper and Eccles' work on the interaction theory of Mind/Brain relationship and gives us an hypothetical *how* this takes place. Further than that, it seems to fit in very well indeed with our analogy of the mind as a skull cap of which the lining is a liaison element between the brain and the mind, the middle layer the mind (self-conscious self) and the outer covering the interaction element between God and the individual person.

Sheldrake also uses analogy to describe the relationship between conscious formation and formative causation. The analogue he uses is his own theory of the relationship between formative and energetic causation which he expresses as follows:

"Formative causation does not suspend or contradict energetic causation, but imposes a pattern upon events which are indeterminate from an energetic point of view; it selects between energetic possibilities. Likewise conscious causation does not suspend or contradict formative causation, but selects between motor fields which are equally possible on the basis of morphic resonance" (p. 115ff).

This analogy coincides well with our analogy of radio fields and resonance (pp. 115ff). The frequency of our own soul putting us into two-way communication with God is analogous to morphogenetic fields and resonance. As

Sheldrake points out this does not prevent our co-operation with the motor fields of our physiology but enhances shapes and selects their activity. His idea of self-conscious selection reinforces the Christian doctrine of "freedom of choice".

In this book, we have again another instance of a refutation of crude Darwinian evolution.

Talking of the role of formative causation in creativity our author says, "This creativity can either be attributed to a non-physical creative agency which transcends individual organisms or else it can be ascribed to chance" (p. 205).

As the evidence for some evolution process having taken place is very compelling at this point of time, our attitude towards it as a probably directed methodology of the Creator seems to stand firm. If we accept the idea of morphogenetic fields, it is hard to agree with Darwin's idea of the evolutionary emergence of new species through gradual small changes over a long period of time. Sheldrake's view seems to favour the emergence of a new species as being a very fast phenomenon. In this he has the support of Popper and Eccles and implicitly of Schrödinger by whom it is suggested they would appear as akin to "quantum jumps".

The *third* widely held theory is that of "the Creative Universe". We dislike theories of this kind because they talk of some creative agency inherent in all things but they never tell us what these agencies are or where they came from. They merely overcome problems by coining new words to describe a phenomenon and then they consider the problem more or less solved by the chosen word. Our author demonstrates quite conclusively that his hypothesis is compatible with this alternative "The Creative Universe".

In his argument he proposes an idea which is of considerable importance to us. He appears to agree with the criticism of the "Creative Universe" just mentioned. We quote directly from page 206 of his book:

"Creative agencies could give rise to a new morphogenic and motor fields by a kind of causation very similar to the conscious causation considered above. In fact, if such creative agencies are admitted at all, then it is difficult to avoid the conclusion that they must in some sense be conscious selves.

"If such a hierarchy of conscious selves exists, then those at higher levels might well express their creativity through those at lower levels. And if such a higher-level creative agency acted through human consciousness *the thoughts and actions to which it gave rise might actually be experienced as coming from an external source. This experience of inspiration is in fact well known.*

"Moreover, if such 'higher selves' are immanent within nature, then it is conceivable that under certain conditions human beings might become directly aware that they were embraced or included within them. And in fact the experience of an inner unity with life, or the Earth, or the universe, has often been described, to the extent that it is expressible.

"But although an immanent hierarchy of conscious selves might well account for evolutionary creativity within the universe, it could not possibly have given rise to the universe in the first place. Nor could this immanent creativity have any goal if there were nothing beyond the universe towards which it could move. So the whole of nature would be evolving continuously but blindly and without direction.

"This metaphysical position admits the causal efficacy of the conscious self, and the existence of creative agencies transcending individual organisms, but immanent within nature. However, it denies the existence of any ultimate creative agency transcending the universe as a whole" (italics mine).

The fourth metaphysical theory on which Sheldrake comments he calls: "Transcendent Reality" (p. 206). Again it seems only fair to quote *verbatim*. Sheldrake says:

"The universe as a whole could have a cause and purpose only if it were itself created by a conscious agent which transcended it. Unlike the universe, this transcendent consciousness would not be developing towards a goal; it would be its own goal. It would not be striving towards a final form; it would be complete in itself.

"If this transcendent conscious being were the source of the universe and everything within it, all created things would in some sense participate in its nature. The more or less limited 'wholeness' of organisms at all levels of complexity could then be seen as a reflection of the transcendent unity on which they depended, and from which they ultimately derived.

"Thus this fourth metaphysical position affirms the causal efficacy of the conscious self, and the existence of a hierarchy of creative agencies immanent within nature, and the reality of a transcendent source of the universe."

This is a fascinating section. The last paragraph is dialectically superb. In a mere thirty-five words, we have a lucid apologia for the idea of a Transcendent Reality (God) simply because it "fits" all the basic notions proposed.

We conclude this review and summary of still another outstanding book, again with a plea that it will be read.

Burr — The Electric Patterns of Life

The idea of "fields" as controlling forces in the formation, operation and maintenance of life, particularly human life is not new; Dr. H. S. Burr, Professor Emeritus of Anatomy of the Yale University School of Medicine published a book called *Blue Print for Immortality* (Spearman) in 1972. As its sub-title "The Electric Patterns of Life" suggests, it is a study of extensive research into the relationship between electrodynamic fields detected within living things, and also external to them, and development, abnormalities and behaviour. It is well worth reading. Professor Burr's research work extends over a period of forty years.

Dr. Sheldrake, commenting on Professor Burr's work, suggests that Burr may not be correct in his assumption that the electrodynamic "life fields" (the existence of which appears to be established beyond doubt) control morphogenesis.

However, without entering into the debate the reading of both books tends to suggest there may be some (at present not discovered) relationship between the work of these two highly trained scientists. Time will tell.

What does emerge strongly is that break-throughs in the solution of many of life's riddles may come from research into the phenomenon of "fields" and their interactions. If fields are the link (or at least part of it) between God and his creatures and also between creatures themselves, they must affect all creation. We know from our research into communications with submerged nuclear-powered submarines that radio waves of very low frequency are effective. As fish are certainly living creatures one wonders whether the research into low frequency communications at present in progress may reveal some secrets pertaining to life fields. From the Christian theological point of view, one asks should we be looking more carefully, perhaps with our scientist friends to help us, at phenomena like inspiration, insight and intuition? It is not impossible that these phenomena may have their origins in field resonances and interactions.

Revelation of God to man was complete in Christ. Sheldrake's speculative work gives us an outstanding example of how *our* understanding of this Revelation may deepen and develop by co-operation between scientist and theologian. How necessary it is that each should know what the other is doing!

CHAPTER 9

CHRISTIANITY

AT the beginning of this book it was made clear that it is the work of a Roman Catholic priest. Some of the conclusions reached in this chapter will attest to this fact. The writer, who is a convert to Catholicism is firmly convinced that the Catholic Church has some gems of faith expression and ecclesial order to offer primarily to our separated brethren in Christ which could prove helpful in restoring the unity of the Church for which all sincere Christians long and pray. This same expression of the Christian Faith may also prove useful to agnostic and atheistic readers who have perchance reached this chapter. Everything that will be included in this summary will be consistent with our touchstone of Christian orthodoxy, the Nicene Creed, and also will be in harmony with the scientific climate of the late twentieth century. Having made this claim let it also be said that the theological conclusions of this chapter would have the support of the vast majority of Christians.

God

We posit without compromise the existence of God. God is Spirit. He is eternal, infinite and omnipotent. God is a Trinity of Persons in a unity of nature; each Person is perfect so each are consequently equal. One cannot add to or subtract from perfection. God is the Creator of all that is, seen or unseen. He *gives* everything its existence and he *gives* the energy necessary to sustain the orderliness of the Earth and the universe. Love in the *agape* sense, always contains the nuance of giving. The creation of the universe and all that can be implied in the widest use of that term is an act of giving. This material universe is the object of study for the empirical scientist. God is *agape*; God is love. All arguments for the existence of God boil down to the necessity for a first cause for created things and to find a source for the necessary energy to account for the fact that everything in the universe is maintained in motion. There is order in our Earth and in the Universe. Apart from the force necessary to initiate movement some energy is also required to maintain order as we understand from our reflections on entropy and the second law of thermodynamics.

Life On Earth

Turning to our Earth as the example of creation nearest to us and looking at it from an existential point of view we see a planet in constant motion in at least three dimensions. It supports a myriad of life forms. Each life form is seen in numerous individuals of the same kind. The individual appears as a progeny of its parent or parents. Its individuality persists through a period of time during which it reproduces its kind in new and similar individuals. The next parent dies and its progeny continue the same cycle. We know in great detail the conditions necessary for the existence and procreation of life but we *do not know* what life itself is. The Christian posits it as originating from God; the "breath of God". Life *per se* has no mass or definition. It appears to be beyond the range of scientific investigation. The mere existence of the phenomenon of life could be the most compelling evidence for the existence of God. All living creatures maintain their existence by a process called metabolism. They absorb energy from the sun or atmosphere and they take into themselves their food, convert this food to maintain their formal structure and dispose as waste any material they consume which is unnecessary or surplus to their requirements. The varying forms of life are shown in outline on diagrams (see pages 43 and 81). Fishes, reptiles, birds, animals and mankind all use other living forms as their food.

Human Life

Mankind is a notable exception to the extent that no other animal preys on him or relies on the consumption of human beings as a staple diet. A human being is outstanding in many ways. While he has an animal body with an elaborate and efficient metabolic system he has a singular spiritual component which is referred to as soul, self or mind. He has a brain, which compared with other animals is disproportionately large and functionally different. This brain has other unique characteristics detailed by Sir John Eccles whose work in this area we have reviewed. A human being's brain and soul interact and his whole being is subject to his self or soul. This soul is not material and so cannot perish as things do in the material order. Each human being has distinct characteristics and tendencies which we call personality. The human race is essentially gregarious because the manifestation of personality requires the presence of other human beings with whom the individual can relate.

There is weighty evidence that the ecology of the Earth is designed to provide an ideal situation in which human beings can exist, grow and procreate.

The human brain relies on its sense organs for all the information it requires to initiate action appropriate to situations in which the person finds himself. The self or soul can however accept, reject or modify courses of action indicated by the brain. As well as receiving messages from the brain the soul can receive ideas from an outside source. This is the phenomenon we refer to as inspiration or insight. The soul is then capable of ordering the brain to produce the appropriate physical response necessary to initiate action in harmony with inspired ideas. The Christian proposes that this inspiration comes from God but is aware that the spiritual line of communication is subject to interference from evil spiritual influences. In all cases of inspiration, insight or sense inspired suggestions the soul has the power to accept, reject or modify the idea which has been generated. This phenomenon involves the use of the faculty we call conscience.

We affirm that a human being can communicate with God and that God can communicate with a human being. As man is a gregarious animal the normal means that God uses to speak to a person is through the words, actions, writings, works of art or music of another human being or the society in which he lives. This communication reaches its maximum efficiency in the like minded community we call the Church.

Man is a psychosomatic creature, body/soul, and therefore is immortal. He has been given the gift of freedom of choice. This is to enable him to love in the *agape* sense; That is by giving himself to the service of God and his fellow men without compulsion in the least degree. This love is a sharing in the divine creative power.

Evil

When a human being uses the gift of freedom to grab, take, exploit or destroy for his own selfish ends he releases a toxic spiritual power which we call evil. Evil is a power like love but it is best thought of as the power of love bearing a negative index. From the beginning of human history man has released this poisonous power, the effects of which we see all around us. True love is the handmaid of order. Evil is the essence of disorder.

The object of mortal human existence on Earth is the pursuit of happiness which is really peace and serenity. Distorted by sin and living in a poisoned atmosphere people often seek escape from the morbidity of sin by exciting themselves through indulgence in acts, which give them pleasurable sensations. Pleasurable sensations are not necessarily morally good or evil but if they are indulged in from a motivation of selfishness they may compound rather than alleviate misery.

The condition of mankind living in an atmosphere corrupted by *hamartia* was hopeless until God intervened with an act of unbounded love. In the incarnation of himself in Jesus Christ, born from Mary and in his human life, death, resurrection and ascension into eternity God provided mankind with a "Way", a method of escape from evil and more wonderful still, he gave us the opportunity to choose to establish a close personal relationship with himself, to become his adopted sons and daughters. This means that having exercised our freedom of choice during our mortal existence by accepting God's offer, we are then able to enter our eternal level of being close to and in intimate association with our Creator, the Father of us all.

Moral Standards

It is from this belief in God and what he has done for us that all Christian moral standards originate. We seek to be like him and to do his will. Because moral standards involve the individual's relationship with other people God instituted his Church, the body of his faithful followers, to be the arbiter and guardian of moral teaching.

Moral codes must perforce relate to a standard. The alternative to relating them to God is to relate them to humanity. This approach is called humanism. It has an inbuilt fallacy in that it is not a consistent standard. Humanity, the standard, is in a sinful condition so we initiate our humanistic codes from a faulty base and they invariably reflect this defect. Very quickly a humanist code degenerates from standards that people ought to accept to standards they want to accept and thus humanism fails inevitably.

The Christian standard is perfection. We are all aware that we cannot achieve this degree of excellence. The Christian is happy to accept the perfect standard because he knows that when he fails Christ will forgive him, reinstate him and encourage him to persevere. Christianity provides a return path, a "Way", back to happiness as long as the individual Christian seeks it sincerely.

The Church

References have already been made to the Church in this chapter and throughout the book. The Church was founded by Jesus Christ two thousand years ago and has remained in existence ever since. In its long history the Church has found it necessary to define certain beliefs clearly and often at length. It was not, however, until the 21st November 1964 that the Church attempted to define itself. On that day the Second Vatican Council issued a document called *Lumen Gentium* or *The Dogmatic Constitution on the Church*.

Dr. Albert C. Outler, then Professor at the Perkins School of Theology within the Southern Methodist University, Dallas, U.S.A., a Protestant observer attending the Council, comments on this document as follows: "The Dogmatic Constitution on the Church may rightly be regarded as the masterpiece of Vatican II. In the first place — and strange as it may seem — this is the first full-orbed conciliar exposition of the doctrine of the Church in Christian history." The full text of Dr. Outler's response to *Lumen Gentium* is well worth reading. It can be found in *The Documents of Vatican II* (Ed. W. M. Abbott, S.J., published by Geoffrey Chapman).

The qotations in English from the Council documents in this book have, unless noted otherwise, been taken from Abbott's edition. The opening sentence of this unique document sets the tone of all that follows. It reads: "Christ is the light of humanity; and it is, accordingly, the heartfelt desire of this Council . . . that by proclaiming His gospel to every creature it may bring to all men that light of Christ which shines out visibly from the Church."

Lumen Gentium is a profound document. Doubtless it will be studied, clarified and expounded for centuries to come (that is, if our Lord does not come again while we are still wrestling with it).

Facing this page is a diagram designed to give an impression of the overall view that the Council produced of the Church.

THE CHURCH. As defined by the
Second Vatican Council.

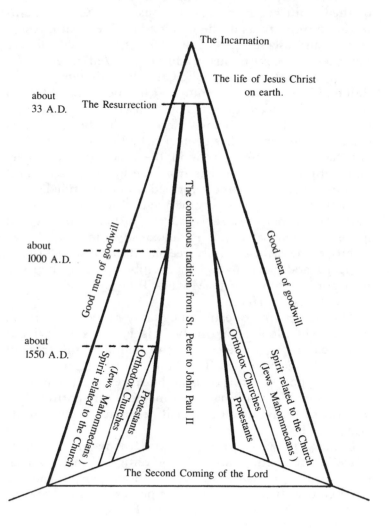

The Incarnation

The life of Jesus Christ
on earth.

about
33 A.D.

The Resurrection

about
1000 A.D.

about
1550 A.D.

Good men of goodwill

Good men of goodwill

The continuous tradition from St. Peter to John Paul II

Orthodox Churches
Protestants
(Jews Mahommedans)
Spirit related to the Church

Orthodox Churches
Protestants
(Jews Mahommedans)
Spirit related to the Church

The Second Coming of the Lord

A study of the diagram shows the essential unity of the Church which on reflection is far deeper than appears from its fragmented presentation of itself to the World. Founded by Christ and vivified and launched by the Holy Spirit on the first day of Pentecost it rests, for its existence on the infinite goodness and graciousness of God in manifesting himself to us in the incarnation, life, death, resurrection and ascension of Jesus Christ. The central area indicates the continuous tradition of what is generally known as the Roman Catholic Church. Although this tradition is historically continuous it has never been free of trouble. It has been subjected over the centuries to adverse pressures both internal and external. It has been ruled by saints and sinners. It has been ravished by military might and has been tossed about in the maelstrom of international politics. It consists from the Pope to its lowliest member of sinners, some reformed, some sanctified, some recalcitrant. The one common characteristic of all its members is that they rely entirely on God's mercy and grace for their salvation. Paradoxically the Church can rightly be described as holy because it has Jesus Christ as its Lord and Saviour and its members are by baptism incorporated into Christ's Mystical Body of which he, God incarnate, is the Head.

The challenging question inevitably raised in the mind of an outsider looking at this body is, how has it survived? There can be only one answer and that is by the grace of God (his graciousness). The Holy Spirit remains as the life giving power of this body and inspires and strengthens its membership continually. Its members are entirely free to leave it at anytime and later if penitent to return to its arms at will.

It has endowed our world with many gifts such as schools, universities, hospitals and refuges. It has given an ugly world glorious treasures of literature, art, music and architecture. It has been and is a power-house of prayer. All the great universities of medieval Europe were founded by the Church.

The great religious congregations have in the last two

centuries awakened public conscience to the point where the State has now accepted some responsibility for social services. Benefits like free schooling, medical care, hospitalisation, homes for the poor and aged, refuges for young women, relief of destitution and poverty and so on were provided by this Church for centuries before governments considered these challenges a public responsibility. In Western civilisation and wherever the Church has spread it is still conspicuous in providing for the needy.

The Second Vatican Council made it quite clear that nominal membership of this central tradition in no way guaranteed the salvation of any member, nor did it cut off the Roman tradition from other Christians, believers in God, or even good men and women who, having never heard of God, strive to lead good lives. If we study the drawing we see that the Church claims involvement wherever God's grace is at work. It claims a very close relationship with other Christians to whom it refers as "separated brethren". After the Council Pope Paul VI made a public confession of the wrongs the Roman Church has committed over the centuries against other Christians and mankind in general.

Religious Unity

There is in the world today a strong movement towards complete re-union among Christians. There are also organised approaches trying to establish closer rapport with our fellow men who believe in God, such as Jews and Mohammedans, and also with non-believers.

The approach to the material in this chapter has followed from the production and study of the diagram of the Church. The central core which many people would call the Roman Catholic Church is determined in shape and continuity by history alone. It is not intended to convey any suggestion of élitism. On the contrary, as a body this central core of Catholicism admits and accepts its share of blame for the many divisions amongst Christians. On the positive side it also accepts as an obligation the duty to do everything to assist in a genuine reunity of Christendom.

These facts, taken together, form the reason why members of the continuous historical core of Christianity do not like being referred to as Roman Catholics. Certainly this body has been governed from Rome most of the time from its inception. The term Roman Catholic is certainly meaningful and convenient. The word Catholic, however, means universal, embracing all. The title Roman Catholic is in a way a contradiction of terms. The members of this body who, like many other Christians, long for the re-union of Christendom, naturally prefer the outward-looking all-embracing nuance of the word "Catholic" without the adjective "Roman" which seems to imply the ideas of introspection and exclusiveness.

Science and Religion

By means of a running commentary in chapter 5 to 8 inclusive it has been shown how the findings of modern science and the teachings of the Christian Church can complement each other to give a rich picture of the universe we live in. More important still is the fact that by applying the knowledge obtained by the revelation of God to man in the person of Jesus Christ, which fits so well with the philosophy of modern science, we are able to see a plan and purpose in the creation and redemption of the material universe.

Further we are given a reassuring picture of the phenomenon of man and his ultimate destiny in eternity, a destiny which can rise to heights beyond imagination.

Religion

Having outlined a picture of the Church and the Christian Faith the question might well be asked: What is it that motivates people to think of religion at all? Some of us have been reared in families where religious beliefs and practices were so much part of our lives that from earliest childhood we accepted religion as part of our existence. Others have gone through life without experiencing religious practice and without giving the matter much thought at all.

In a large proportion of cases where individuals have accepted religious beliefs with conviction or have alternatively arrived at a considered decision that the idea of God is untenable, the catalyst evoking either decision has been the intrusion of some evil of startling enormity into the life concerned. In the world today there is only one effective anti-toxin to the poison of evil and that is Christianity, the Christian religion.

What do we mean by religion? Answering this question the *New Catholic Encyclopedia* says "A precise but comprehensive definition is difficult. The problem can be examined best by considering religion from several points of view or under several distinct aspects." (Vol. 12, p. 240.)

For the sake of simplicity it is proposed to define religion from the point of view of a Christian whose faith, in the objective sense is expressed in the Nicene Creed. Acceptance of the tenets of this creed does not in itself make a person a Christian. There is much more to Christianity than that. The creed however does provide a useful reference point from which a relative assessment can be made. One could designate the Lord's Prayer (the Our Father) as the universal prayer of Christianity and in this sense the Nicene Creed could be regarded as the National Anthem of Christians. In the baptismal rite of the Roman Church, after the candidate has indicated assent to the creed, the celebrant says, "This is our faith. This is the faith of the Church. We are proud to profess it."

Taking the standard suggested one could divide the human race into five broadly based categories:

1. Those who accept explicitly or implicitly the tenets of the creed (We include Eastern Orthodox Christians in this category).

2. Others who call themselves Christian but would exclude themselves from Category 1.

3. People who accept religions other than Christianity.

4. People who have never made a decision in regard to religion. They have neither positively rejected nor accepted the idea and are not interested in the subject. They would normally describe themselves as agnostics.

5. Those who have arrived at a considered opinion that belief in a god or a religion is an illusion and an error. These people accept that the complete span of personal destiny lies between birth and death. This is the atheistic class.

In the five divisions detailed above it is easy to recognise a clear line of demarcation. Categories 1, 2 and 3 assert the existence of God as defined in the creed, or other gods. With few exceptions the deity would be recognised as the creator of all that is, seen and unseen.

Classes 4 and 5 would in most cases assert that all creation as they see it came to be by random chance and natural selection. In the case of the agnostic most would agree with the random chance/survival of the fittest approach but would hedge their decision with the proviso that if there be a god then he is unknowable. Religion to both groups is a futile exercise.

Christianity is a dynamic missionary religion. It's thrust and purpose is well expressed by St. Paul in his first letter to Timothy where he says: "God wants everyone to be saved and reach full knowledge of the Truth". This statement enunciates an important principle; the initiative in the saving act lies with God.

The Creed

As we intend to use the Nicene Creed as a reference point for the objective context of Christian Doctrine it is necessary to point out that a number of modern philosophers and theologians dislike the ancient creeds. Their objections can be summarised simply. They propose that a credal statement compiled to refute some heresy in the fourth or fifth century is not necessarily relevant to modern times. Most of them press for a constant re-expression of truths in the thought patterns of the present. This sounds plausible but the phenomenologist, existentialist approach appears from our studies of time, space and light to contain an inherent fallacy. In summary, what these thinkers are teaching is that *truth* is a function of *time*. Modern physics denies time the status of a constant and proves it to be variable. Hence if we make truth a function of time, it too becomes a variable and immediately Pontius Pilate's question arises in our minds *Quid est veritas?* (What is truth?).

If on the other hand we see truth as a function of *light* we have a constant. On reflection the idea that truth is variable is nothing less than a contradiction in terms. This intervention is a very brief reference to a very large and complicated modern problem in epistemology. The subject is handled at length and with much wit by Jacques Maritain in his book *The Peasant of the Garonne* and by Vincent P. Miceli S.J. in his work *The Gods of Atheism*. Nothing in this comment is intended as a bar to the idea of the *development* of Christian doctrine. St. Paul encapsulates the notion of a determined faith coupled with deepening of understanding in his letter to the Ephesians. Speaking of the role of teachers in the Church, he says of their work: "In this way we are all to come to unity in our faith and in knowledge of the Son of God, until we become the perfect Man, fully mature with the fullness of Christ himself" (Eph. 4:13).

It will doubtless have been noted that not one of the scientists whose works we have reviewed states explicitly that God is the Creator yet Copernicus, Galileo, Newton, Einstein, Sherrington, Schrödinger, Sheldrake and Eccles are obviously theists. In view of this fact, why do they make no mention of God as Creator? The answer is even more important than the question. All the men whose books we reviewed were writing as empirical scientists. No scientific experiment yet devised can produce direct evidence of the existence of God. Yet these scientists believe in God. What has happened is that each has recognised a boundary beyond which modern science cannot proceed. Obviously reacting with awe and wonder at the results of scientific experiments all these great men have reached out beyond the limits of their laboratory work. The wonders revealed by their experiments and observations have led them to look for an ultimate cause or origin and obviously they have received the grace of faith enabling their minds to cross the bridge between the two great realities, the physical and the metaphysical. Schrödinger's remark when this happened to him is worth repeating, "we know, when God is experienced, this is an event as real as an immediate sense perception or as one's own personality". Sir John Eccles epitomises the limitations of empiricism when he says, "Science is very successful in its limited field of problems; but the great problem, the *mysterium tremendum*, in the existence of everything we know, this is not accountable for in any scientific manner" (*The Self and its Brain*, p. 564).

From all we have studied and read of these authors it seems reasonably certain that if the proposition, "We believe in one God the Father, the Almighty, Maker of heaven and earth, of all that is, seen and unseen" were put to them the answer in each case would be "Amen".

All the authors we have studied are restless about the limitations of classical physics. We are so well served by this approach to science in our life on Earth that there is a kind of disappointment evident that the language of mathematics lacks a form of expression to carry our thinking over into an area in which our minds posit that "matterless" realities exist.

God who made us and designed our curious minds comes to our aid here through the force the Christian refers to as revelation. Revelation became complete when God became incarnate in Jesus Christ. In the mystery of Jesus Christ all the frustrations resulting from empiricism defining its own limits are resolved. In the God/man Person we have more than a union: we have a fusion of a mortal, time/space, highly intelligent, spirit filled, material being with the infinite, omnipotent, all wise, pure Spirit, God. In Jesus Christ we have an inexhaustible source for inspiration, research, admiration and wonder.

All the ideas set out above emerge in the second paragraph of the Nicene Creed where the union of God with his creature man is set out with an economy of words so remarkable that there is a danger that they may be read without full comprehension.

The third paragraph of the creed sets out the climax of the Good News, the Gospel. It tells how Jesus worked out his life on the Earth, how he passed through the experience of human suffering and in his resurrection and ascension assumed our humanity into the eternal timeless mode of existence. It stresses the extreme power and disorder of sin, in that this evil force accounted for the death of Christ in his human nature, despite the fact that that same nature never contributed by actual sin to maintain the power of evil. Christ's death was absolutely unjust and illogical as so many of our personal experiences are. In his resurrection and ascension, however, is demonstrated the supreme power of the love of God over sin. It is so necessary to remember that the narrative of the ascension includes the human body of the Lord. The witnesses to this event were people who knew that body well, his mother and the eleven apostles. The entire Christ, body, blood, soul and divinity moved upwards into the timeless existence of eternal life. The story does not end there but assures us he will return again in the same way as we saw him go, human/divine, and identifiable as a man. His second coming introduces the phenomenon of the eternal kingdom which scripture calls the new heaven and the new earth.

Finally the creed tells us of the third Person of the Blessed Trinity, the gift of God given to Christ's followers to the end of time. He speaks through the prophets and works through the Church. The Church is not just an aggregate of Christians; it is the operative human part of a Mystical Body, of which Christ is the Head and we Christians, the members. It is vivified and empowered by the Holy Spirit working through men. It continues Christ's saving mission till the second coming. Like Christ, her Lord, the Church on earth is continually harassed and wounded by sin. Damaged and wounded though it may be, it remains indestructible as it, like Christ before it, is inseparably united to God by the life-giving principle, the Holy Spirit. The Church continues on earth the saving work of Christ by forgiveness of sins and it waits and hopes for the second coming of the Lord, when the dead shall be raised and we who are alive shall be caught up to be with the Lord and his friends in the eternal level of existence.

Sources of Christian Knowledge

If we desire to find out something about Jesus Christ, how do we proceed? The ideal method is to approach some well informed minister or layman of Christ's Church. As already stated Christianity was intended to be taught and learned. The basic truths about Jesus Christ are contained in four books called the Gospels of Matthew, Mark, Luke and John. These together form the first section of the New Testament of the Bible.

The personal and individual acceptance of Jesus Christ as one's Lord and Saviour has a tremendous effect on any-one making that choice. That person becomes convinced of his or her own immortality, aware of personal wrong doings and accepts the freely given forgiveness of all sins contritely confessed. In Baptism the candidate becomes aware of a re-conception in the womb of Mother Church. He sees himself conceived as a new creature by the union of his own mortal life with a germinal share in the life of Christ, risen from the dead. This life is of course the life of the Blessed Trinity. The baptized becomes actually not figuratively a child of God.

All this and more flows from the Gospels and the other books of the New Testament. It therefore becomes im-perative to face the question: Do the New Testament and the teaching of the Church have for us men and women of the twentieth century a true objective basis that gives us the right to commit our lives and our intellects to the words of Christ and of the Church? The question is a serious one, for if faith is a truly genuine faith it binds our whole intellect and our whole life to this revelation; it is also

serious to the extent that once we know it to be true, we
have not only the right but the duty to bear witness to it
before others and to urge of them that adhesion of the
intellect which is owed to all truth.

In our last few pages we have made many claims for
Christianity. These rely for their authenticity on that part
of the Bible known as the New Testament. Christianity is
essentially a religion to be taught but the Bible is available
for all men to read.

The New Testament was written about two thousand
years ago. That is undeniable. In this fact alone lies the
reason why it should be taught by some person qualified to
do so. It is hard to imagine in our time when we are
inundated with paper and printed material that in Christ's
time there was no such thing as paper. Everything that was
written was inscribed either on papyrus or parchment. If·
copies were required of any written work it would be
necessary to re-write it in manuscript. Obviously in that
era there were many great scholars. If text books were not
available to all, how did they acquire their learning? The
answer is of course by attending lectures, by debate and
above all by using the art of learning texts by heart. Classes
would spend most of their time reciting together phrases
and sentences first enunciated by the teacher and then
repeated over and over by the pupils.

It was from this culture that the four Christian Gospels
and the rest of the New Testament emerged. The Church
classifies these writings as inspired. The important question arises as to how reliable these documents are and to
what extent can they be regarded as history.

When reading the Gospels one must always remember
that they were not written as biographies or histories but as
sermons. Their authors wrote them to different groups of
people and in doing so selected the narration of events and
presented them in the manner most likely to influence
those to whom they were addressed. Owing to the difficulties of reproduction they were written to be read aloud to
an audience rather than to be studied privately and at
leisure. As in many cases members of the audience would

be curious, critical or hostile it would be certain that questions would be asked and criticisms levelled. The only Gospel that appears to have been written to a particular person is that of St. Luke but wc know that it was not long before this narrative was used publicly. Many attempts have been made to write the history of Christ's lifetime using the Gospels as source material. One of the first of these efforts was that of Tatian who wrote his *Diatessaron* towards the end of the second Christian century. One of the last efforts would be the *Knox-Cox Gospel Story*. None of these works have been really successful. They always suppress the genius of the original authors, part of whose skill lay in the selection and presentation of material in a way that gave thrust and colour to their message.

A much more fruitful way to study the Gospels, at least the first three of them, is to arrange them set out in parallel columns. An excellent study aid using this method is *Gospel Parallels* ed. B. H. Throcmorton, Jr. (Nelson).

Bearing these facts in mind we present the view that the Gospels present data which are basically and substantially historical.

During the last thirty or forty years we have rediscovered so much valuable material which gives us the historical and geographical context in which Jesus lived and of the social climate of the Jewish people of his time, that any assessment of the historical value of the Gospels made before these discoveries needs to be updated. Of prime importance in these discoveries is the finding of the Dead Sea scrolls from the library of a Jewish community contemporary with Christ. These scrolls give us an account of life in Judea quite consistent with the picture we obtain from the Gospels and the New Testament. Palestine, occupied by the Romans as an outpost of their empire, was in a constant state of revolution and subversion. The Jews were divided amongst themselves. There were the Sadducees who collaborated with Rome, the Zealots who incited violent revolt, the Essenes who were disciples of non-violence and the conservative theological group, the Pharisees. It is interesting to realise that the Palestine in which Jesus lived was socially very little different from what it is today. This is most important as it places Jesus in an atmosphere almost identical with our own.

Let us examine the sources from which our knowledge of Jesus is obtained. The events of his public life are recorded by men who were eye-witnesses of them and who in turn were prepared to proclaim them to crowds many of whom would have either direct or reliable knowledge of them. Here is incontestable evidence of authenticity. What about the stories of Jesus as a baby and as a boy; should we doubt them? Again they were proclaimed openly and in the context of a sermon which reflected the literary and preaching styles of the authors. The obvious fact that comes through is the divine power operating effectively in a human situation as genuinely human as the society in which we live today.

Based purely on evidence available there is more material accessible testifying to Christ as an historic figure than there is for Nero or Julius Caesar. We have manu-scripts of the New Testament centuries older than any of Julius Caesar, or for that matter, of any of the Roman classical authors.

Form Criticism

Claims have been made in recent times that the narratives of Christ's infancy, his public life, his miracles and even his resurrection were not necessarily based on historical events but were literary devices designed to paint a picture or to convey a message.

Bible scholars some years ago devised a method of study of scripture known as *form criticism*. This was first applied to the historical works of the Old Testament. The inten-tion was to attempt to separate the original material, much of which had been transmitted orally, from alterations, additions and glosses made by various editors. As much of the historical and legendary content of the Old Testament came from sources lost in antiquity the application of form criticism aroused considerable interest. The same methods were later applied to books of the New Testament.

Here it is necessary to make a re-assessment. The writings of the New Testament are in a completely different category from those of the Old Testament. They were all compiled in the early days of modern history and the events they describe occurred less than 2000 years ago. Further they were obviously written by eye-witnesses of the events. If we examine the four Gospels it is immediately obvious that each was written by a different author. They were compiled in different localities over a period of about thirty or forty years in the later part of the first century A.D. Some of the events they record are mentioned in contemporary non-religious literature. All these facts alone place the Gospels in a class apart from any Old Testament writings with the possible exception of one or two of the Wisdom Books.

We posit Jesus Christ as an historical figure. Further, that in his Person are united inseparably the natures of God and man. There is no authentic reason to doubt the veracity of the gospel stories as long as we see them as first learnt by rote, handed on this way and finally committed to writing not as history but as hermeneutics (sermons).

The physical resurrection of Jesus Christ and his ascension into the eternal state as God/man seems to be an essential "tile" in the great mosaic of God's purpose in the creation and redemption of mankind. St. Paul saw this point and enunciated it clearly in his first letter to the Corinthians when he wrote: "If Christ has not been raised (from the dead) then our preaching is useless and your believing it is useless". In Christ's ascension we have the prefiguring of our own assumption into a higher level of existence (cf. Chap. 2). Modern physics proves to us conclusively that all matter is in motion. The authors whose works we have reviewed concur in supporting the notion of the eternal, non-material element in every human being. The evidence from science for the existence of God as a Creator of unlimited intelligence is overwhelming. If we accept the incarnation of God in Jesus Christ, and Christ's life, passion, resurrection and ascension as an indication of the eternal destiny available to every man and woman then we can see a clear plan in which the power of evil is overwhelmed and men and women are caught up in the universal movement characteristic of all created reality. This is the type of movement typified by all our studies of evolution. It is always an upward movement towards greater potential coupled with the "falling out" of individuals or species which tend to remain static. If we regard the "resurrection" of our Lord merely as an idea we frustrate our own destiny. If our personal bodily resurrection is not among the things we hope for then we revert at the best to a Platonic dualism in the notion we have of ourselves. Worse still we undo the whole purpose of the incarnation, we separate the soul of Jesus from his human flesh. We destroy the majesty both of the personhood of our Saviour and of ourselves.

The Problem of Christian Reunion

In the opening pages of this volume will be found a prayer from the Divine Office recited on the feast of St. Albert the Great which includes the petition "Help us so to follow his teaching that every advance in science may lead us to a deeper knowledge and love of you".

Conspicuous in modern Christian activity is the strong movement towards reunion of all Christian denominations. This is occurring simultaneously with the dramatic change in the relationship between leading empirical scientists and theologians.

Amongst Christians there is still another force which must be recorded and that is the current advancement and renewal of biblical scholarship at a more profound level than has ever been known. This revival is not peculiar to any one denomination. There has evolved a sort of brotherhood amongst modern scripture scholars irrespective of their denominational loyalties. An excellent monument to this movement is the École Biblique at Jerusalem. It was founded in the late nineteenth century by the Dominican Order. In this school lectures range over subjects like form criticism, history, geography, archaeology, Oriental languages, epigraphy and exegesis. Any genuine scholar sufficiently advanced to benefit from or contribute to biblical scholarship would be considered by the school. Not only does the *École* teach in the conventional way but it undertakes practical work in archaeological excavation, identification and repair of ancient texts and so on. It has produced a fine modern French translation of the Bible called *La Bible de Jéru-salem*. An English edition of this work has been published under the direction of Alexander Jones (*The Jerusalem Bible*).

The simultaneous emergence of these three forces, the desire for unity, the reconciliation of science and religion and the common Christian interest in profound biblical scholarship seems to invite a new approach to the problem of reconciliation of the dogmatic teachings of various Christian communities.

From a study of documents issued by various committees and councils engaged in ecumenical dialogue it appears, to those of us not actually involved in the task, that the system proceeds as follows:

1. Some important topic such as baptism or the eucharist is selected by mutual consent.

2. An effort is made to define the limits of complete consensus and to pinpoint remaining differences.

3. A document is circulated indicating the widest possible area of agreement at the time of issue.

4. Doctrinal differences not resolved then become the subject of study and prayer by all concerned during an adjournment preceding a further meeting.

Much progress appears to have been made by the groups of men working on this all-important task. Most of the older generations of Christians living today learned their doctrine from catechisms. In many ways this was an excellent system of learning. We memorised the questions and answers and then our teachers would expound the doctrine concerned and quote selected passages of scripture to support the dogma proposed by the catechism.

The Second Vatican Council in its document on revelation, *Dei Verbum,* seems to invite a different approach when early in its constitution (para. 3) it states "God who through the Word creates all things and keeps them in existence, gives men an enduring witness to himself in created realities".

Why not start from this point now that science has so much to offer us in its overview of created realities? Here Christians of all denominations and for that matter agnostics and atheists too could share common ground with modern science. It is necessary to realise that science has now reached a stage where it is tending to define the limits of legitimate empirical research, and at the same time admitting the reality of existence outside the material world. Christian scholars of all denominations could certainly deepen and develop their faith in the Creator, by studying the view of created thing presented by biologists, neurologists, micro- and macro-physicists, astronomers and in fact any modern scientist in his particular discipline. At this exercise Christian scholars would find a unity in philosophising and theologising from a common source of inspiration.

It is a natural step from a study of God's works to move next to God's Word. The method used by most of us when we are challenged on a point of doctrine is to enunciate our understanding of the question raised, then, if possible, to quote from any authoritative source expressing the mind of the Church and finally to search scripture for texts which appear to justify our position.

The alternative method would appear to be to work through scripture prayerfully and let the dogma flow from that source. This approach would have the advantage that all proceedings at this stage would issue from a firm universally accepted basis.

The combined approach to scripture will allow the Bible itself to determine the next areas requiring examination. They are of course the validity of tradition and the exercise of that authority committed to the Church by it founder. The obvious route in these areas is the study of Church history. Most dogmatic definitions have been crystallized and formulated in the face of threats to the existence of the Christian faith or of the Church. The Nicene Creed quoted at the end of this book is a typical example. Very useful work in the historical approach has been done by Monsignor Philip Hughes in his book *The Church in Crisis* (Burns & Oates). This is a study of all the major councils in Christian history from the First Council of Nicaea (325 A.D.) to the First Vatican Council (1869–1870). The author died in 1967 two years after the Second Vatican Council. For the first thousand years of its history the Church maintained a discernible unity. There were, of course, differences as there always will be where human beings are involved but the historical unity remained intact. For another five hundred years the Church in the overall picture was divided into two major groups, the Roman and Orthodox allegiances. Between these two groups the differences in dogmatic theology are, even today, not very widely divergent. In very important areas such as the sacramental system, particularly baptism and the eucharist, orders of ministry and mariology, practice and teaching are remarkably close. It was not until the early sixteenth century with the emergence of the Protestant movement that the fragmentation of the structure of the Church so obvious in our times commenced. Without reviving controversy in any way the Roman Church has accepted without reservation that drastic reforms within its own structure were imperative at that time. With all other Christians today we regret that divisions occurred which exist substantially to this day.

Looking back over the scene that history records we see that for 1500 out of its 2000 years of existence few differences emerged in the area of dogma.

There is no doubt whatever that many of the differences which finally found expression in terms of dogmatic theology, were in origin more political than theological. A typical example would be that of the Queen of England in her position as spiritual and temporal head of the Church of England. As the Queen is a constitutional monarch the final authority in the Church of England appears to an outside observer to vest in the British House of Commons. Irrespective of allegiance to the Queen as Head of State it is most unlikely that either the Christian people or people of other religions in the British Commonwealth of Nations would be prepared to accept the House of Commons as the final court of appeal in matters of faith.

If recourse in ecumenical debates were to take the path outlined above from the starting point of God's works then through God's Word and Church history we could traverse the ground from the beginning of the Church up to the Great Schism and freed from the pressures of politics from age to age, deal only with differences in dogma *per se*. In these days it would appear to be obvious that the chances of resolving problems in an atmosphere freed from the heat of the moment would be much better than the recorded discussions contemporary with the various rifts would indicate.

The same process could be applied to the sixteenth century situation right through to the emergence of recent sects. All along the line the main problem to emerge would be some form of fundamentalism, a negative mental attitude, which has already been discussed. How necessary it is for all of us Christians to focus our attention on Jesus Christ above and beyond any other value.

To Whom It May Concern

I can remember as a boy hearing my elders say "I don't know what the world is coming to!" The reaction of my generation was that such remarks were early indications of the overall syndrome of senility.

Having entered the ranks of the elders myself I would never be guilty of saying *I don't know* what the world is coming to, for the simple reason that *I do know* what it is coming to, and so does every thinking person. A crisis is immanent and it appears to be unavoidable.

We have the world divided into three distinct camps, ideologically and socially incompatible. We have the enormous Communist bloc consisting of Russia and China together with their European, Asian, African and South American satellites. The United States of America combined with the NATO alliance countries and their scattered allies form another bloc and then we have that mass of people we refer to as the "Third World". In the main the third world people consist of the native populations of the huge European colonial empires which disintegrated after World War II.

It is common knowledge that the United States with their allies and the Communist bloc between them have more than enough nuclear weapons to eliminate all life on earth. Obviously war is avoided by both camps because of stark fear of the consequences. Fear or rather terror is the most debasing motivating force a human person can experience. Terror and love cannot co-exist. This is the overall scenario from the militaristic point of view.

If we examine the world scene as a human problem the divisions are on an even more frightening level. Men and women in numbers approximating half the world's population and living under Communist rule suffer the degrading experience of loss of true freedom. In religion particularly, they are severely hampered in its practice. There are restrictions on what they may read, on the religious education of children, on what they may proclaim in public and on the assembly of people for religious exercises and worship. The schools and universities teach atheism and the Marxist varieties of philosophy. There are almost complete restrictions on travel to other countries. We have established that to love in the *agape* sense a human being must be absolutely free. Theoretically at least the Communist states are making it superficially impossible to love God and very difficult for their people to love each other in the divine *agape* level. Nevertheless evidence is continually coming out that God's grace is still operative under these conditions. The work being done by Keston College in Kent and its branches and affiliates in Australia and elsewhere makes it known that the stuff of which martyrs are made still exists in Russia as it does wherever the Church is persecuted.

The so-called Free World has a similar problem with a different cause. The plague there is materialism. If a person's object in life is to become rich in the sense of possessing material goods, if one's life ambition is to have a large bank account, sumptuous living quarters, cars, television and stereo sets, a plenitude of food, clothing and entertainment then again that highest of all human potentialities — love in the *agape* sense — is inhibited. The true materialist might be a pleasant person to meet but the motivating force in his life is to acquire, to possess: the very antithesis of giving. Christ emphasised this danger when he said "it is easier for a camel to pass through the eye of a needle than for a rich man to enter the kingdom of heaven".

A study of the so-called third world reveals a strange mixture of idealism and pragmatism. Here we have tribes of people recently released from generations of colonial rule. In many instances these folk lost their tribal culture as they were relegated to servile duties by the colonisers. In the interests of self-preservation many of these people appear to be seeking loose alliances either with the Communist bloc or nations of the Free World. The memories of colonial oppression are fading slowly. In numerous instances power hungry individuals have found that people accustomed to colonial rule and exploitation are ideal subjects for dictatorships. Most of the third world people are desperately poor and many are undernourished. Extreme poverty has fuelled many a war in human history.

All the above material sounds like a prophecy of doom. It has been stated at some length as a background against which to examine the status of an atheist, an agnostic and a Christian in the last years of the twentieth century.

To the Atheist

Atheism is by no means exempt from the challenge issuing from modern philosophies of science to re-examine its axiomatic bases. It is hard to see how a genuine conviction held say thirty or forty years ago can be maintained today. Many of the key premises on which early twentieth century atheism relied for its logical development no longer exist. The crude Darwinistic concept of evolution by random chance and natural selection is in our times mathematically, scientifically and logically untenable. Yet as a methodology for the creation of the living bodies of the world today evolution is generally accepted. The factor that has been destroyed is the *random chance* element. There is only one alternative to random chance and that is a *planned development*. Planning needs a Planner. The concept of a planner immediately suggests the notion of design. Darwin and his contemporaries knew nothing of the DNA molecule which can be posited as an example of design *par excellence*. There is so much evidence, a little of which we have reviewed, that mutations in species are not gradual processes but resemble quantum jumps. This phenomenon supports the idea of intervention by a "Designer". Einstein's work in destroying the idea of time and space as static constants and the emerging philosophies on the physics of light all suggest that we have a lot of re-thinking ahead of us.

Modern physics' demand for a source of energy for initial motion and for overcoming the inherent tendency to disorder in matter poses another question to be answered. Supporters of the "big bang" theory for the creation of the universe have a problem here, for if the hypothesis be correct we are faced with a question: whence the energy to initiate and maintain the obvious and predictable order found for example in our solar system?

Atheistic philosophy finds support for its rejection of God in the problem of evil. No doubt inexplicable and superficially horrifying events occur regularly and these appear to the atheist to negate the idea that any divine power directs the destiny of mankind. On the other hand we frequently observe or hear of beautiful and noble achievements by men and women. These paradoxical observations must be seen together. In the Christian context they explain each other.

Christianity adopts a noble view of the human race because it sees in *homo sapiens* a creature capable of the unique potency to love. Nowhere else but in men and women can we see this phenomenon in action and no one would deny its power. Here we are talking of the *agape* concept, pure unselfish, irrational if you like, self-giving. It is in the use of this divine power in a reversed or negative sense to grab, take or destroy that we are able to comprehend the spectre of evil. If we discipline our minds to contemplate the *problem* of evil simultaneously with the *problem* of good we develop a mental attitude which can comprehend them both and assist us to appreciate the one factor that distinguishes the human race from all other observable life and that is our freedom of choice.

In the review of Professor Schrödinger's book it will be noted that he used the term "negative entropy". This is analogous to the Christian's concept of the role of Christ. He supplies the energy needed to overcome entropy in the spiritual sphere. He draws his energy from obedience to God, resonance or tuning in to the will of God to the extent that his human will and the will of God operate as one. It is essential to remember that during his short sojourn with mankind Christ "laid aside" the power of his own Godhead. This in no way diminished his power. When the Father wished to use him, the two wills, that of God and that of the man Jesus, were in perfect resonance. This fact would account for the phenomena of his miracles. It can also be seen as the source of energy required for his bodily resurrection. God willed that Jesus Christ should be born, live, suffer, and die as we do. His suffering and death were demonstrations of the immense power of evil, while his resurrection demonstrated the omnipotence of the power of God operative through a man who freely made his will coincide completely with the will of God. Jesus in the garden of Gethsemane extended his will to accept an agonising death. Here he met fully the ultimate test. His human body died and then his obedience and resonance with God's will produced a reverse effect, a negative entropy. The omnipotent God cannot die so the Father's will became operative and the humanity of Jesus, the perfectly obedient man, was restored indestructibly. As St. Paul expressed it: "Christ as we know having been raised from the dead, will never die again. Death has no power over him any more."

The atheist who wisely decides to re-examine his position in these days of challenge is advised to do everything possible to obtain a modern concept of material reality as it is understood today. The bibliography at the end of this book makes fascinating reading. It is by no means complete. It has been selected to give an overview rather than detail. Some of the reading suggested will introduce the dialogue at present proceeding between prominent scientists and equally capable theologians. The wealth of divine revelation is accessible only from the Church.

In an encounter with the Church today in its sadly divided condition there appear superficially at least as many reasons to ignore it as to examine it. A closer look at what it really is produces a quite different reaction. St. Paul presented a fascinating analogue of the Church when he referred to it as the Mystical Body of Christ. St. Paul's view makes Christ the Head and the countless millions of its members the Body. If modern knowledge of the cell had been available to him there is no doubt St. Paul would have seen his analogy extend to embrace individual Christians as cells of the body. In our reference to Christ we saw how the power of evil affected him. It affects the Church in the same way. Christ, God/man, is its Head so it is indestructible but on its journey through the mortal time/space situation to its end in glory it shows the same disfigurations that Christ endured. Carrying his cross along the Via Dolorosa to Calvary the crowd saw a body flayed, stripped and bleeding from flagellation, bruised and broken by assault and disfigured by blood from his crown of thorns. Yet substantially this was the same body which was the subject of the resurrection, the complete triumph over evil. In the Church the enquirer will find excellent people who occasionally behave in a way falling far short of perfection, together with wayward folk who will suddenly perform admirably. Its cohesion in spite of the scars of evil is due solely to the power of its Head. Any atheistic enquirer will never reach intellectual certitude in religion with respect to Christianity or the Church and this is by design. Jesus Christ is a Person. He desires a true relationship of sincere and loving friendship with every man and woman born or yet to be born. During his life on earth he made himself available to every person who called to him for help. He requires this prayer from each of us. The acceptance of Christ as our Saviour demands an act of courageous self-surrender. Having established the relationship, the effect is overwhelming. Sin and death have no longer any dominion over *us*. At this point the serious reader could with profit recapitulate the concept of eternity outlined in Chapter 2.

To the Agnostic

All the material in the section addressed to atheists could be of use to an agnostic. The challenge here is to abandon preconceived fixations of the mind and assess the claims of Christianity on the basis of a balance of probabilities. The alternatives available to the agnostic are a confused uncertain frame of mind, a lifetime faced with the prospect of certain death to be accepted with as much courage as despair will allow. The other choice offered by Christianity is a lifetime stimulated by a well founded hope worked out in the company of like-minded people of every race, colour and nationality. The Church universal exists everywhere for everybody.

To the Christian

The great problem for every committed Christian is how to develop a true and sincere concept of the grandeur of his or her calling and then of course to adjust one's lifestyle to be consistent with the reality of one's being. To be a son or daughter of the Creator of the Universe is hard to comprehend but that is what we are. We are not limited by time or space; we are children of light and of the day. This dignity was not conferred on any of us in our mortal existence just for our consolation. Christianity is dynamic, for the Mystical Body of Christ is alive. Its life is the life of Christ risen from the dead which is the life of the Trinity. As individuals we may assess our capacity as small but in the strength of the Body, the Community which is the Church, we form part of a power which is invincible. One of the greatest and most effective Christians of all time was St. Paul. He worked out his life in harmony with three great principles which any Christian could adopt with profit. They are:

> Of myself I can do nothing.
> I can do all things in Christ.
> Nothing can separate me from the love of Christ.

> O Strength and Stay upholding all creation,
> Who ever dost thyself unmoved abide,
> Yet day by day the light in due gradation,
> From hour to hour in all its changes guide,
>
> Grant to life's day a calm unclouded ending,
> An eve untouched by shadows of decay,
> The brightness of a holy death-bed blending
> With dawning glories of the eternal day.

> Verses from the Divine Office.

The Nicene Creed

We believe in one God, the Father, the Almighty, Maker of Heaven and Earth, and of all that is, seen and unseen.

We believe in one Lord, Jesus Christ, the only Son of God, eternally begotten of the Father, God from God, Light from Light, true God from true God, begotten not made, of one Being with the Father. Through Him all things were made. For us men and for our salvation He came down from Heaven; by the power of the Holy Spirit He became incarnate from the Virgin Mary, and was made man.

For our sake He was crucified under Pontius Pilate; He suffered death and was buried. On the third day He rose again in accordance with the Scriptures; He ascended into Heaven and is seated at the right hand of the Father. He will come again in glory to judge the living and the dead, and His kingdom will have no end.

We believe in the Holy Spirit, the Lord, the giver of life, who proceeds from the Father and the Son. With the Father and the Son He is worshipped and glorified. He has spoken through the Prophets.

We believe in one holy Catholic and Apostolic Church. We acknowledge one baptism for the forgiveness of sins. We look for the resurrection of the dead, and the life of the world to come. Amen.

International System of Units

For those interested the following are the SI equivalents of measurements expressed in other terms in the text (see Introduction p. vi ff).

"Speed of Light" (*in vacuo*): Symbol c, Value 299792458 ms^{-1}, with degree of uncertainty of 0.004 parts per million.

"Planck's Constant": Symbol h, Value 6.626176 × 10^{-34} JHz with degree of uncertainty 5.4 p.p.m.

"Atomic Mass Unit": Symbol 1u, Value 1.6605655 × 10^{-27} kg with uncertainty of 5.1 p.p.m.

"Electron Rest Mass": Symbol m_e, Value 5.4858026 × 10^{-4} u, with degree of uncertainty of 0.38 p.p.m.

"Proton Rest Mass": Symbol m_p, Value 1.007276470 u, with degree of uncertainty 0.011 p.p.m.

"Neutron Rest Mass": Symbol m_n, Value 1.008665012 u, with degree of uncertainty 0.037 p.p.m.

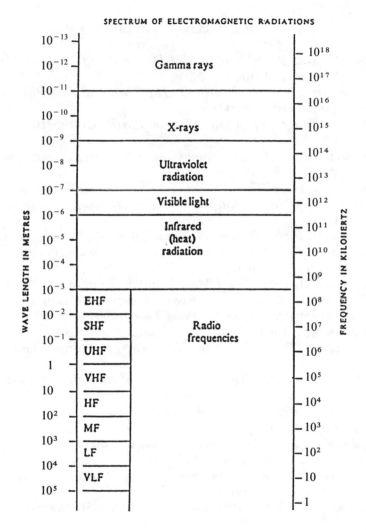

SPECTRUM OF ELECTROMAGNETIC RADIATIONS

BIBLIOGRAPHY

ed. Abbott, W. M. 1968. *The Documents of Vatican II*, Chapman, London.

Angel, R. B. 1980. *Relativity. The Theory and its Philosophy*. Pergamon, Oxford.

Attenborough, D. 1979. *Life on Earth*, Collins/B.B.C. London.

Bassett, B. 1976. *And would you believe it?*, Sheed and Ward, London.

Boros, L. 1972. *The Moment of Truth*, Search, London.

Burr, H. S. 1972. *Blueprint for Immortality*, Spearman, London.

Capra, F. 1976. *The Tao of Physics*, Bantam, New York.

Coleman, J. A. 1969. *Relativity for the Layman*, Penguin, Harmondsworth.

Day, M. H. 1969. *Fossil Man*, Hamlyn, London.

Eddington, A. S. 1920. *Space Time and Gravitation, Cambridge University Press, Cambridge*.

Einstein, A. 1961. *Relativity*, Bonanza, New York.

Guardini, R. 1954. *The Last Things*, Notre Dame, Paris.

Harre, R. 1972. *The Philosophies of Science*, Oxford, London.

Jaki, S. L. 1974. *Science and Creation*, Scottish Academic, Edinburgh.

Jaki, S. L. 1978. *The Road of Science and the Ways of God*, Scottish Academic, Edinburgh.

Leon-Dufour, X. 1973. *Dictionary of Biblical Theology*, Chapman, London.

Lonergan, B. J. F. 1957. *Insight*, Longmans Green and Co., London.

Mackie, J. L. 1972. *The Miracle of Theism*, Clarendon, Oxford.

ed. Mitton, S. 1977. *The Cambridge Encyclopedia of Astronomy*, Cape, London.

Peacocke, A. R. 1979. *Creation and the World of Science,* Clarendon, Oxford.

Peacocke, A. R. 1981. *The Sciences and Theology in the Twentieth Century,* Oriel, Stockfield.

Pieper, J. 1979. *Death and Immortality,* Burns and Oates, London.

Pirsig, R. M. 1979. *Zen and the Art of Motor Cycle Maintenance,* Corgi, London.

Popper, K./Eccles, J. 1977. *The Self and its Brain,* Springer, New York (see Chapter 7).

Schilling, H. K. 1973. *The New Consciousness in Science and Religion.* S.C.M. London.

Schrödinger, E. 1944. *What is Life? Mind and Matter,* Cambridge University Press, Cambridge (see Chapter 6).

Sherrington, C. 1938. *Man on his Nature,* Cambridge University Press, Cambridge (see Chapter 5).

Sheldrake, R. 1981. *A New Science of Life,* Blond and Briggs, London (see Chapter 8).

Simpson, M. 1971. *Death and Eternal Life,* Mercier, Cork.

Smart, N. 1981. *Beyond Ideology,* Collins, London.

Stannard, R. 1982. *Science and the Renewal of Belief,* S.C.M. London.

Torrance, T. F. 1969. *Space, Time and Incarnation,* Oxford, London.

Torrance, T. F. 1976. *Space, Time and Resurrection,* Handsel, Edinburgh.

Torrance, T. F. 1980. *Christian Theology and Scientific Culture,* Marshall Pickering, Basingstoke.

Troisfontaine, R. 1963. *I do not die,* Desclees, New York.

Ward, K. 1982. *Rational Theology and the Creativity of God,* Blackwell, Oxford.